# IT'S ALL
# IN THE
# NAME

## The Hidden Power within Words

## SHARITA STAR

### Foreword by Crystal Bush
Author of *Linda Goodman's Star Cards*

PORTAL BOOKS
AN IMPRINT OF STEINERBOOKS, INC.
610 Main St., Great Barrington, MA 01230
www.steinerbooks.org

Cover design: Aarathi Ventakaraman
Book design: William Jens Jensen

LIBRARY OF CONGRESS CATALOGING-IN-PUBLICATION DATA

Star, Sharita, 1971–
It's all in the name : the hidden power within words / Sharita Star ;
foreword by Crystal Bush.
    p. cm.
Includes bibliographical references (p. 302).
ISBN 978-0-9831984-0-6
1. Astrology. 2. Language and languages—Miscellanea. I. Title.

BF1711.S755 2011
133.3'3—dc22

2011014239

eBook ISBN: 978-0-9831984-2-0

# CONTENTS

To My Poppie

EARL

*The first person that taught me how to be REAL.*

# ACKNOWLEDGMENTS

There could be an entire book written on the people that I extend my heartfelt gratitude to. The journey that has brought this project to fruition has been one of the most rewarding experiences I could ever imagine being on.

Life itself is the inspiration behind the words within all of the chapters to follow. But, without my own having crossed the path of learning a most uncanny method of how to interpret some of the mysteries surrounding us all—in such a way that Lexigrams can—I'd not know the joys of this lifelong passion that I found.

## WITH EXTREME GRATITUDE....

TO the legacy and work that Linda Goodman left to us. Without question it is the source of what took my life by the hand during my 1st Saturn Return and led me to the calling of what I must do.

TO Rick Jacobs, as forecasted to me, you entered my life and opened the door that most certainly has allowed my creativity to soar.

TO Gene Gollogly, for having the ultimate faith that I could be onto something here.

TO William Jens Jensen, for your patience with one of the more eccentric editing projects I am sure you've ever seen.

TO Crystal Bush, for your encouragement and continued support to carry on the incredible wisdom Linda Goodman left to us, the magical gift that must still be shared.

TO Aarathi Venkatataram, whose graphics brilliance has made my work shine beyond any expectation. How amazing it has been to be together on this co-operative artistic journey.

TO Mark Gregor, for your strong involvement and advice since the beginning. You have shed clear light on this path.

TO Alice O. Howell, for your sweet encouragement and impeccable knowledge that the heavens above indeed do declare is a blessing.

TO Daniel Iliescu, for always seeing inside us and being the beacon of light from which the creative can emerge.

TO Kristin S. Kopp, who taught me how to truly manifest when it was the perfect timing in my life to learn it.

TO my Grammie, Kathleen Kern, for everything you have brought to my life, always.

TO Elma Krumwiede, who taught me so long ago to never stop searching for the truth.

TO Kathy and Burton Lanzi, my parents; I am happy I chose you both so I learned how to appreciate freedom and never ever take anything in life for granted.

TO Jimi and Christine Harrington, Mike Di Mesa, and Zai Jawat Ali: my beacons of light for Grammie when I have to be away.

TO Magick, my beloved feline friend, who has been purring by my side every step of the way, since before my Saturn Return.

TO ALL of my honored Clients who have granted my imagination the endless outlets to continually affirm there is always a tale to be told from a name.

TO ALL of my beyond fantastic Friends, every single one of you, for all of your priceless gifts of love, support, and help.

TO You, The Reader, for opening your mind and allowing the possibility of Lexigrams to enrich your life and see that the truth is, more often than not, right in front of you.

TO The World, tremendous appreciation goes out for what has been created in thought and action for me to interpret. The power of words is something to behold with integrity.

> With Much LOVE to EVOLVE,
> *Namaste,*
> *Sharita*

# FOREWORD

*Sharita my dear,*

You have been talking about this book for several years and I have been waiting patiently for the day you would call me to tell me it was completed.

I never had any doubt that it would be done, for your passion of astrology, numerology, and lexigrams is second to none.

What a gift!

You are opening up and sharing a whole new world of understanding by educating the masses on the secrets hidden within our birth name, married name or the name of any entity in our lives.

Most of us walk through life blinkered, focused on getting through the day, with family priorities, work demands and rarely understand where the road is taking us. Few have the privilege of time to explore in any depth the world around us, to search for the reasons why things are happening and to question how to change.

You are offering explanations, guidance and a fun way to uncover the journey conveyed within a name, sometimes dictated to us by our birth parents, at other times by personal choice.

My journey of discovery was way back in the eighties when I was introduced to lexigrams and numerology through reading Star Signs by the guru Linda Goodman. My friendship with her and her unlimited knowledge of all things metaphysical unveiled many mysteries of the Universe to me, including the magic of a name and the joy of knowing what my own name held for me.

Thank you my dear for your perseverance and commitment and in taking this step to further educate the planet by continuing to explore Linda's passion of Lexigrams. Writing this book and sharing your insights with us has my heart smiling and I am sure that Linda is smiling, too.

*Crystal Bush (The Irish Tara/Sharita)*
Author of *Linda Goodman's Star Cards*

# PART I:

# THE WHY'S AND HOW-TO'S OF LEXIGRAMS

# AN INTRODUCTION

# Chapter 1

## WHAT YOU WANT TO KNOW
## IS RIGHT IN FRONT OF YOU

*"If there exists any phenomenon or miracle it is in the power of words."* —HAZRAT INAYAT KHAN

People throughout history have always been intrigued by a phenomenon of one kind or another. Add to that the seemingly endless obsession with needing to know what goes on in other people's lives—whether that be of a neighbor, family, the latest headlines in the news, and, especially in today's society, what our famed politicians and celebrities are up to. In the end, one may wonder if you ever really do hear the actual truth of the matter at hand, being that most news today rarely comes from the actual horse's mouth. But allow me to share with you a new concept of revealing the essence of truth—surely one, by the time we are finished, you'll more than likely find to be another phenomenon in life. This one just so happens to demonstrate that what you may have been looking for has always been right in front of you.

Have you ever played the word jumble in the newspaper or a fun game of Scrabble? We have all, at one time or another, played around with words, maybe even through what is known as anagrams. Anagrams merely take a word, for example—HEALTH—and simply spell other words from it like—HATE, HEAL, THE, LET. I've only stuck to utilizing the letters within HEALTH. Yet when I phrase these anagrams in a form of prose, I can get a message: HEALTH: LET THE HATE HEAL. Welcome to the world of Lexigrams.

Within the following pages of this book, you'll be ever amazed at just how far this intuitive form of language analysis can take any open mind beyond the simplicity of rearranging letters from one word and making new ones. This poetic phrasing of anagrams is an all too telling star secret that lends itself to be an incredible way to tap into the true meaning behind the words we think, hear and speak everyday. What becomes even more of a phenomenon is when we take the art of Lexigrams from the simplicity of words to our names or anything with a title. Thus, the ability to gain self-knowledge from the analysis of your own name or whatever you may choose to entitle in life is usually right there, eagerly waiting for you to explore it. But before we get too ahead of ourselves, let's take a journey into what you may not have already known some of those words that are contained within the average dictionary are really able to tell you, shall we?

Why not start with WORDS? It's a wild thing to realize that they can often be a SWORD when we use them, like throwing RODS at some one. Words can hurt us; there is no doubt about it, and they can potentially leave deep emotional scars when they strike, which can later lead to physical ones. So, right away in our newfound understanding of language, let us all realize that our TIME is nothing but MITE, and we can be so much more productive with it when we remember not to allow the precious words we have to communicate with to go down a harmful path. Besides, if we truly are to EVOLVE (and I bet you might already know this one), there isn't another way to do so other than to LOVE.

As individual souls we are all here on our own JOURNEY—and that would be YOUR ONE RUN ON EON. Yes, that surely means you are tied to all the other lives and experiences you've had every time you've come back again as another EARTHLING. It's because of the revelations within this very word that I wonder why people on this planet are still looking for Aliens and UFOs out there, when we know for a fact it is too hot to live on Mars or the Sun and too cold to live on Uranus or Pluto (and who, by the way, has not been dwarfed by any means in its powerful presence astrologically). Take a look at the messages this seemingly simple word really has to tell us:

## EARTHLINGS

- ARE THE REAL "STRANGE" ALIENS SENT TO SING IN A GREAT HEART
- ARE THE ANGEL STARS SENT TO HEAL THE EARTH
- AS THEIR HEARTS HEAL THE EARTH IS IN GREAT GAINS
- THEIR EARS HEAR HATE IN THE ANGRIEST LIES
- THE REAL RELATING IS IN TRINES, IN TRIANGLES— IT REALIGNS THE EARTH
- THE GAINS IN LEARNING A HATE HEALING ARE GREAT
- THE TIES IN HEALING HEARTS ARE GREAT
- HEARTS GET IN RAGE, IN HATE AS EARS HEAR LIES

- AS THEIR HEARTS SHARE IN THE LIGHT THE ANGELS THEN HEAL THE EARTH
- SENT IN A STAR SIGN IN REAL STRANGE TALES
- SENT IN STAR TRAIL TRIALS, HE IS SHE=SHE IS HE
- ARISE IN THE EIGHT AS IT GRANTS THE EARTH AS IT EARNS THE REAL GIANT GREAT GAINS
- INHALE THE AIR, IT HEALS, IT REALIGNS
- SING IN ENGLISH, IT HEALS THE HEART=THE EARTH
- THE EARTH IS AS THE GREAT HEART
- HEARTS SENT IN GREAT HEALING GAINS
- THEIR HEARTS ARE IN GREAT GAINS IN ART
- ARE ANGELS IN GREAT GAINS IN HEARTS THAT SHARE
- LISTEN IN A SILENT AIR, THE HEART LEARNS THE LARGEST GAIN
- EATING GRAINS IS THE GREAT GIANT GAIN IN HEALTH
- LEARN THE RELATING ANGLES; IT IS A RELIANT ART
- 'NEATH THE NIGHT STARE AT THE STAR'S LIGHT, IT IS RIGHT AS IT GLISTEN
- LEARN THE HEART ALIGNS IT RIGHT, LIGHTENS IT, LETS IT SHINE
- THEIR TEARS, AS THE RAIN HEAL THE GREAT EARTH, HEAL THE HEART
- THE EARTH IS IN A GREAT ANGER IN TRASH, NEAR IRATE LIARS
- GATHER THE HATE, THE RAGES, AS IT IS THE ANGRIEST SIN
- RISE IN A GIANT GAIN IN SHARING THE HEART, IT HEAL THE GREAT EARTH
- IN A GREAT GAIN AS HEARTS GATHER IN AN INTEGRAL HEALING

Quite the mouthful from a word with only ten letters! And certainly there's more to come with that one (you'll have to read on to chapter 3 to learn of Lexigrams and their intricate tie to the planetary connections of Astrology and Numerology). One thing to say right away, however, is that Lexigrams are truly a never-ending story. So, now that we don't have to wonder any longer where the Aliens really are, and that we here on earth have a lot more work to do, let's move on to ponder another word that has some needed wisdom to share with us.

Back to those soul journeys and time and those other fun lives we've all lived before, have you ever wondered if they are all SIMULTANEOUS? You bet they are all connected...

- MENIAL MINUTES ONSET AT SAME TIME
- UNITE EONS AT SAME TIME, TIES IN ONE TO ONE
- ALIENS SEE EONS AT SAME TIME
- ATOMS SEE EONS AT SAME TIME
- SOULS SEE EONS AT SAME TIME
- SOULS SEE EMULATIONS AT SAME TIME
- SOULMATES SEE EONS AT SAME TIME
- SOUL'S NAMES TIE ONE TO MULTI-EONS
- SOMETIMES SOULS NO LISTEN IN TIME MISS OUT
- SOULS NOT MEANT TO TAME TIME
- LISTEN, TIME A LESSON TO ATONE, TO TUNE US IN
- TUNE IN TO A SILENT TIME TO LISTEN IN
- LUMINOUS SOULS SEE MULTI-TIMELINES IN NO SINS
- MEAN SOULS SEE MULTI-TIMELINES IN SINS, IN TOILS
- TAME SOULS IN SMILES SEE ELATIONS
- LET A LOTUS IN TO SMILE IN A SILENT TIME

- UNTIL SOULS UNITE IN SILENT MUTUAL ELATIONS TIME UNTIES US
- TIME IS MITE, TIME IS MILES, TIME IS MASS
- TIME IS SET TO LAST EONS ON

No doubt, it is one of those mentioned phenomena that indeed indicates that the past, present, and future are all one. Yet, when you consider a word like *simultaneous,* there are so many clues within the word that share with us the truth about time, beyond the fact that we know it to be short. That's one thing my own dear Mother was certainly right about when I was young—that it goes all the faster the WISER you get as I RISE (the word *older* for this description does not exist in my vocabulary). Ask anyone over 30, and they'll say that this is ever so true! Father TIME is definitely not joking around when he says he is MITE. As souls here upon Earth, we are each here with special gifts, but as you'll read further in the upcoming chapter 3, it is always our choice to allow them to emerge in whichever lifetime we are in. Each and every time we decide to choose another set of parents to continue on in our soul's spiritual journey, it is in deep connection with the lives we've already had. But there I go getting too ahead of myself again, so let's get back to your introduction to this insightful way of looking at simple words.

One Lexigram I always need to personally remind myself of is the message within the word BREATHE: BEAT THE HATE, THERE THERE—BATHE THE HEART RATE, HEAR THE THREE. It's amazing that, in all of the schooling we have as children (at least, in the U.S. public system), one is rarely taught any proper way of being mindful of the breath as a way to remain calm and collected. When we BATHE THE HATE, we give our heart a bath of sorts! If only all souls learned this lovely tool at a young age. HEAR THE THREE is the natural rhythm of life of our body, mind, and spirit. While our spiritual beings are here in each life in our human experiences, as we learn the benefits of breathing properly (whether we find out about this later on or are blessed enough in our childhood), one cannot question that once they BEAT THE HATE, it will have no room to hang out and bother anybody.

While we are on the topic of bodily functions, here's another one about the only two things we have upon our face besides ears, THE EYES. Well, it's a no-brainer to let a Lexigram tell you that YES THEY SEE! And how many times have you ever gotten that kind of look from someone you'd rather avoid? YET THESE EYES SEETHE. Well, my apologies for ever having to deal with that kind of indecent behavior, but you'll have to take it up with the person who owns the eyes. That's their choice.

After all, eyes are only one small part of what makes up an entire HUMAN BEING. Unfortunately, there is a tendency to BE INHUMANE, to BE MEAN. But we are so much better off trying some other potentials from our existence while we are trying so hard to "get it right" in this specific lifetime. We'd be taking a much better step in the right karmic direction if we in our spiritual beings embrace the true clues behind the experience of embodying a:

## HUMAN BEING

- ◉ BEAM IN A HUMANE ENIGMA
- ◉ BE IN A BIG BENIGN GAIN
- ◉ BE IN A HUGE BEAMING IMAGE
- ◉ BEGIN IN A MAGI GAIN
- ◉ MAN BE INHUMANE IN A GUNMAN GAIN

- A GUN NUMB MAN IN A BIG HUGE MEGA MEAN IMAGE
- A GUN NUMB MAN IN A BIG GAME AIM BINGE
- IMAGINE I AM A MAGI
- I AM A HUMAN IN A BENIGN MEANING
- NAMING MAN A MAIN ENIGMA

Even though we lived multitudes of years upon this planet without guns to fight our battles, it is interesting to note they found the human race eventually. That's one current political topic of controversy I just won't bother to touch any further, and we'll just let the Lexigrams in the chapters to follow speak for themselves. They do have every right to their own free speech, just like everyone else!

So it would seem silly and even more controversial to move forward to the topic of RELIGION, but you'll find this book is not about adhering to the normal kinds of boundaries. And this one lends some very simple advice on how to proceed with whatever your soul chooses to believe (or not) in this life: LORE IN NO EGO OR LIE, ORIGIN IN NO EGO OR LIE, LINGER IN NO EGO NOR LIE, RELIGION IGNORE EGO, RELIGION REIGN IN NO LIE, GO ON IN ONE LORE IN NO EGO NOR LIE. There is plenty more to explore here but this is about opening your mind as well, so always know I will leave you plenty of Lexigram fun to do on your own from the examples you'll see. After all, how would you learn anything if I told you all the answers?

Guess it is the perfect time to ask the question if you have learned anything yet, because that is the whole goal behind writing this book for you. How fun that when we do our LEARNING we ARE IN A REAL LARGE INNER

GAIN, NEARING A REAL REALIGN, EARNING IN A RANGE, and LEANING IN ON A REAL EAR. Well, people wouldn't learn a thing if they weren't lending their ears to LISTEN, because then I IS SILENT, I LET IT IN, I LET IT SIT, I LET IT INSET, I LET IT TIE IN, I ENLIST IT. Now you know exactly why some people can be so insistent when they are talking, as they only wish that you not impolitely interrupt them so you can intake these very qualities from whatever lesson they are granting you wisdom to absorb.

When you've been good and silent, no doubt then you've let the LESSON in, for once we tune in our learning and listening skills, then NO LOSES SO NO LOSS, and surely here the LESS ONE LOSES EONS ON. After all, we only have this LIFETIME within this incarnation to learn what is requested of us on this particular Karmic Path. There is a MITE TIME LIMIT on this particular FILE, and we shouldn't delay adhering to our needed lessons early so we can MEET ELITE TIME. LIFE is never to be about the what IF. Why not in this LIFETIME, LET IT LIFT ME?

That's where some good old healthy DREAMING can be a wonderful way to lift a soul up to where it belongs. Whether it be your daytime fantasy of leaving your current job and doing the "crazy thing" all your friends and family tell you can't be done, or the kind the majority of us do over a good night's sleep, DREAMING urges us: I DREAM BIG AND DARING, I IN A BIG GAIN IN A DREAM, I IN A MAIN GAIN IN A DREAM, A MIND GAME IN A MIRAGE, I DREAM A GRAND ENIGMA, I REIGN IN A MAGI AIM, ADMIRE A BIG MAIN DREAM, I AM IN A GAIN IN A GRAND IDEA.

So let them flow, those IDEAS of yours; they for certain are your AIDES. Keep in mind that, while we can all be dreamers, there must also be the balance of being RESPONSIBLE to ourselves while we make real the dream we are meant to fulfill. When we are on this path, we are a SENSIBLE SOBER PERSON, SEE NO BILLS IN BINS OR PILES, SEE EONS POSSIBLE, BE OPEN IN RESPONSE, are NOBLE PIONEERS, say REPLIES IN POISE, and are OPEN IN LESSON SO NO ONE LOSES SO NO LOSS, and for sure to be responsible ONE IS NO LOSER!

Now, the human means to be responsible can come from various sources, depending upon what your lifestyle prefers. Yet certainly one proven method up till now to help us remain poised is:

## MEDITATION

- I AM IN A TAME IDEA
- I TAME A MIND IN TIME
- I AM TIED TO AN EON TO ANOINT IT
- ME MIND DO NOT INTIMIDATE ME
- I DOMINATE ME MIND
- ME MIND DO NOT TAINT ME IN A MEAN IDEA
- I OMIT A MEAN IDEA
- I OMIT A TIMID DEMON IDEA
- I NOT TO TOTE A MEAR OR DEMON IDEA
- I ADMIT I AM IN A MIND DOMAIN
- I DONATE TIME TO TAME ME MIND
- IN TIME I ATONE IT TO AMEND I AIM TO ATTEND TO ME MIND
- ANOINT TO A TIDE TIME AND I TIE ME MIND TO A MAIN TAME IDEA

Meditation has existed for all-time, yet in this world of "insta this" and "I wanted that done last week that," the average soul can be lost in knowing where to begin to calm the mind with all the entertaining choices that modern-day society offers for a "healthy" mind relaxation. Remember the gifts that can be bestowed upon us when we listen and are silent. Well, it's an idea to toss around at the very least on what may be a wise choice as to how to adhere to the energy of responsibility.

Well, I've become so serious with you that it's obviously time for us to explore LAUGHTER! One just has to love the messages here—because underneath all the proper things that a soul does in life, this one is by far one of the most needed. You know those times when you are laughing so hard it hurts so much that it brings tears to your eyes, while it is a wonderful high all the same? That's because the LAUGHTER: ULTRA HEAL THE GREAT HEART; A REAL LAUGH HALT THE HATE, ALTER THE ARGUE; GATHER A GREAT TRUE HEAL, THE REAL ULTRA EARTH HEAL, URGE THE REAL LARGE HEAL, LET THE LAUGH RULE THE EARTH. Truly pause here for just a brief moment. Can you only imagine an entire planet full of laughing souls? Mother Earth would only be sooooo pleased.

My sincere apologies to you, Dear Mother Earth, for not mentioning you and the messages you would like to have heard. You are actually getting some special attention from our American Indians in the chapter "For Any New Age" later on, because as we already are quite aware of, you surely have some inherent wisdom to share with us to help your pressing needs at present. What would the world do without a MOTHER? Here we see THE OTHER HERO, THE HOME OHM, and although we no longer get a chance to watch mothers like those in *Leave It to Beaver*, there is MORE TO HER—MORE TO THEM—than a child ever really knows. There are typically a vast number of years preceding the time when any woman becomes a mother, and this is what her child does not know directly about her and, indeed, should not. Surely even a dear mother is entitled to her privacy.

But ask the average mother or parent who has CHILDREN, and they'll surely tell you that they ENRICH and are IN NICER NICHE. They like to be HELD and told no LIE that will HINDER them. DRENCH them in love and they'll always be NICE. One thing every PARENT is warned not to do in the role is to ENTRAP.

By now you may have noticed that some words have some peculiar messages they'd like to relate to us. There are plenty of words that you'll decide to ponder upon that will tell you some truths one may never have ever realized are right there to be heard. MESSAGES are SAGES, here to SEAM SAME MASSES AS MEGA GEMS, yet can also relay SEES MEGA MESSES. When we are open to them, they EASE us to SEE the real issue at hand, as they have known the right side of life we should be adhering to for AGES.

Like recognizing when one is FORTUNATE, as then one can see that their FATE NOT OFTEN ROTTEN, but TRUE TO ATTUNE TO AN ORNATE NATURE, ON A TRUE ROUTE OF FUN, as well as typically ONE OUT OF TEN to be so blessed TO EARN A TON (and if you like the more mystical telling kind of fortunes, it's equally fun to note here: TO TUNE TO A TRUE TAROT ART). But surely, to be fortunate our RESOURCES in life SURE ARE SECURE, and most certainly RESCUE OUR CORE SOURCES. We shouldn't allow them to USE OR CURSE US, where we would then have to refrain from becoming too MATERIAL. Better that I AM A REAL TAME REALM; I REMIT A REAL TAME MERIT. Otherwise, one may find LATER I IRATE, LATER I LIE AT ME, I LET A REAL ALTER EAT ME and IT AIM AT A REAL MARITAL ALARM.

Speaking of marital material things, there's no question the divorce rate around the world today, especially within the United States, is the highest it has ever been. One of the biggest reasons for divorce—aside from the fact that the majority of people marry before their first Saturn Return and First Period Cycle have allowed them enough time for self-discovery (which will, for any soul, fall around 28 years of age and then vary personally from 26 to 35 years of age)—is the obvious fact that the two people lack HARMONY. When it's there, MY MY NO HARM ROAM, NO HARM A NORM, ANY MAN MAY OHM, NO MANOR HARM, NO MAN MOAN ON, A MANY MAN HYMN MANY AN OHM, and here's one that is especially a message to listen to: NO MAN ARMY MAY HARM NOR MAR ON ANY MAN.

I guess if the world is to become totally harmonious, we ought to have quite a bit of ROMANCE involved. It is truly then, when romance abounds, that NO MAN MOAN OR CAN ROAM MEAN. Now you'd have to admit it is completely true that ONCE A MAN OR MEN COME NEAR A MARE, MAN CAN CARE and ONE MAN CAN MOAN NO MORE. All same-sex unions excluded, one has to wonder where would men ever be upon this earth without WOMEN by their side. Oddly (perhaps because of karmic ties), ladies in history often have felt NOW WE OWE MEN; or maybe it isn't that way, and the reverse option is chosen by WOMEN: WE OWE NO MEN, WE OWE NO NEW OMEN NOW, NOW WE OWN ONE: ME. It may have taken centuries of work, but the motto of the WOMAN in today's modern world can be heard similarly to say: NOW OWN NO MAN, NOW WOMAN WON MAN. Guess our sexes better get back to working on those romantic endeavors.

And how TRIUMPHANT you can be at anything including romance if you only try! I HIT IT IN TRUTH, I AM IN A MAIN PART IN TRUTH, I AM A PURITAN, I AM APT IN A MAIN PAIR, I AM A MAIN PART IN A PAIR TRUTH (*see*... just be triumphant and it's possible!), I AM A TITAN IN TRUTH, I AM IN A MAIN HUMAN INPUT IN A TRIUMPH, I AIN'T IN PAIN, I AIN'T IN RUIN, I AIN'T IN RAIN, I AIN'T IN HURT, I AIN'T IN HARM, I RUN IN A MAIN PATH THAT TURN IN TRUTH. That's right, now I sense you may be beginning to understand like never before what energy encompasses the words we speak and gives a voice to the Universe.

You'll probably agree more after realizing that it's a pretty safe and smart thing in life to make the choices that avoid the DISASTROUS from occurring. Seemingly, when we see the kinds of outcomes that particular choices made in life can fall to this kind of energy potential, you may notice: OUTSIDERS DESIRES ARE SATIRES, A SERIOUS ISSUE AROSE, A SAD IDEA DIES, EDITORS STORIES SOAR OUT TO ASSORTED RUDE SADIST ROUTES, STARS TRIED A RESIST AS IT RIOTED, SERIOUS ISSUES ARE

RAISED, A STAR RAISED A TRUE IRATE ISSUE, IT IS
SO SAD AS A TRUE STAR IDEA DIES.

Now I hope I haven't gotten too heavy on you. But like I
noted from the very beginning of this chapter, some words
can be like a loaded gun. Well, words have been around
a long before guns; so pardon me—let me rephrase that
one. Too bad we couldn't keep on fighting our real wars
(if we must) like our word wars, with those swords still
in their sheathes, all ready to be drawn to slice and dice.
Well, I still haven't gotten out of heavy. Time to lighten up
the subject matter again. What enlightening topic shall we
investigate next?

INVESTIGATE! There should be no harm in check-
ing this one out. I GET IT IN A SEVEN GAIN (follow
on to chapter 3, and you'll learn that the planet ruling the
Number SEVEN is one true lover of investigation). I GET
IT AS I GIVE IT A SIT, I GET IT AS I GIVE IN, I GET IT
AS A SAGE, I GET VAIN IN NEGATIVES, I GET VAIN
AS I INSTIGATE, I EVER IN A GAIN AS I INVITE IN
A VISAGE, I SIT IN A VAST VINTAGE AGE AS I SEE, I
IGNITE IN A GIANT GAIN AS I SEE IT IS GETS EVEN, I
SEE ENTITIES IN GIANT GAINS AS SAGES, SAGE TIES
GIVE GIANT GAINS, GET IN A GIANT SEVEN GAIN.

As usual, I could write a short book alone just from that
word (and many others, as you may have already noticed), but
I am supposed to be letting you do some of the look-seeing into
the magical tales within words. My apologies if I seem to be
giving too much away, but trust me, you won't find the entire
dictionary analyzed here. And besides, as I also have mentioned previously, the Lexigrams never cease, oddly enough,
in what they want to tell you. It'll become more apparent as

you continue to do them, however, that Lexigrams only tell you what you need to know when you are ready to receive the message. They don't always reveal it all at once.

In my experience since this seemingly bizarre ability was bestowed upon me, I can go back to a word, name, or title at any moment after giving it a first real examination and each new time find all sorts of other goodies that stream-line out of it. That's the beauty of Lexigrams, they can be a never-ending journey of mind-filled fascination. Truly it is what makes them so much fun to be telling you about. I'll admit now, there's no doubt I found my "hook" in life. Never before has there been one true formula with which I can find the truth of the matter, and I am ever again and again and AGAIN (and ah, oh yes, that would also be seen as I IN A GAIN!) completely endlessly amazed by what's within the apparent straightforward English in front of me! We'll get into Lexigrams and some current events over the past 10 years in the later chapters, but let me just say I had a slight problem watching the news on television once Lexigrams showed their validity to me. So it became obvi-ous I had to write this book to let you all know about this way of looking at the world. What eventual good would it do me to keep this star secret all to myself?

KNOWLEDGE is truly meant to be shared. WE NOW KNOW an OLDEN GOLDEN LEGEND NEED. For me, it's like being a kid in a candy store to now understand I can dive into a word, name, or title and be able to figure out the truth. And don't we secretly all LONG to KNOW the truth in life? WE NOW WON ONE GLOW, WE WOKE ONE NOW, WE WOKE NEW EGO, WE KNOW EGO GO DOWN, WE NOW ENDOW NEW GOLD, ENDOW

NEW NEED, WE KNEW EGO DONE NO ONE NO GOOD. Again, there's much more to the tale within this word here, so don't be shy, go ahead.... give it a try, what messages are waiting to be told to you?

Now, please don't get frustrated if things may not magically come to you right away. English teachers everywhere may be cursing me for letting this cat out of the bag, causing too much confusion in future classrooms, because, of course, our very language is already one of the most complex to learn. Remember, my dear brilliant ones, that this is a new way to exercise your brain, so one does need a bit of I CAN from the word PATIENCE when trying something new. I IN AN ANCIENT PEACE, I CAN ENTICE PEACE, I CAN PATENT IN PEACE, I AIN'T IN A PANIC, I AIN'T IN AN ANTIC, I AIN'T IN PAIN, I IN A NICE PEACE, I CAN ENACT PEACE, I CAN EAT IN PEACE, I CAN PACE IT. So always remember the wisdom within PATIENCE, and that yes, I CAN!

What just may happen to you that happened to me is you'll be DAWNING as a soul into all of these incredible marvelous revelations in life that you will now be able to have at your very fingertips. Sooner than later, you'll DAWN IN A WIN IN A GAIN AWW GAWD, and your new WING will allow you to go wherever the mighty WIND takes you in those clever derivations that will come. Like a fairy godmother (or father), you'll wave your magic WAND over words and presto: I DIG A GAIN IN A WIN. The WADING through words will have you WANING any doubts that Lexigrams are indeed for real. It is always before the DAWN that we GAIN IN WANING. It's beyond uncanny and ultimately mysterious, but if you want some truth in life, you'll probably want to keep reading. The evidence is pretty fierce once we dive into those full names and other titles later on.

By the time you close the back cover of this book, you'll have more than likely reached a TRANSFORMATION of one kind or another. ROTATIONS IN STAMINA such as these occur in these times OF MOTION, OF MAIN TRANSIT. I AM SORT OF IN TRANSIT, I AM A STAR STAT STATION IN MOTION, I AM A MAIN STAR (more on the telling of your star stats in chapter 3), I SORT OF TAINT IT IF I AM IN NO FORM, SO TO A MAIN STAR TRANSIT I ATTAIN TO ANOINT IT. There are many times as souls where we are always meant to be reaching in life so that we break through to a new ground. That would also be linked to the adherence to your true self through what the two other star secrets, Astrology and Numerology, can tell you, not resisting the keen advice they are each here to bless us with.

You know, whenever we fall to RESISTANCE that I CAN'T INCREASE IN IT, I CAN'T SET TIES IN IT, I CAN'T CREATE IN IT, I CAN'T RISE IN IT, I CAN'T SEE IN IT, I CAN'T SEE A STAR SAINT IN IT, IT'S IN AN INSINCERE RAIN I CAN'T RISE IN, IT'S IN NASTIES I CAN'T RAISE CARES IN. Well, now I don't know about you, but that sure seems like an unhappy place to be hanging out in life, huh? And not that any of us don't ever find ourselves in it in life, but back to those times we are within transformation, we just may need a polite nudge or, for some, a good swift kick to get us out of feeling stuck in the mud. But when people around you may choose to WALLOW in resistance, ALLOW them A LOW WALL in the WOW ALL LOW LAW—it's best to run quickly out of their way.

To the next INTERSECTION that grants you new choices. I SORT IT TO ATONE, I ENTER IN INTEREST, I SEE SINCERE EONS, I CONSENT TO SEE IT IN EONS, I SEE EONS IN SECRET TRINES, I NOTICE TONS IN NICETIES, I SEE IT IN INTENSE INSTINCT SINCE I SEE TIES TO ESOTERIC, I ENTICE TONS IN CONSENT, I ORIENT IN SINCERE INTEREST, I ERECT IT IN ENTIRE CENTER CORES. A further telling here is the very phrase CITIES RISE IN NOISE. Aren't just those kinds of places chock full of intersections and the busy-bee buzz of life?

Truly, if we don't allow ourselves choices of direction, how can we ever be LIBERATED? I RELATE IT, I ABLE AT A DEBATE, I ALTERED IT, I RELATE A REAL TRIBAL ART, I A REAL LEADER, I LEAD A REAL IDEA, ALBEIT I A DEAR ABLE ELATED LEADER. Now that you've gone into the intersection of liberation, no doubt your ALIGNMENT may have begun. I AM IN A GIANT MAIN GAIN, I AM MELTING IN A TAME TEAM, I LEAN IN AN ANGEL LITE, I TINGLE IN A MAIN GAIN, I AM TAMING ME, I MINGLE IN A TEAM, I AM IN A MENTAL ALIGN, I AM AN INNATE GAIN MAGNET, AGAIN I AM IN AN ENIGMA.

Ah and doesn't the beauty of alignment bring one to be quite COOPERATIVE? Now the CREATIVE VOTE can be cast TO PROVE TO REAP A VICTOR. I OPERATE OVER A CAPTIVE PEACE, I CREATE A POETIC VOICE, I COVERT A REACT TO A PEACE ACT, I VETO IRATE TO TIE TO A TRAP, I ROOT TO A CREATIVE ACT. So, if you have attended to your personal homework, let's just move on to ponder what genuine fun will be had with others as you have reached this new RELATIONSHIP:

- I SHARE IN REAL POLARITIES TO SHINE ON
- I SPENT IN A PERSONAL HEAL AS I ALTER IN A SILENT SPACE
- AS I HEAL THE PAST I LET IN A REAL SPIRIT IN HOPE
- SO AS I SHARE IN PAIRS IT IS IN REAL HOPES TO HEAL THE EARTH
- IT'S SHARP THE POINTERS I LEARNT ALONE TO SHARE IN REAL PAIRS
- PERSONAL PAIRS SHARE IN REAL HOPES AS HEARTS LISTEN IN EARS
- PERSONAL PAIRS ORIENT IN A REAL HOPE TO SHARE IN THEIR RELATIONS
- LIPS IN POLITE AIRS SHARE HOPES TO THE EARS TO HEAR TO INHERIT IT
- A HEART PAIR IS NOT TO LAST IN AN IRATE, HOSTILE OR PHONIES AIR
- A HEART PAIR IS NOT SET TO LAST EONS ON IN LIES
- REAL HEART PAIRS ARE SET TO LAST AS AN ELATION SET TO INSPIRE ONE ANOTHER EONS ON
- LISTEN IN, THE PLANETS ARE RELIANT AS REALIST STAR PAIR PLANERS
- THE PLANETS ARE THE HEART SPIRIT TO THIS EARTHSHIP
- THE PLANETS RELATE THEIR LINEAR ART TO THE EARTH'S HEARTS INERTIA
- RELATIONSHIPS ARE SET TO ASPIRE ONE TO A REAL HEAL IN SPIRIT THEN SET TO SHINE ON

We are undoubtedly responsible to the relationship to ourselves before we can make those relationships to others become successful, and even more importantly AUTHENTIC. I CAN ATTUNE IT, I CAN UNITE AN ANCIENT TIE, I CAN ENACT AN ETHNIC TIE, I CAN TEACH IT IN A UNITE. What a delightful OFFERING to be sending out to the world. I OFFER IN ONE, I OFFER NO EGO, I REIGN IN ONE EON, I GO ON IN NO GRIEF, IF I GO IN EGO I a GONER, I GO ON IN FINER FIRE. Once that inner fire is roaring you know you're on your way.

To continue on in a MOMENTUM which TUNE ME UNTO ONE MOMENT TO MOUNT ME. And there you are with all of your COURAGE that really brings forth OUR GRACE as, once more, another word is here to advise that it's best we CAGE OUR EGO OR GO ARGUE, ERGO OUR URGE A EGO CURE, as it must be that OUR GRACE CURE OUR CORE, GRACE URGE OUR CARE. Sounds like our words, yet again, are onto something as another divine plan for us Earthlings to take into consideration.

The messages that lie within honoring our courageousness come from making sure we do not give up our own INDIVIDUALITY in life. I IN A VALID DIVINITY DAILY, I AIN'T IN AN INVALID DUALITY, I AIN'T INDIVIDUAL IN ANY VANITY, I DANDILY IN AN AVID LITANY, I IN A VITAL VAULT IN ID, I LAY IT IN A TIDY UNITY DUTY DAILY. Maintaining this important notion comes from the choice to take OWNERSHIP of it. I NOW WORSHIP IN NEW WISHES, I OWN NEW NEWS, I NOW OWN IN POWER, I HONE IN ON POWERS, I NOW SHINE IN PERSON, I NOW SHOWER IN WISE

NEW POWERS, I NOW IN NO PRISON, I NOW HERO IN POWER, I NOW RISE IN WISER PROSE, I NOW OPEN IN HOPES, I NOW WIN.

To be true to our ownership, HONESTY has just asked if it could make one remark to you: YES THOSE HONES SET THE TONES EONS ON, HEY ONE NOT TO SHY TO ONSET TONS. That one may take a bit more mind-bending to reach into it, but it's obvious already that honesty isn't quite the open book we all might prefer. Taking some time in CREATION is A CERTAIN IN TO AN ACTION, to help undo what may be stopping us from being true. I CAN RETAIN IN AN ORIENT TO ORNATE IT, I NOTICE IN A CARE, I NOTICE IT IN A TRINE, IT CAN COIN AN EROTIC ACT, I CAN TONE IN CARE, I REACT IN A NICER AIR, I CAN'T ENACT OR EARN IN AN IRATE AIR OR ANTIC, I CAN ATONE TO A CERTAIN CORE, I CAN TRACE IT IN A TRANCE.

Once the creation is on, we can keep on in the MANIFEST. Here our FATE IS IN A MAIN FEAST and maybe even IN A MAIN FAME IF I AT ME FINEST. When it's on, IT'S A MAIN FIESTA IN ME, A MAIN FIESTA IN TIME, TIME IS FAST, so it may be best to FASTEN IT so we remain TAME IN TIME. Then we can really enjoy the BLESSINGS that are meant to be counted IN BIG BLISSES, IN BIGNESS, BEGIN IN BLISS, BEINGS SING IN BLISSES, yet not to ever get carried away LESS I LIE IN BIG BINGES, LESS I IS IN LIES IN BIG SINS I BE IN BLISS.

Bliss, by the way, will probably only encourage more ENTHUSIASM, which wants you to know it's extremely important to have around in abundance as often as you can, as IT SUSTAIN US IN HUMAN TIES, IT IS A MESSIAH,

IT TUNES US IN, IT ISN'T IN HASTE, IT ISN'T IN HATE, IT IS A MAIN THEME THAT UNITES US HUMANS, IT IS IN A SUNSET, IT SHINES AS HUMANS MATE, AS MEAN HUMANS MISUSE IT IT UNTIES THEM, THE MAIN SAINTS SHINE IN IT, HUMANS IN TIME USE IT AS A TEAM IN A HUMAN UNITE. Doesn't that make you just totally in love with the idea of having more of that in every nook and cranny of your life?

Well, as the age-old expression *carpe diem* goes, and whether to do so or not every waking new day is totally a personal choice, yet know IT UP TO YOU TO TURN INTO YOU, to take that chance and seize any OPPORTUNITY. Bet you didn't ever think that was actually waiting in there to let you know that truth of the matter. But as I've discovered with words, they're not lying to us. They are so blatantly honest it's almost too good to be true. But true they are. So back to when you're manifesting things to come your way, when OPPORTUNITY knocks, it is so wise to TURN INTO IT PRONTO, IT UP TO YOU TO OPTION IT IN, IT UP TO YOU TO POINT IT IN TO YOUR UNITY, IT YOUR TIP TOP PRO TIP IN YOUR INPUT, IT NOT TURN TO YOU TO RUIN YOU, IT TURN UNTO YOU TO TRY IT OUT.

We've already said that LIFE is not about those what-IF's, and so how else will we ever reach the goal of ILLUMINATION if we don't grab hold of something really good when it's right in front of us? Just imagine A NATION IN A MILLION MULTI-UNION, A NATION IN A MULTI-ANOINT TO OMIT TOIL. Well, before that happens, we can on our own, I AM IN A MAIN UNION IN A MILLION, I ANOINT IN A NATION, I AMOUNT

TO A LOT, I AIM IN A UNIT IN ALL, I AM ON A TALL MOUNTAIN UNTIL ALL INTO A MAIN UNION. On that mountain it will be where we come to STILLNESS. I IS SILENT, I LET IN LISTEN, LESS I ENLIST IN LIES I LESS ILL, LIES SET IN ILLNESSES, LIES TELL ILLS, I TELL LESS, I LISTEN IN, I SIT IN SILENT, LISTEN—IT IS SILENT. I SIT IN IT.

Once we are *silent,* we can *listen* and bear WITNESS. ITS NEW WISE NEWS, IT TWINES IN TWINS IN ITS WINS, I IS WISE, I IS NEW, I SET NEW WISE TIES, I SITE NEW WINS, I NEST IN ITS NEW WISEST NEWS, I IS NEW—I SIT IN IT.

Words are powerful. What amazing messages from the simple utterances we speak or think! Our words are choices that should be made with benevolent intention. They have hidden mysteries swirling within them that yearn to be seen and deeply understood so all the less we find them in life to be our sword. Our words are energy. They are here to be wisely adhered to within the choices we make with them. Being kind with words, and all laws of the Universe will be kind to us in return. Yet they will equally let us know when we need to perhaps change our direction. Again, I welcome you to your journey of Lexigrams. We've truly just begun.

# Chapter 2

## BUT FIRST… SOME RULES

*"The deeper we dive into the mystery of life, the more we find that its whole secret is hidden in what we call words."* —HAZRAT INAYAT KHAN

By now, you might have gotten the urge to go out and test the Lexigram waters on your own and may have already found a word that doesn't say much of anything to you. Well, there are some rules and guidelines that this art form does request of us. One is not everything, nor does everybody wish to be analyzed in this way. Certain things that are meant to remain unknown is the prevailing force here, and you may not always find what you are looking for when you think you need it most. As the element of mystery will always be part of our existence, some souls and entities wish to keep to themselves. There is a definite trail of evidence that leads to the conclusion that the shorter a name is, the more that word, person, or thing does not wish to be explored. When we journey into how the magic of Lexigrams can tell just about any person's story and purpose here on earth, we'll see that certain souls are practically an open book. Yet, as action in life continually validates one's planetary analysis, it is those souls whose charts typically indicate a tendency toward privacy who have their name in alliance with this, as well.

But let's not get too ahead of ourselves without getting back to those rules. I don't know about you, but even with the best set of rules that can be laid down in life, these, due to the natural process of EVOLVING (which, of course, is accompanied best by some GIVE and LOVE IN NO EGO), just seem to at one point or another—become BROKEN. Then, once that occurs, OK ONE EON BORN is the new energy to emerge. Hmmmm... how many times have we seen this to be apparent in life? Now, I have to ask, don't you think these Lexigrams so far are nothing short of fascinating? Many times I have been asked, "*Why* is this so?" Now, while I am intuitive and have tapped into a most unusual artistic form of analysis to discover the truth, I will tell you that I don't have an exact explanation. I will be making plenty of reference to the marvelous woman who is responsible for opening the awareness to the ultimate marvels of Lexigrams to me, the late Poet and Astrologer Linda Goodman. I'll let you know Linda's take on the situation, which is far better from the horse's mouth. So, please also find some time to read chapter 8 of her book entitled *Star Signs* for her direct opinion on this.

You've undoubtedly noticed by now that I haven't written a Lexigram yet without the use of capitalization. My sincere apologies if you thought I was shouting at you. Certainly the question, "Why are these Lexigrams all in capital letters?" more than likely has crossed your mind already. This was the most important rule I learned from Linda, and this is definitely one that is not meant to be broken. I have become accustomed to posting my endless Lexigram messages on things like Facebook and Twitter, where I often have my friends engaging in the conversation. I am always thrilled to see others opening up their own Lexigram ability, but I must admit, when they return the reply in lowercase letters, my head wants to explode. So to make rule number one, if we are to start formulating a list, Lexigrams must be written in CAPITAL LETTERS. Pardon the tangent here, but it does relate to the subject matter:

### CAPITAL LETTERS

- ALL LETTERS TELL A REAL SECRET
- ALL LETTERS SEEP REAL LIES
- ALL LETTERS SET A REAL PACE
- AS LETTERS ARE RESET, LETTERS TELL A REAL TALE
- ALL LETTERS LET A PEACE TALE SPIRAL

The SPIRAL here is ever so important, and it is no coincidence why that particular word is hidden there, which we'll get to in just a few more moments. But, why then is it so necessary to use all capital letters? Well, aside from the obvious messages that CAPITAL LETTERS alone reveal to us, it is from the basic understanding that we are not reading our English like we normally do, such as how you are reading the words upon this page right now. When we are exploring the mighty mysterious truths of Lexigrams, we are in essence taking what is already in order, and shaking our alphabet up a bit. Yes, we are still writing out our phrases and prose-like spirals utilizing our English language, but it is not the same understanding as writing like I am writing to you now. When we write in Lexigram mode, we are decoding what has been presented to us "properly." The use of capitalization allows Lexigrams to be heard and seen, so that we don't miss any of the messages they want to reveal. Because everything in our lives seems to be so visual, there is an attention CAPITAL LETTERS get that lowercase letters simply do not. Look at the difference:

> capital letters
> all letters tell a real secret
> all letters seep real lies
> all letters set a real pace
> as letters are reset, letters tell a real tale
> all letters let a peace tale spiral

Just doesn't "grab" your attention as well, does it? Lexigrams are not normal ways of looking at things, so the capitalization is a true must when one wants to spiral those uncanny derivations that you'll more often than not find within your searches. Oh yes, there is that "spiral" word again. Linda Goodman coined this word as what the art of Lexigrams is truly all about, "spiraling." While some may consider Lexigrams just a fun and entertaining form of phrasing anagrams, this couldn't be further from the truth. As Linda clearly stated about them: "Lexigrams are not for amusement or intellectual exercise. They probe behind anagrams to uncover higher knowledge and wisdom, hiding—in-plain-sight, where many esoteric mysteries hide, unsuspected and therefore undiscovered. Most satisfying to those who master them, Lexigrams can verify what intuition has only hinted at concerning history, science, and people."[1] So when one spirals, it is the uncoiling of the real truth behind the subject matter at hand.

Over my years of research and personal consultations, probably the second most popular question I hear is, "Do you need to use all the words you anagram from the original title or name in every Lexigram phrase you derive?" Good question! The answer is no. Yet when you find yourself revisiting investigations, the next time you might be ready to see how some new message awaits to be revealed to you, and previously left out words may just come in handy in that next moment. By understanding that the art of Lexigrams is the phrasing of anagrams from a simple word, name, or title like poetry or prose to tell the true story or clues, one can simply begin by seeing how many different words can be listed from the topic at hand. While plenty of examples have been already revealed on how the phrasing works, let's get your Lexigram brain trained in the proper way.

Before getting into the rules that are meant to be broken that are behind the artistic analysis of Lexigrams, it is important to learn more on the fundamentals before engaging in your very own spiraling. Trust me, once you get savvy and awaken your own innate Lexigram ability, you'll be bound to spiral faster and faster. As with all things in life, practice in this case keeps you on the endless journey to PERFECTION, that I PRONE TO FREE IT, I CREEP INTO ONE FIT, ONCE I FREE IT I FREE TO TOP IT.

In beginning to allow you to become a poetic psychic of anagrams and then an ultimate Lexigram Master, it is best to approach how to utilize your PATIENCE, once again that encourages I IN A NICE PACE, I TAP IN AN ANCIENT PEACE, I CAN PACE A PAIN IN A TIE-IN. So as the real simple rules go, start with what will seem to be the act of playing a MEGA word GAME that will intrigue for an AGE. We are keeping it SIMPLE, so let's stick to starting first by listing the anagrams within. Remember, anagrams *only* utilize words from a word or title utilizing the same letters within. SIMPLE: SMILE, LIPS, LIP, PIES, PIE, MILES, PILES, PILE, ME, I, IS, LIES, LIE, LIMES, LIME, I'M, PIM, PIMS, PI, LIMP, LIMPS, SLIME, SLIP.

Now, it's obvious all of these anagrams do not have a relevant connection to the classic definition of what SIMPLE is known to mean. But, after taking the time to just look at the bigger picture of the word, I start to see things that come together that lend to the clues I was figuring I might find, thus the art of spiraling comes to aide in what I am meant to discover, keeping in mind as Linda told us about what is bound to happen when that Third Eye opens:

**SIMPLE**

- I'M SMILE PILES
- I SLIME LIES
- ME LIES SLIP ME LIPS
- MILES I PILE ME SMILE
- LIES LIMP ME
- LIES SLIP ME
- I PILE ME SMILE

What you'll learn is that it isn't necessary to utilize all the anagrams from any given word or names, as we'll have some truly uncanny Lexigram fun with in later chapters. But, it is essential to find positive ways to phrase your anagrams into messages that may not be classic English, though don't worry about sticking to the grammatical rules that apply in normal writing. Once more, to all you English teachers out there: my sincere apologies for any disruptions in your classrooms. This is all more of a relatively new SPIRITUAL adventure of tapping into our SPIRAL talents.

Oh, speaking of, let's look at this example: SPIRITUAL: SPIRIT, STAR, RITUAL, I, IS, ITS, IT, LIST, LIPS, TRIPS, TRIP, LUST, RUTS, RUT, ARTS, TRAILS, TRIALS, PAST, LAST, STRIP, PITS, PIT, RUST, RIPS, APT, TIPS, TIP, SIT.

### SPIRITUAL

- I IS A SPIRIT AS IS IT A STAR TRIP RITUAL
- I TRAIL ALL STAR ART
- I APT AS I SIT A SPIRAL TIP TRIP
- I PASS A PIT, A RUT, LUST & TRAPS
- I LIST PAST SPIRIT STAR TRIP RITUALS

The SPIRITUAL and the SPIRALing it brings is oh so much joy, isn't it? Definitely one of those words that can bring us such lovely potentials to choose from that blossoms rituals that serve the soul. Which now brings us to those choices once more. Free will is always any soul's option, and you'll discover that just like our astrological and numerological guidance proclaims, so too is free will granted from Lexigrams by being aware of them. So, now you should have a better idea on how Lexigrams do not need to use every anagram to be valid in their spiraling revelations.

The third most common question I get asked is, "Can you use the letters more than once in the anagrams you derive?" Now, I have seen how the original rule I learned that answers this question is one of those rules that seems to get bent just slightly more often than not. Just to be clear, you can always use letters over again in different words that originate from the subject at hand. Taking our example of SIMPLE: when I anagram MILES and SMILE, or PILE and PILES, I am utilizing the same letters again in separate words. When you phrase them, yes, the same letter absolutely can and will appear within the different anagrams composing the entire Lexigram phrases.

Now comes a chance to be a little rebellious. What you'll discover in your Lexigramming spirals is that often within the word or name you'll be examining, in certain cases, seemingly a letter or two is "missing" that would complete a thought or derive an anagram that makes sense to what those spiraling thoughts will be pointing to the truth about. One example of this is within PATIENCE. As we looked at before, I can derive the phrase I TAP IN AN ANCIENT PEACE. Now when you look at the word ANCIENT, notice the two N's. There aren't two N's in the original word PATIENCE, logically. Continuing on that logic, when one thinks of the word PATIENCE, we are indeed led to the thought—IN AN ANCIENT PEACE. Isn't utilizing PATIENCE something the "ANCIENT," meaning our dear wise and elderly souls, seem to have and teach to those with less experience?

The original set of rules states that when adding a letter that is not already there within your word or name subject at hand—that the additional letters you may wish to add to make up a complete thought or more flowing one should be in parentheses. So, from PATIENCE, I should have put the second N as so: ANCIE(N)T. We also see this in the SPIRITUAL example when phrasing I TRAIL ALL STAR ART, and I PASS A PIT, A RUT, LUST & TRAPS. The ALL and PASS don't have the second L and S in the word. Yet, these two words are important to convey the hidden messages SPIRITUAL wishes to convey to me. The SPIRTUAL certainly covers ALL and with the interesting derivations of PIT, RUT, LUST, and TRAPS, my guess is the SPIRITUAL recommends surely it is best that we PASS them.

In the beginning of my Lexigram days, I did apply this rule. But over time, I soon realized this was where I had to question what I had learned and develop my own theories. It became more and more apparent to me when that second letter you may be looking for is already found within your name or title, the need to put it in parentheses is not necessary. Why? Because the letters' energy already exists in the word, and when we add another of the same, we are only intensifying that existing energy. Doubling up on a letter that the word already contains isn't something you'll always need to do, yet it is "safe" to make on occasion (and these should be rare, but if your spiral goes there, see how essential it may be to the truth at hand), to get the point across you see that the original word wants you to discover. I find in relating the flow of the messages, the added parentheses in these same letter cases breaks up the phrase unnecessarily. See the differences here from PATIENCE and SPIRITUAL:

1. I IN AN ANCIENT PEACE PACE
2. I IN AN ANCIE(N)T PEACE PACE

1. I TRAIL ALL STAR ART; I PASS A PIT, A RUT, LUST & TRAPS
2. I TRAIL AL(L) STAR ART; I PAS(S) A PIT, A RUT, LUST & TRAPS

It may seem silly, but the visual of reading the first options is smoother and doesn't break up the word, so it becomes more challenging to receive the importance of the given Lexigram message. Now, this is just one small tweak that I have learned works well when explaining Lexigrams to others, and believe me, once the spiraling bug gets you, you'll be telling everyone you know about it. Remember, this particular "tweak" only works with adding additional letters that match one that already exists within the original word, name, or title you are examining. It is important to keep in mind, as well, that you don't necessarily want to add those second letters unless you find it is important to completing the thought and message that your subject matter wishes to communicate. I will repeat, *adding a possible second letter should only be utilized when it is essential to making a phrase more clear, while emphasizing the truth that the word, name, or title is about.*

Let's see how it works to add letters that aren't already part of the word you are looking at. You'll find especially when you get to investigating people's names and longer titles that this will also come in handy. So, sticking to our present example of PATIENCE, let's explore how adding letters can be of benefit, and when it is best to just allow a mind to stretch itself and be open to the possibilities. PATIENCE, as we know, derives the phrase, I IN A NICE PACE. Going back to the list of anagrams we can list from PATIENCE, IT is a smaller word that pops out at me. Now, IT alone doesn't reveal much about PATIENCE. Yet, when I want to make those easy flowing phrases to compose my Lexigram prose, by taking the word IT and adding a letter that cannot be found in PATIENCE, I can get a little more savvy to smooth out a thought.

◉   I (S)IT IN A NICE PACE, I (S)IT IN A NICE PEACE, PEACE
    I(S) PATIENCE.

Back to the visual of it all. In as much as we can get over the parenthesized S's in this case and still receive the messages from PATIENCE here, I have learned that altering the parentheses rule can be done, while not breaking up the flow of our minds absorbing the real truth at hand. So, I have adapted the simplicity of underlining the additional letter(s) you may need to utilize to make those phrases just as appealing to the eye.

⊙ I <u>S</u>IT IN A NICE PACE, I <u>S</u>IT IN A NICE PEACE,
PATIENCE I<u>S</u> IN PEACE.

Better, right? The very word PATIENCE leads one to <u>S</u>IT down and be in that PEACE place, IN A NICE PACE. And there it sits! There are plenty of times you will need to interject missing letters to make a point more clear. Should it so please you to choose not to underline them, and you like the parentheses method instead, then it is your total free-will to do so (and if you like the optional use of lowercase letters in these cases, this can be done as well). As much as any given RULES LURE US and may be SURE things, the importance of this indication in your Lexigram spiraling needs to be implemented in the way that is most comfortable for you. While I also began using parentheses in my beginnings of the art of Lexigramming, I have had great results in the simplification of underlining them when necessary. This rule is one that may not necessarily need to be totally broken, but in how I like to tweak, this option still is in alignment with what guidelines we do need to follow in all of our Lexigram fun.

Now that we've covered some basics, let's move on to some other important things you need to know before you are endlessly fascinated to want to continuously dive into spiraling your Lexigrams as much as I am. Linda Goodman noted some other guidelines that are not to be overlooked. We all know there are only 26 different letters that make up our English alphabet. With the examples we have displayed thus far, the words we have used have had, at most, 9 different letters, taking CAPITAL LETTERS for instance.

It's obvious there are more than 9 letters within, but when you see how many double up, or triple up in the T's case, in essence you are dealing with only 9 separate letters. Most words you'll choose to ponder will be within this same understanding. Going back to our example of SPIRITUAL and PATIENCE, the first has 9 total letters, but 8 different ones, while the latter contains 8, and only 7 are different.

Why are we worried about the number of letters? With only 26 letters to choose from in the alphabet, there is another rule we do need to follow. This will come more into play later on when you get into the intriguing tales you'll be spelling from longer titles and people's names that you know, but we are stating the rules here, so remember to keep track of them for the best results! In any name you will find yourself examining, it must contain no more than 15 separate letters. You can have over 15 letters in any given name or phrase, but the count on the ones that do not repeat, such as in our previous examples, need to be kept to the 15 limit. Otherwise, going over that letter confines, you can spell all sorts of things, as you will have over half of the alphabet at your disposal. As Linda also noted, with "more than fifteen separate and different letters of the alphabet, you could form just about every word in the dictionary, and your Lexigram won't reveal anything personal or reliable."[2]

However, in knowing how those rules can be bent, it is interesting (as you'll see in the historical evidence) that, even with longer titles or names, the energy of a name can still tell the tale when it is over the limit of 15 separate letters. We may be getting a little ahead of ourselves, but consider the title given to our Gemini 29 President, whose life was taken so tragically—just 3 letters over the 15 different limit once he attached his position to it:

### PRESIDENT JOHN FITZGERALD KENNEDY

◉ TAKES SHOTS IN HEAD ON A FRIDAY IN A CAR PARADE TO HIS DEATH

I'm sorry if that revelation is a bit too shocking, but history has proven itself that this is indeed true. You are going to see just how intimate Lexigrams can get in the many pages to follow, and how terribly important choosing a name or title is in life. But in getting back to how the rules ultimately work, there are 18 different letters that compose JFK's title as PRESIDENT. By the way, after opening my awareness of Lexigrams, I have always wondered how anyone would eagerly sign up for a title that has the word DIES IN DEEP SIN, TIED IN PRIDE DESIRE in it, but I won't tangent too much on that one. There will be a little more political chatter later on in chapters 4 and 11. So we find 18 separate letters making up JFK's title, which is 3 over our limit. Yet, this is another example of how those rules can be bent. Why in the world can I derive that phrase? It's just plain eerie, yet it is the complete truth.

Before we move on to other fundamental rules, there is an essential rule when you are Lexigramming that I have implemented into my own practice, and this is one

I consider to be one of the most important rules to follow. It is evident that Lexigrams tell us the bare truth, as the historical example above proves. But, *it is against any spiritual law to predict or indicate death and dying when examining a living entity.* Later chapters will reveal how history backs up the uncanny truths Lexigrams can unfold, but those are only able to be written and talked about after those actions leave the present moment, and become part of the past. When you decide to seek the hidden truths beyond the words that can be found in any dictionary, and you are examining a living being, should you find that Lexigrams reveal and indicate death, these are not meant to be focused on or presented as a prediction. With any living person, this art of telling the tale from the name is meant to discover the truth that lifts the soul up to its highest purpose.

Back to the lighter rules that you still need to know to open up your Lexigramming talents. We've covered the letter limits that keep us from getting too lost in not understanding the messages we will receive. Now, our alphabet is also divided into what we all know from English class as consonants and vowels, where our consonants are 21 or 20 when we use the alphabet law that there are 5 vowels with the possible 6 (with the sometimes Y). So, when we look at our names and titles, the number of these is also to be taken into consideration. There is a vowel limit as well. The more vowels in any given name or title will also, as Linda told us, allow us to spell almost any word that doesn't make the truth be seen in clarity. She laid down the rule that if there are more than 4 out of the 5 normal vowels (not including Y), then you shouldn't consider your Lexigams to be valid.

"If the original word, name or phrase contains five vowels, it does not want to be lexigramed, and is too complex to allow you to learn anything from it,"[3] stated Goodman on this point. Once more, I discovered numerous times how this rule is another that just didn't always apply in my spiraling, as the Lexigram revelations I could derive most definitely *did* validate the truth I was searching for. Keep reading to chapter 4 and beyond and there are more than enough examples where this rule proves itself that indeed it can be broken, as history has already been written.

Linda also noted the presence of being able to spiral the words YES or NO from the subject you may be seeking the truth of. When the word YES is in the phrases and prose you compose, then the phrases derived are all true. You'll most certainly notice you can derive both the negative and the positive from the subjects you'll examine. Equally from being able to anagram the words NO or NOT, then the phrases are not true about that word, person, or entity. However, going back to how these rules are meant to evolve and change, let's look at examples of how this may not always apply.

When we look to the word ASPIRATION, one can easily see the word NO within. But look what happens when I Lexigram some truths about ASPIRATION: I ANOINT IT IN SPIRIT, I TRIP ON A STAR, I TRAIN TO SPIN ON A SPIRIT STAR, I POINT TO SPIRIT AS I SOAR. Here's where I question the validity of this yes or no rule Linda brought to our attention. The phrases listed are indeed the truth about ASPIRATION and I do not believe because we can spell NO from this word that this means these derivations are to be cancelled out. Again, the countless examples within the pages to follow will have you equally questioning this as well.

Let's take the word DESTINY, a word that spells YES. DESTINY is a tricky word I find, for so many people always want to find their own. Be careful with this one, as DESTINY: TIES IN SIN, DIES IN SIN, TIED IN SIN, IN NITE I SIT IN SIN, YET I DIE IN SIN, YES? If the YES here supposedly affirms these messages may be true, then I for one, definitely have no need to seek my destiny. That's about as silly as wanting to be in PARADISE. I REAP A RAPE, I DIE AS I ASIDE IN PRIDE, I REAP A SAD ERA, I PARADE AS I RAID. How many times have you heard someone say that they want to be in PARADISE? Not exactly a very happy place for one's aspirations, is it? One thing you'll be very aware of by the time you finish this book is the wisdom of our words, and that we have all the power within our free will—and most importantly within our free thinking—to make proper choices that will attract the energy to make our lives more fulfilled and enriched.

Ok, we've almost got you fully prepared to go on our Lexigram safari. But first, you need to have the two other star secrets that are vitally important to open your ever-spiraling mind to how you'll be able to make the most out of the wisdom Lexigrams are here to share with us. Without tuning into our mighty planets above that govern both our astrological and numerological data, the tales we will see from within the names and titles to follow won't make entirely as much sense to you as their truths are shown. So, we've got one more piece of the star secret puzzle to reveal. Before we journey to all sorts of places, people, and things where the truth has been hiding upon our great earth, let's take a spin around our galaxy and see what mysteries are awaiting for us to find them.

Chapter 3

# THE INTRICATE LINK OF LEXIGRAMS TO ASTROLOGY AND NUMEROLOGY

*"Lexigrams revive your sixth sense, which will in turn, gently coax your Third Eye—allowing you to then uncover layer after layer of mysteries swirling around you—and the enigma of Heaven and Hell and everything in between, including the intricacies and complexities of human relationships."* —LINDA GOODMAN

So, Dear Reader, you've got the rules all in place, and now, we are ready to really dive into some of the more ultimately fascinating ways Lexigrams are here to serve us in their uncanny wisdom. It is so nice that they wish to be of SERVICE to us in this way, granting that I RISE, I SERVE, I RE-VERSE VICES, I SEVER VICES, I REVISE, I EVER SEE. The time is now to focus on your Third Eye abilities and be open to the possibilities, for when one decides to IMAGINE: I AIM IN A MAIN GAIN, I AIM IN A MAGI GAIN, I AM IN A MAIN GAIN, I AM A MAGI, I AM A GENIE, I AM AIMING IN AN ENIGMA, I GAIN A MINI GEM, IN A GAIN I AM! You just can't deny the magical energy here!

As your Lexigram abilities become stronger and stronger, undoubtedly you'll find yourself spending more time in REFLECTION: I FREE TOIL IN RELIEF, I LET IT

FREE, I ENTICE IT IN CENTER TO LIFT IT, I LET IT ENFORCE, I LET IT REFINE, I ORIENT TO FEEL IT FREE. The joys of your freedom that will emerge as you are CREATING will grant that I IN A GREAT GAIN, I ACT IN A NEAT NICE GRACE, I AIN'T IN A CAGE, I AIN'T IN A RAGE, I RING IN A GREAT GRACE. I really shouldn't be giving you all the answers, but it should excite you in any case to know how much this energy will allow you to CREATIVELY discover anything you wish: I CREATE IT ALIVE, I LIVE IT REAL, YEARLY I TRAVEL, I CREATE VERACITY, I CREATE A VERY VERY ACTIVE REALITY.

In this day and age that we are presently living in, we are preparing for one of the greatest shifts in our collective consciousness at the time this book is now published, getting each and every one of us ever closer to ENLIGHTENMENT. Attaining it is more important that ever, and for all you Ladies reading right now, the Lexigrams sincerely apologize for excluding you from being mentioned: GENTLEMEN— LET THE LIGHT IN IN TIME, MELT TELLING THE LIE IN INTENT, MINGLE IN THE LIGHT, LET ME LET LIGHT IN. While I understand that either sex is completely capable of enlightenment, perhaps our feminine population probably was purposely left out here due to their innate nurturing abilities, so in that KNOWING: I NOW WON, I NOW OWNING IN A WIN, I KNOW I NOW GO ON IN A WIN, I NOW KNOW I OWN IT.

Now, aside from the endless magic Lexigrams shower upon us, there are other sources of knowledge at our fingertips that are intricately linked to this form of seeing the truth. For certain you've already heard about them, I'd imagine.

Allow me to re-introduce two other elixirs in life that are equally here to serve us, Astrology and Numerology. As I have learned from the legendary Linda Goodman, it is an invaluable benefit to understand how these two wisdoms are undeniably important when we want to make the most out of our Lexigram adventures. If you are interested at all in truly becoming your very own psychic in life, then keep on reading, because the relationship between how Astrology, Numerology, and Lexigrams work together is nothing short of miraculous.

What, you may ask, makes this statement true? How in the world does the art of decoding names, words, and titles have anything to do with the ancient knowledge that Astrology and Numerology provide? I am so happy, number one, that you'd ask these important questions. Number two, it is my pleasure to share the answers that I can translate to you within this chapter. Number three is the pure fun and wild ride through the cosmos that we'll be taking showing the ever-fascinating connections between these three wisdoms. Now it is absolutely time to have your Third Eye open to the possibilities and ready for action! While I will not explain every minute detail that relates to Astrology and Numerology, my hope and intention is you'll definitely have a much clearer understanding of how to be your very own seer in your own life. So let's not waste anymore of that MITE TIME, shall we?

Anytime I talk about the connection of Astrology and Numerology, the first place to start is with THE PLANETS: THESE SEE ALL TALES, PLANETS PLAN ALL AS they TELL ALL PLANS, THESE HELP AS A HEAL, SENT AS A NEAT PLAN THAT HELPS. What binds these two ancient forms of self-knowledge is those mighty planets above. Whether you are looking at things such as a Sun Sign, Moon sign, ascendant (rising sign), Karmic Path, Lifepath, or Personal Year cycle, you are in essence tapping into the channel of a particular planet that governs over that star guidance energy (like a frequency does over the radio waves). The planets are very special tools that are here to serve us, equal in weight to the insights Lexigrams ultimately provide. When you begin to understand the true relationship between the three star secrets as I have come to coin them—Astrology, Numerology, and Lexigrams—furnish any one with an undeniable advantage to discovering all the hidden mysteries from our vast Universe that cast their affects and energies to us here upon the earth.

"The Star Secrets Wheel" diagram on page 48 is a helpful guide to aide you in the visual of seeing how Astrology and Numerology are practically inseparable subjects. These should always be considered alongside your Lexigram derivations, as you will undoubtedly find the planets' messages within names that you choose to spiral from. Over my years of utilizing these three forms of analysis, the value of seeing how they work uncannily together has proven itself time and time again. But, as I was once told, don't just take my word for it. There is no better teacher than what personal experience and application can give anyone. So, without further adieu, let's get to it and bring you into a better understanding so you can go out there and seek the truth and find the answers to the mysteries in the Universe you are looking to solve.

What became apparent to me through how Lexigrams speak to us is that they certainly are tapped into a deep

# The Star Secrets Wheel

*The wheel highlights the connection between astrology and numerology,
and demostrates how they relate through planetary energy.*

INTERACT and EXPLORE The Star Secrets Wheel at:

## *www.sharitastar.com*

*Wheel design by Aarathi Venkataraman*

awareness about our mighty planets above. You'll find plenty of examples in the later chapters of how people's names, more often than not, when Lexigrammed, will derive phrases that indicate such things as their particular Zodiac guidance and, coincidentally enough, their individual numerological analysis as well, aside from the tale of the life. It is said that when we come back to this earth and choose another KARMIC PATH (and pardon me if I extend the idea of past lives; I won't ask you to believe this, but recommend keeping the mind open to the possibility of them), that we do, through our soul's agreement, indeed choose our date of birth, our parents, and guide them to the names we are given. Our KARMIC PATH: A RICH KARMA MAP I TAP, THAT I MARCH; A CHART I CHARM AT; I PICK A KARMA TRIP, is the very calendar date of the day alone that we are born to in any given month. Lexigrams also have an uncanny way of depicting past lives from the present name we carry in this life. But, before I yet again get too ahead of myself, back to how those planets work, because time is of the essence here.

Planets, as you more than likely know from somewhere in your previous schooling, are always in motion above us. These more than heavenly bodies in our Universe move through a system known as the Zodiac. Planets travel through the constellations, the very patterns and pictures our ancient masters depicted from the night sky. They do this through the very specific mathematical calculations of a 360-degree circle as they orbit in their varying ways (minus Pluto, who encompasses all in his elliptical orbit). So, in case you haven't already heard, The Zodiac, or Astrology, is indeed a mathematical science. If you've ever picked up the newspaper and read your horoscope, you may even already know what sign you are. Tying it all into Numerology, we will discover these same planets shed quite a bit of light upon this less mathematically complicated science of self-knowledge.

There are 10 planets that cast their energies on the 10 single digits and 12 different Zodiac signs, and each of these occupies a 30-degree space upon the Zodiac Wheel, which is measured from 0 to 29 degrees. You'll notice on the Star Secrets Wheel that the 0 is represented and watched over by, yes, the still-dwarf planet Pluto. (I won't start a heated discussion with an astronomer here, but Pluto was always the smallest planet examined in Astrology anyway. We'll come to learn, however, his affects are quite the opposite in their magnitude here on earth.) PLUTO is undoubtedly the one TO PULL OUT. Wherever Pluto is, he is the mighty transformer and he brings us regeneration and long-term changes through his seemingly "small" energy.

Have you ever met a SCORPIO soul? These beings have come incarnated as the mighty Eagle to soar above it all and manage every detail of the big picture in life. Whilst they are wise to ignore the potential of that deadly sting best given by a Scorpion, they come to know the intensity of transformation in their lives. Lovers of all that is esoteric and mysterious, these natives see more than their fair share of death and rebirth in a SCORPIO lifetime. Funny to note that many police officers and detectives seem to fall under this sign, and wouldn't you know IS PRO COPS, IS COP PROS await to be found. With the secretive and protected lives most Scorpio Eagles lead, you won't get too much more information out of this one.

Let's bring it back to center with the SUN. Oh yes, that's US! The Sun is the center of it all, the "planet" that is really a star, but the one that when looking at anyone's birth chart is the place to look for your identity, your Sun Sign. Astrologers interpret the Sun, even though technically it is a star, just as they do a planet. Our life force, which aids in the survival of the earth as a whole, comes from the Sun, the being around which all other planets align. I'll bet you might already know which number has the privilege of being governed by the one in the center of it all. That would be the ONE! Looking to the Sun, it's all ONE EON. Remember from chapter 1 when we talked about the real meaning behind what being as ONE EON is all about.

Surely you've seen those people in life who take charge and center-stage who are LEOS. Gravitating to a little Spanish, SOL is the same meaning as the Sun, and Leos get the honor of being in some kind of spotlight in their life. SOLE also can mean being solo, or one, and thus you'll find those ONE Karmic Paths acting out their roles in life alone, as they know nothing else but how to bring forth initiation as they carry our their karmic agreement. Now, maybe I've just said something that confused you. Did you ask what's a ONE Karmic Path? Oh, I am so glad you asked! One Karmic Paths are anyone who is born on a calendar date of the month that reduces to one, thus 1st, 10th, 19th, or the 28th. These natives, no matter what Sun Sign they are born to, will carry the energy of the Sun with them, just as our Leo Zodiac pals, as they radiate warmth through their outward persona and talents in life. Now, as much as I know Leos and Ones love getting all of this attention, it's time to move on, as we've got a lot of ground to cover to get your planetary thinking caps in order.

And off to the MOON we go! Things definitely shift to the realm of EMOTIONS whenever we are heading to the MOON. Well, how could they not when those EMOTIONS: TIES ME INTO MOON, TIES ME IN NITE TIME, SOON I EMOTE IT IN ONE EON. But of course the Moon also falls into the same understanding as our Sun Star, which isn't technically a planet either, but a satellite of our earth. Yet, like the mighty affects of Pluto, have you ever been just a wee-bit emotional or "loony" on a Full Moon? Now, if you are a TWO, you may find you TOW your emotions around with you a little too much. You are a Two Karmic Path if born to the calendar date of the 2nd, 11th, 20th, or 29th. As a Two, you are ever-guided by your sensitivity and your urge to nurture, and what a fascinating imagination you have! You can truly make all the other numbers jealous, especially if they are Scorpios. But I'm not here to single any sign out; let it be known that we are all affected by every sign in the Zodiac in our own individual ways.

Some of the most family-oriented and emotional people you may know are also CANCERS, who CAN RACE AS CARERS. One of the things they need to avoid is thinking they ARE NEAR SCARES. Moon influenced natives are in the soul struggle to combat their emotions, calm their fears, and, for heavens sake, stop worrying about everything! Now, not all Cancers nor Two Karmic Paths are basket-cases, but they do, in that way their symbol THE CRAB, who BARE A RARE CARE with HEART, is depicted, have a tough exterior that they present, but on the inside they are so sensitive and need to cast off emotional issues more often than not. Then, they can let their free will guide them to all of the wonderfully charitable acts of kindness you always can find these natives behind. While they do love to spend their time taking care of others in need, they are more than eager to go back to home base, the place they cherish most in life.

Which is not what you'll find when looking to JUPITER. This planet, who rules over expansion, idealism, higher education, good fortune, and foreign travel, is the one to PUT IT/U RITE, TIP UR JET TRIP, UP U RITE. Whenever Jupiter is present, there are luck and blessings abounding, and there are trips you definitely take, whether physically or in the mind. Just ask any THREE Karmic Path, who adores moving from HERE TO THERE. Those born on any calendar date that falls on the 3rd, 12th, 21st, or 30th will surely tell you they are always in movement uniting it all in three, as they innately grasp the connection of mind, body, and spirit. These natives are the philosophers as well as our comedians, who cannot stand a lie and will always tell it to you straight rather than in circles. They can excel and multi-task in their constant state of movement, and there is a healthy dose of optimism that accompanies this ever-growing energy. Jupiter allows us to reach far beyond our comfort zones, and will with brutal honesty bring on new ways of expressing what we truly believe.

If you've ever been near a SAGITTARIUS, undoubtedly they have left you in brighter spirits through an act of their generous nature. A STAR RAISES US, GAITS START US, A STAR AT ARTS, A STAR AT TRUST are just a mere glimpse at what any ARCHER, who can REACH while aiming those arrows high, has in store for you. Next to

Leos, Sagittarius energy is by far the next in line to excel at creativity, and where it goes is as limitless as Jupiter, the largest planet we study, can go. Again our Lexigrams are on their mark as we see that the word GAITS is within SAGITTARIUS, as The Archer's symbol is the depiction of the half-man/half-horse, whose movement is recognized in this way. You'll find any Jupiter native, whether they be a Three or an Archer, equally excelling in the area of sports, especially those where running is required. Above all else, Jupiter always wants to have oodles and oodles of fun wherever they adventure in the big wide world that they consider their home.

Now, are you ready for the unexpected that URANUS wishes to bring to the planetary mix? RUNS "UR" SUN, RUNS US. Hmmm. Here's an example of how Lexigrams can truly stretch the mind—I take this as when Uranus casts the unusual our way we typically need to RUN! This original planet loves breaking up the normalcy of things, and is not afraid in any way of throwing around surprises. You may feel like running when Uranus is present, for he will bring on obstacles, but in the ultimate lessons that all FOUR Karmic Paths are here to learn, any challenge is only an opportunity to jump over another hurdle. FOR OUR whole human race, these natives deeply seek to unite people in a sense of brotherhood and sisterhood, and typically keep their judgments to themselves. Perhaps you know these calendar date folks, those born on the 4th, 13th, 22nd, or 31st of any given month. You can recognize a Four easily because they are well ahead of their time, always prophesying about the future with their innovative minds. They possess a tolerance that the rest of the numerical Karmic Paths only dream of. This is why they can take on the sudden changes that the energy of Uranus unpredictably brings and typically overcome them with a smile.

Our AQUARIUS natives equally share the unusual gifts that Uranus brings. Sometimes seen AS A SQUAR<u>E</u>, like the Fours, these air sign souls bring structure and foundation to our lives. When you are a WATER BEARER, you are most certain to BREA<u>K</u> A BARR<u>I</u>ER, BE A RAW BEAT, BE A BREWER, REAR A RARE ART. It's amazing to realize the break-through inventions Aquarius arrives at with their innate ability to bring new life to what is old and stale in the world. They are so busy at times in their individual way of seeking improvement, they can appear to be raw to others, and are not exactly your touchy-feely types. (Best to bring in a Cancer if you truly want to be held and rocked to sleep). Aquarius time is when we get into the deepest part of winter, so it's really not their fault they present a cold front at times. Besides, when you are the sign responsible to make the world a better place, intimacy wouldn't be your strongest point either. You'll always find The Water Bearer willing to share in an airy, intellectual, and friendly conversation about life, but don't expect them to want to hold your hand.

If you really want to carry on an endless conversation, don't be shy and simply ask MERCURY to come on over for a visit. He'll definitely CURE UR MERCY while he CUE U MERRY and bring on a MERRY CURE. Now, you may want to logically toss him out the window when he's retrograding and playing his typical tricks (we'll be getting to this backward understanding in just a few more pages), but then you wouldn't be adhering to the mercy he is meant to shower upon you. Our Messenger planet is the one to have around to make sure you get all of your communications, thinking, and mentality in order. Think of the people you know born on any FIVE Karmic Path, those that VIE to be clever and adapt to just about any kind of change that comes their way with a big smile on their face. They won't be shy to display their FIE when something needs fixing either, as they question away with a what IF. You know exactly whom I am talking about if you know someone born on any calendar date that vibes to the 5th, 14th, or 23rd of any given month. These Mercury souls are here to move the masses and bring permanent changes that require a swift energy you may find hard to keep up with.

You may also know some other Mercury natives as THE TWINS: THE HE IS SHE/SHE IS HE TWINES, SENT IN WINS, SET IN THE NEWS, SEEN IN THE WISE WINS; otherwise known as your dear GEMINI friends. Linda Goodman was first to call them a MINI GEM. Even though you may see them for periods of time and then wonder where in the world they have disappeared to, you'll have to realize you've got two mini gems that you are dealing with. But how else could just one person come up with all of the innovative ideas they are here to let us know about that bring such positive change to our world? They'll be the first person to tell you the latest news, trends, and wisdom that needs to be shared, as the thoughts they receive come from everywhere. You'll find they'll practically go anywhere that air exists. Ever friendly, you could talk about anything with a Gemini, who'll be probably doing (and more than likely analyzing) something completely different as they converse with you. Talk about clever!

When you need Mercury's energy to be in a more grounded form, you should seek out one of your VIRGO friends, who will undoubtedly bring you some VIGOR. They will politely be a true GO-GIV<u>E</u>R, as the placid VIRGIN GIV<u>E</u> IN any moment they can to be of service. While a Virgo can possess a shyness not found in Gemini, you can be sure the winds of change still will find them traveling where they may upon the earth. You'll typically find a genuine purity within a Virgo, who enjoys keeping everything neat, tidy, and as healthy as possible. When they aren't nit-picking over some small detail, wallowing in self-doubt, or turned off by rude behavior, Virgos will gladly help serve you and bring order to your life in the most efficient way possible. That just sounds perfect, doesn't it?

But if it is not logic and perfection you seek, and you prefer to indulge in romance and beauty, then it is VENUS that you should invite over for tea. S<u>A</u>VE SUN VENUES, VENUS S<u>A</u>VE SUN, VENUS S<u>A</u>VE US (again, a little shy she is to reveal much). While Jupiter may govern over the numerical vibration of the very word LOVE (carrying a Name Expression of the 21/3; keep on reading to find out what a Name Expression is), Venus, of all the planets, values it highly and denotes how you will feel it in the natal birth chart. Whatever it is that you adore and honor in life, Venus is there to attract you to it. Holding to the finest tastes in life, going beyond the material you'll find the lover of harmony planet to be blessing everyone surrounding her with fairness and diplomacy. Find a SIX Karmic Path and they can show you the way to find peace with what simply IS. These natives are born to any calendar date of the month that falls on the 6th, 15th, or 24th. Like our

Cancers, you'll definitely get plenty of affection and absorb some femininity when spending time with the number of compassion. There won't be any fighting or fuss, and if you are looking for a companion to go to museums with, take a romantic Six with you.

Or just ask one of your TAURUS friends along. With these souls, UR A STAR, STAR R US, as they'll surely get you grounded and rooted into something resourceful and persevering like the ARTS. They have all the patience in the world coupled with a practical, tranquil, and conservative nature that deeply enjoys what is down-to-earth. Spending time in Mother Nature's pleasures equally suits THE BULL'S stance, who can most often be found enjoying THE BEST while standing in front of art, or anything extremely beautiful, classical, and sensual. Rare to take risks, you'll find that your Taurus alliances will show you how to proceed with caution. Looking at the present state of the mighty changes that are speeding up our world, will all Taurus leaders please stand up?

Then take a LIBRA with you so together you can BAIL ALL AIL, BAIL ALL LIAR, with the freshness of this AIR sign. When you have THE SCALES balanced, then we can all SEE THE HEAL, LET THE HEAL SCALE, LET THE HEALS LAST. While a Libra can find themselves to be a bit wishy-washy when those scales are tipped, you definitely want to have their typically friendly and diplomatic way of reaching idealism handy. One way to peace is through this air-guided intelligence that truly only desires to bring harmony and grace to all that they touch. Venus gracefully influences these natives to enjoy musical pleasures, relationships, and all kinds of cooperative acts. Whenever you need the fair judge in life, make sure you have the negotiating talents of a Libra by your side.

Then you can move on to take just about any inner psyche situation by taking solitude in NEPTUNE, who can surely PUT IT IN TUNE. The one on one love you learn from Venus then can be showered out to the Universe as this planet sympathizes with all of humanity's sorrows. When you need to tune in, the mystic planet will grant you the seclusion to meditate and gather up your inspiration while your intuition is surely next to unfold. You, too, can become clairvoyant and tap into those higher states of consciousness. Just ask your SEVEN Karmic Path friends who SEE EVEN, those born on the 7th, 16th, or 25th day of any given calendar month. A SEVEN always EVENS it all out because they are brilliant at knowing how valuable it is to spend time on the self, and if you want to learn how to be SILENT and really LISTEN, these older souls are capable healers ready to help you turn dreams into reality.

If you need further help in the spirituality department, call upon a PISCES to put the PEACE PIECES together with you and, like a Six, just be with what already IS. PISCES make fantastic SPIES, as they are complete addicts when it comes to any mystery to be solved. The energies within their Zodiac playground is as vast as the waters of any ocean, and the deeper the better so THE FISHES can escape. THE FISH SHIFTS IT, THE FISH SETS IT, THE FISH SEES IT (just like their Neptune Seven pals). But when these natives come back from their psychological dives, they are always ready to perform and entertain you with their mysticism. When they aren't confused or in self-deceptions, the psychic channels they can bring are profound and may be hard to believe; but, more often than not, their intuition is right on the money.

Oh, did someone mention money? You better TURN to SATURN to be able to save it. TURNS A STAR ART, RANTS AT "UR" SUN, SATURN STUN US. Whatever needs responsibility, discipline, toil, and endurance in life, you'll find this karmic adjustor planet right by your side (hopefully not cracking a whip over your head). Ambition is Saturn's passion, for how else can things be established that are truly meant to last? While you'll find those Neptune souls chock-full of wisdom about how to be with the self, the wisdom that Saturn grants will structure your life with complete efficiency and a thoroughness you'll find with no other planet in our vast Universe. You know them, your EIGHT Karmic Path worker-bees in life. These born on the 8th, 17th, or 26th of any given calendar month innately TIE THE "HITE," GET THE TIE, HIT IT. When you need a bit of strategy and organization, you'll find the perfect connection with the Eight, who will lead the way to showing you how to have self-control, maintain financial security, and learn from all of your lessons in life. These careful counselors always need to balance more fun with the work they are in a constant direction to achieve, and it might be your karmic obligation to help them, in return, to lighten up!

If you need a further dose of authority, turn then to a CAPRICORN. They'll appear that they are IN NO PAIN, IN NO PAIR, because that hard work is the realistic thing to focus on. Like our Scorpios, a many CAPRICORN become a COP IN NO NAP. Whether a cop or not, you'll rarely find a GOAT snoozing, for they just GOT TO GO GO AT IT! Going back to that IN NO PAIR revelation, that's another typical Goat trait, to be single, because if all they do is stay self-absorbed in their reserved and prudent lives, the perfect partner is rare to fit in. Yet, if you need some focus, you can depend on this fatherly sign to give you the most reliable and professional advice. Those Goats that don't labor in pessimism will always be the ones that bring the material into established forms that serve the social classes on earth with structures that are meant to last.

And last, but certainly not in the slightest way least on our planetary journey, is the courageous MARS! We'll talk about those RAMS in a minute. The mighty MARS who eagerly is at ARMS when anyone else says I AM here! Wherever the pioneer planet is, you'll find plenty of impulse, self-starting, force, exertion, and motivation. If only Mars had an E we'd see the ME there too, as Mars knows all too well about the self when it comes to the ego. The virtue of patience is something you may not want to learn from a Mars native, till they truly have a grasp on it themselves. But if you are looking for action, competition, strength, and adventure, it'll be easy to distract them with the right argument. Conflict can be enjoyed by any NINE, who will just dive right on IN! (Usually head-first.) Yet, these people you know born on the 9th, 18th, or 27th day of any given month will penetrate right to the core of any situation with their strong leadership skills and, hopefully, without too much defiance or obstinance. That Mars energy needs to be switched to that of courage for these natives to ever succeed in their ultimate finalizations. You'll find a Nine behind anything that is about to be completed, and if you honestly appreciate them, their determination to finish gets motivated all the more.

Which slightly differs from the energy that guides their Zodiac starters, the ARIES. You all know those "I" types I'm talking about. But you will find the MARS RAMS out there, those ARIES souls, to RAISE ERAS AS I RISE, for these souls tend to start way more things than they ever seem to finish. AS AN ARIES I IS I, and you'll typically find the Ram in a flourish of self-assertions. Equally in competition with a Nine to get over their anger explosions, patience is the key to keeping their compulsive and rash energies from becoming too foolhardy. An Aries is best to put on any task where exploration and adventure will be part of the fun. You know that friend of yours who is always asking A LOT of questions? Ask them when their birthday is and you more than likely will find they've got Mars driving them to satisfy their curiosity. They love anything that deals with their own head, and often even into their wiser and elderly years, carry on with a childlike wonder that is still thrilled with taking on daring pursuits.

Well, I don't know about you, but I think that was a pretty daring pursuit we've just been on! Now, do planets, signs, and numbers make a bit more sense in their innate connectedness? There is even more that numbers have to share with us that undoubtedly could fill up a whole other book alone. But one more thing that will be handy for you to know, to understand better the endless Lexigram examples to follow in this book, is one other numerological understanding known as your LIFEPATH. This number, will tell you how I APT TO FILE THE PATH, THE PATH I HELP FAITH and where you find THE PATH I HEAL LIFE that you are walking down in this incarnation. You'll notice the Karmic Path influence will denote the energy behind your personality, abilities, and health, kind of like a "numerical Sun Sign." But with the Lifepath—which is simply determined by adding up all of the digits in your birthday and then reducing to a singular number—you'll find your own "yellow brick road" (which you may, if on a 9 Lifepath, for example, want to instead paint a brilliant fiery red) that you are meant to follow for your best results all throughout your entire life.

Even though these planets affect each and every HEART that has ever lived upon this EARTH, they still make up a small part of the entire Universe at large. When we tap into what is UNIVERSAL: I LEARN I LIVE IN REAL VALUES, I SAIL IN A REAL SUN AS I LIVE. Here's to living up to what all our planetary guidance requests of all of us, which truly starts by recognizing what talents and abilities your Sun Sign is here to illuminate your identity with. But we definitely don't stop there. There are layers and layers of channels and energies guiding you from your personal planetary strings. We are going to dive into more goodies and need to know star secrets about our names and titles, but first let's finish up with our conversation about those planets that, since the time any of us were born, have always kept moving in forward motion.

Well, okay, I told a little white lie there, and I do hope you will forgive me. Planets don't *always* move in forward motion as they spin in their orbits around their perfect 360-degree circle. With the exception of our Sun, who is the star of the whole Zodiac show anyway, all planets have periodic transits in which they actually will reverse in the degrees that they are traveling through in any given sign. Our Moon (even though she's not technically considered a planet, either) does a sort of retrograde understanding, too, but through a whole other concept called Moon-Void-of-Course. Again my sincere apologies for getting too ahead of myself, but I am always looking to make sure the information you read here is totally accurate. You'll have so much to explore along your spiraling journey once we reach our destination. But first, let's see what those planets do and what Lexigrams advise we should be doing when our heavenly bodies aren't exactly looking where they are going.

From Mercury all the way to Pluto, you'll find our channels of guidance to take action in what is called RETROGRADE. These are especially the times when our inner planets closest to us urge that we GO REDO EGO, GOT TO REDO EGO, GOT TO GO TO ART, GO TRADE A<u>N</u> EGO, GO TO A GREAT DEAR READ. Any astronomer can properly explain to you how it is that even though the planetary measurements will reverse their direction in their degrees, they aren't in actuality going backward at all. One thing for certain is that they aren't moving forward when one is in the awareness of any planet's retrograde motion. Oh and by the way, the RETRO you can also obviously see here is not some new trendy thing from the past. However, the RETRO you do witness under these reflective planetary periods certainly does take you back to fix what it may be screaming for you to take—that pause to chill out, slow down, and finally pay attention to it.

Now here's where, in my years of research about what the mysteries of Lexigrams can tell us, I began to realize there are incredibly valuable messages not only in our given names and simple words, but in the phrases and titles we give to things as well. Truly it is nothing short of remarkable to have this kind of examination at your fingertips to weather any storm in your life. Because, let me tell you, the average retrograde period for a planet such as Mercury can stir the winds of change upon the earth with the unexpected, delays, and illogical events. Any planet's retrograde period requests us to go back, refix, redo, and reassess what we've already put into forward motion in our lives. It is best, too, to have your birth chart properly done by a professional astrologer at some point in your lifetime so you can know exactly what area of your life any given retrograde urges you to retro on back to. I've written many *RE*'s for some of our planets retrograde periods, and the rule of thumb always REmains to stick to those words that start with RE, and you'll have a fine time with whatever the planet (or possible planets) at hand have to dole out.

## MERCURY RETROGRADE

- DAY TO DAY, GREET YOUR URGE TODAY
- GOT TO REDO, GOT TO RETRACE
- GOT TO REROUTE YOUR GAME
- GOT TO RECREATE TO REORDER
- GOT TO RE-EDUCATE
- GOT TO GO TO A GREAT ART
- GO TO A GREAT COMEDY
- GO REDECORATE
- GO READ, TRY A REREAD
- GO DO YOGA
- GO EMERGE, RECORD A RARE DREAM
- GO MEET A TAME COURAGE
- GOT TO REDUCE OUR TERROR
- GOT TO REDUCE A RUMOR

- GO TO REGARD TO REDUCE A REGRET
- GO! TRY TO AGREE—GO TO A TRUCE
- GO MEET A TRUE EGO CURE: TRADE OUTRAGE TO GRACE
- TRADE OUTRAGE TO A COURAGE REMEDY
- GO TO A MERCY TO CURE A GREEDY EGO
- GO GREET A MORE MATURE AREA
- GO TO A REMOTE AREA TO MEET A GREAT REMEDY
- GO TO A GOD—ADORE YOU!

The last and extremely intricate link before we officially dive into what will be more than enough substantial evidence from history about how important it is to carefully choose the names we give to ourselves and to titles in life deals with Name Numerology. The *Chaldean Hebrew Kabala Alphabet* is the letter to number match-up system that we utilize for all Name Expression calculations. While we all have oodles of things that numbers share with us within the mathematical calculations of our birth dates, there is yet another handy star secret to clue you in on. Any word, any title, anything at all with a name, has, as it's known in Numerology, a Name Expression behind it. This form of analysis takes the same letters of the alphabet that have been amazing us thus far with their Lexigram tale-telling abilities, and attaches a numerical value to them. We then, through the simplicity of math, can determine how a name "vibrates," otherwise known as a Name Expression.

While you may have already heard that there is also a Western Numerology System to calculate our Name Expressions, the system utilized in our analysis only uses the *Chaldean Hebrew Kabala Alphabet*. This system doesn't stretch the Alphabet out from A to Z and simply attract the numbers 1 to 26 to them. This would cause the number 9 to have a singular letter value. The Chaldeans' deeply understood how the words we speak create sound like the tones within music. Take the 8 natural notes in a given scale or octave. Is there a 9th natural vibration in there? You won't find the 9 attracted to any letter value in the Chaldean system, because it isn't part of our natural understanding of sound. As you'll see, Name Expressions will add up to a 9 vibration, but a single letter cannot vibrate to the 9. Western Numerologists may want to argue with me, but do your own research between the two systems, and you, too, will learn the uncanny accuracy that the Chaldeans' still have to share with us to this very modern day.

Our Name Expressions provide another layer from the numerological vantage point about our soul's purpose here on earth, just as our astrological guidance does. Soon, you'll understand just how important the art of Lexigrams supplying the final validation of insight about any life or entity. While Name Expressions indicate another layer of our personas, the specific area of life they affect is our career and public standing. Like the 10th house in the natal birth chart, this is the section of any life where we will find the kind of energy behind the types of tasks we will excel in and how the world at large will view our ambitions. Many people change their name from the given one at birth, and 9 times out of 10 their new Name Expression grants a shift in energy to the individual.

How we choose to spell our legal names is completely significant to how much ease and flow we will see in the career and work path, and ultimately this determines the kinds of energies we will attract to us all along the way. We have the choice in how we legally document our names, verses the permanence of the moment we first drew breath, thus casting our star secrets map. It is the purpose of this book to demonstrate not only how planets affect us through Name Expressions, astrology, and other areas of numerology, but also the wonders that Lexigrams are here to share that provides us one more star secret to be in awareness of.

Okay, there's just one more thing you should know about. You'll be seeing reference after reference to the Chaldean understanding of Numerology all throughout the remainder of this book. Unlike Western Numerology, the Chaldeans held that there is an ancient *Chaldean Karmic Mystery* to unlock in each number, 10 and above. These, you will soon agree, are another timeless source that, like our Lexigrams, completely reveal their precise truths about whatever subject we are investigating. You'll see these noted as we arrive as the various Karmic Paths, Lifepaths, and Name Expressions (and, where applicable, I couldn't resist sharing other astrological and numerological connections you will enjoy). Some calculations will be the pure energies of the 1 to 9, and while all numbers over 10 will be reduced to a single number to find their planetary guidance, it all in the end boils down to the planets' frequency coming through any entity.

You'll find along our Lexigram journey in the remaining chapters that there are various times when a person or entity's numerological and astrological information will literally be able to be spelled out within the spiraling messages that are derived. Not in all examples, but I'll let you be the judge of the apparent coincidences that seemingly occur. So... are you ready to take on the world? We're about to travel to all kinds of places far and wide to tap into a sixth sense that you will be so happy has found you. It's been waiting for you to find it, right in front of you, all along.

# PART II:

# BEYOND THE SIMPLICITY OF WORDS:

# THE HISTORICAL EVIDENCE

# Chapter 4

# PEOPLE IN HISTORY

*"Your word is the power you have to create.*
*It is through the word that you manifest everything."*
—DON MIGUEL RUIZ

Now that you have gotten used to the idea of Lexigrams, understand the guidelines, have tied them into some Astrological and Numerological insight, and have perhaps already been streamlining and spiraling some of your own, it's time to open up our exploration further into notable names and historical figures. As we have explained in chapter 3, whether it be a person or anything with a date of origin, it is always wise to be aware of the Astrological and Numerological guidance when one examines Lexigram derivations. More often that not, you'll typically find reference to that entity's Sun Sign, Karmic Path or other planetary goodies within the name in front of you. (This isn't an absolute rule, as we have noted, depending upon what the particular subject at hand is willing to reveal.) So, are you ready for the mysteries of Lexigrams to validate what history has already told us?

One more thing before we start. To get you into the understanding to how the numbers and signs work alongside Lexigrams, this chapter provides an outline of sorts for

each of these notable people in history that are about follow. You'll find the calculations of their Name Expressions,
through both the birth name and what they may have
changed it to along the life. You'll also find their key
Astrological and Numerological data, with an overview of
how all is connected to that person before their Lexigrams
are revealed. I know you're more than anxious to continue
to be mystified by what is next, so off we go!

❂

## ALBERT EINSTEIN
<u>Name Expression:</u> 19 *The Prince of Heaven*
<u>DOB:</u> 14 March 1879
<u>Sun Sign:</u> Pisces
<u>Karmic Path:</u> 14/5 *Movement–Challenge*
<u>Lifepath:</u> 33/6 *Love and Magic*

*"Astrology is a science and contains an illuminat-
ing body of knowledge. It taught me many things,
and I am greatly indebted to it. Geophysical evidence reveals the power of the stars and the planets in relation to the terrestrial. In turn, Astrology
reinforces this power to some extent. This is why
Astrology is like a life-giving elixir for mankind."*

*"At any rate, I am convinced that God does not
play dice."*—ALBERT EINSTEIN

When one is born to a 19 birth Name Expression, one cannot help but be bound for greatness, as the Chaldeans noted
this to be the most favored Compound Number. Surely
Albert Einstein reaped the benefits of the *The Prince of
Heaven's* and singular 1's Sun guidance in his lifetime, as he
remains in the honor of being the greatest scientist to date.
He undoubtedly was the One's channel of *The Initiator* that

opened up the understanding to the concepts of how force and energy works here on earth.

Aside from his other scientific gifts, the world's most famous scientist of the twentieth century sought out to disprove the subjects of Astrology and Numerology, where he found a common element in their teachings—they both are based upon and utilize what he already so deeply understood—Mathematics. One should not be surprised Einstein first looked upon these ancient sources of personal analysis as invalid, being born to the Karmic Path of the 14, where the 5's logic and reasonability guide the individual. No doubt it was the opening of his endlessly searching Piscean nature that granted him the intuition to tap into the true gifts one's star secrets are here to offer to humanity. Before he tapped into his planetary understanding, the infamous $e=mc^2$ of logic theory is one credit we all know Albert Einstein for. The ability to have reaped his seemingly endless famed achievements is readily seen as we look to other planetary influences in his charts.

When Einstein was born in 1879, his Pisces 14 soul was given the gift of the masterful 33 Lifepath of *Love and Magic,* denoting do what you love in life and the magic will soon follow. As Venus guided him with the singular 6 throughout his Lifepath, the duality of expansive Jupiter ruling 3's philosophical ideals allowed him to express these inner workings that brought harmony and balance to man's understanding of energy and matter. Venus is also a pretty big fan of money, and certainly Einstein saw his fair share of financial rewards, as well as the multitudes of recognition he received for the magical masterful conclusions the 33/6 Lifepath requested of him.

What can be seen from Einstein's tale within the name is many of the things we know him for today. In this case, the name indicates glimpses at the Name Expression qualities, the combination of the Sun Sign and Karmic Path relationship and the Lifepath energy. With only 9 letters utilized from the alphabet containing three vowels, what a magnificent story is here to be shared.

### ALBERT EINSTEIN

- ALBERT IS SENT AS A BRILLIANT ETERNAL STAR
- ALBERT IS IN AN EASIER STABLE LINE AS ALBERT RELATES IT
- ALBERT IS A REAL RELIANT STARTER AS ALBERT INITIATES REALITIES
- ALBERT IS IN A REAL LINEAR BRAIN, IT RETAINS
- ALBERT A REAL ABLE LEARNER
- ALBERT IS RITE AS ALBERT RELATES
- ALBERT IS A REBEL AS ALBERT STARTLE
- ALBERT IS REAL INTENSE
- ALBERT'S INNATE TALENTS ARE BEST AT LINEAR ARTS
- AS ALBERT LIBERATES ALBERT IS IN LIBERTIES
- ALBERT ENTERTAINS ENTITIES
- ALBERT'S INTENT IS RESILIENT
- ALBERT REINSTATES AS ALBERT RELEASES REALITIES
- ALBERT ENTITLES AN ANTI-INERTIA INTEREST
- ALBERT IS A REAL LISTENER
- AS ALBERT EARNS ALBERT BETTERS ETERNITIES
- LATER ALBERT REALIZES A TRANSIT STAR ART IS REAL RELIABLE
- ALBERT IS SET IN AN ETERNAL LITE

## HELEN ADAMS KELLER
<u>Birth Name Expression</u>: 11/2
*A Lion Muzzled–A Clenched Fist*
### HELEN KELLER
<u>Second Name Expression</u>: 7 *The Seeker*
<u>DOB:</u> 27 June 1880
<u>Sun Sign:</u> Cancer
<u>Karmic Path:</u> 27/9 *The Sceptre*
<u>Lifepath:</u> 32/5 *Communication*

*"The most best and most beautiful things in the world cannot be seen or even touched. They must be felt with the heart."*—HELEN KELLER

What history has already told us about this particular example of a 11/2 Birth Name Expression, is that divided goals can be unified. This granted Keller with the Master Number 11's influence over the career path, and one that through the singular 2's Moon influence showed us her *Nurturer* qualities, which were only intensified by her native Cancer Sun. Aside from her longtime companion Anne Sullivan, Keller did spend her private life in solitude. The Second Name Expression guidance of Helen Keller alone granted her with the 7, where she also sought the role of *The Seeker* in her career.

This is one of many human stories that show how determination and commitment can pay off with handsome rewards. Keller's 32/5 Lifepath of *Communication* urged her to travel, communicate and reach the masses. Her fiery Mars ruled singular 9 influence over her 27 Karmic Path and struck her with a severe fever at only 19 months of age—Mars is no stranger to dealing with health-related problems of this kind. Still, Keller remained in the energy of the 9 as *The Pioneer,* and luckily with the karmic blessing of the 27, the fever that nearly took her life resulted in the turning point of how she was about to change the world in a way no one had ever seen before.

One might have thought in 1887 that a young girl under these conditions would become a non-functioning part of society, being both deaf and blind. You couldn't tell such nonsense to a girl born on a 27 Karmic Path with a Scorpio Rising. With her Sun in the 8th house in the natal birth chart—the one also ruled by Scorpio, who governs over regeneration—it was inevitable that she was meant to transform this apparent burden into brilliance

Concerning the 27, *The Sceptre,* the Chaldeans stated, "People or entities represented by the 27 should always carry out their own original plans and ideas, and not be intimidated or influenced by the diverse opinions or opposition of others. 27 is a number of karmic reward."[4] Couple this star urging with a 32 Lifepath, and there was much communication through her fame and celebrity to bring to the masses that needed to be done by her courageous Cancer 27/9 soul.

Helen's life changed permanently in her 14/5 Personal Month and 1 personal day of new beginnings upon 05 March 1887. Anne Sullivan had already begun teaching Helen how to understand words by tracing letters on her hand, while having her literally touch what that word was with the other. Yet it was the infamous moment at the water pump that allowed Helen to ultimately grasp the concept of what we all know as language, as she describes her:

> We walked down the path to the well-house, attracted by the fragrance of the honey-suckle with which it was covered. Someone was drawing water and my teacher placed my hand under the spout. As the cool stream gushed over one hand she spelled into the other the

word water, first slowly, then rapidly. I stood still, my whole attention fixed upon the motions of her fingers. Suddenly I felt a misty consciousness as of something forgotten, a thrill of returning thought, and somehow the mystery of language was revealed to me.[5]

It should be no surprise that a Cancer with a Scorpio rising and Pisces Moon could relate through the element of water as these are the very three signs that represent it on our zodiac wheel.

With the power of transformation innately within her, Helen's progress rapidly grew, amazingly and astonishingly, day after day. No doubt the influence of Mars governing the 27/9 Karmic Path blessed her with the ability to quickly rely on her courage, while that 32/5 Lifepath insisted that she adapt to be able to communicate. Fame and celebrity are part of the potential of any 27 energy, as the positive influence of 9 is known to attain Universal appeal.

Helen quickly became known all over the world for her accomplishments. By the time she was 10 years of age, Ms. Keller already had met Alexander Graham Bell and the President. Anne taught Helen to read Braille, and to use Braille typewriters so she could also write herself. She became the first deaf and blind person to graduate with a bachelor's degree from college. Described as a phenomenon, the world up till then had never seen such remarkable accomplishments from a person who not only could not see, but could not hear, as well.

Helen became a genuine leader in our history. An inspiration to the world, she was a person anyone could have complete admiration for. True to her star secrets, she rose above the greatest odds. Proving to the entire world, no matter how much strife life may place in your path, it is your choice in how to deal with it, as Helen stated:

> The public must learn that the blind man is neither genius nor a freak nor an idiot. He has a mind that can be educated, a hand which can be trained, ambitions which it is right for him to strive to realize, and it is the duty of the public to help him make the best of himself so that he can win light through work.[6]

We note in Keller's full name at birth the Second Name Expression energy, her Mars guided Karmic Path, the Lifepath ability, and again the uncanny story that we know to be true of this infamous woman that left her distinct footprint in history. We have 10 letters from the alphabet containing 2 vowels that grant the telling of the tale within this well-known name.

### HELEN ADAMS KELLER

- A MAD MARS HELL MADE HER A NEEDER
- A HELEN KELLER NAME MAKES HER A SEEKER
- HELEN A REAL MARS LEADER AS HELEN MAKES HER NAME HEARD
- KARMA MADE HER A SEEKER, A LEADER AND A LEARNER
- ANNE ENDS HER HELL AS HELEN LEARNS
- ANNE HEALS HELEN AS HER HANDS LEARN HEAR AND SEE
- HELENS HANDS HEAL HER
- HELENS HANDS ARE HER LEADER
- HELEN A REAL DEAR SHARER AS SHE LEADS
- HELEN SHALL SEE ALL LANDS
- SHE MAKES HER DREAMS REAL
- HELEN MAKES HER HALLMARK SEEN AND HEARD

◎

## MICHAEL LUTHER KING
Birth Name Expression: 40/4 *The Recluse— The Hermit*
## DR. MARTIN LUTHER KING, JR.
Second Name Expression: 35/8 *Partnerships*
DOB: 15 January 1929
Sun Sign: Capricorn
Karmic Path: 15/6 *The Magician*
Lifepath: 28/1 *The Trusting Lamb*

*"Everybody can be great. Because everybody can serve. You don't have to have a college degree to serve. You don't have to make your subject and your verb agree to serve. You don't have to know about Plato and Aristotle to serve. You don't have to know Einstein's theory of relativity to serve. You don't have to know the second theory of thermodynamics in physics to serve. You only need a heart full of grace. A soul generated by love."* —DR. MARTIN LUTHER KING, JR. (February 4, 1968)

The man who changed Civil Rights forever in the United States has many numerical complexities surrounding all of the seemingly many names he had in his short lifetime. All of his Name Expressions dealt with the ancient Chaldean deep understanding of the karmic ties that surround the combination of the 4 and the 8 vibrations, as we see Uranus and Saturn in the usual defiance of respecting the other one's identity. In as much as these numbers gravitate to one another almost irresistibly, their combination more often than not denotes sacrificial tendencies, along with the requirement of kneeling to education all along the life.

All of Dr. King's name changes are riddled with this uncanny 4/8 phenomena, as their singular energies are known to cause their very 4 + 8 combination of the 12's sacrifice and victimization to occur when combined. The Chaldean Karmic Mysteries of the compound numbers for each of his names display the very lessons he was to adhere to. Even in Dr. King's final days, the numerical cycles he was experiencing tie into the continual mystery of the energies of the 4 and the 8.

His original name, MICHAEL LUTHER KING, vibrates to the 40/4. The Karmic Mystery being the 40's *The Recluse—The Hermit* requires the time necessary spent in solitude, away from the world, to develop one's ingenious ideas and express the singular 4's energy here of the Innovator. The 4, as inventive and original as it is, should always know the unexpected is right around the corner for them to eagerly undertake as their next challenge.

MICHAEL, alone, vibrates to the 22, a Master Number reducing to 4. The 22 represents *Submission and Caution*, stating that the spiritual must be upheld in the life in order for the masterful successes to emerge. In a matter of sorts, all *t*'s must be crossed and *i*'s must be dotted in life in order for the path to become less obstacle-stricken. One must be cautious in all dealings with others—and beware of deception.

His first name of MICHAEL was changed to MARTIN at the age of 6. Only MARTIN vibrates to the 17/8 and is coined the *The Star of the Magi*. It is known as the number of immortality, denoting the person's name will live on long after they pass on. This increased King's influence of Saturn through the singular 8, and allowed him to work extremely hard and spread his needed wisdom to the world.

Oddly enough, MARTIN LUTHER KING, vibrates to a 26/8, while DR. MARTIN LUTHER KING, JR., vibrates to the 35/8, which carries the same meaning as the 26, *Partnerships*. Either of these vibrations of the 8 grants one the immense ability to help others, yet indicates the need to watch for troublesome partnerships in the life. The Chaldeans deeply understood this energy and that these compound numbers are "full of contradictions. If 26 or 35 is the Expression of the name, it might be best to change the name to a more fortunate influence."[7] Dr. King did not utilize the analysis of Numerology to have this knowledge to possibly ease his path. No doubt there were plenty of untrusting people partnered with Dr. King that resulted in his assassination becoming an unfortunate reality, while his true intention was to unselfishly help others.

His 28/1 Lifepath has the Chaldean Karmic Mystery of *The Trusting Lamb*. The 28 brings incredible achievements and responsibility to the person influenced by it, while at the same time it asks for adherence to careful planning to secure what one has gained. One is advised to be watchful of trusting the wrong people, as intense resistance can occur in career or business matters. The singular influence of Dr. King's 28 Lifepath is the 1, *The Initiator,* and he adhered to this kind of energy along his short yet extremely worthwhile journey. There is no doubt it would be a sadder world to live in today had Dr. King not started the awareness and movement that he did. The benevolent qualities of this 1 Lifepath blended well with the leadership of his Capricorn Sun Sign.

Dr. King was practical, grounded, chock-full of wisdom and innately understood the concept of hard work.

His Karmic Path of the 15 represents *The Magician,* which granted him an undeniable charisma in public speaking. Venus influences the singular 6 here, indicating a soul that is driven by love, compassion, and is urged to bring harmony to the human heart.

There is no question Dr. Martin Luther King, Jr. sacrificed his precious life by bringing inspiration and change to humanity. With Saturn governing his Capricorn soul along with his 8 name vibrations, he showered us with lessons to be learned, while the minor expression of his first name left his eternal mark upon history. Dr. King's *The Magician* Karmic Path did not fail him, as he forever remains famed with compassionately addressing issues with the intention to bring balance to humanity's differences.

It is not only the tale from Dr. King's birth name, but also from the known Second Name Expression he grew into, that lends us further insight into the "name tale" of his short yet incredibly meaningful 39 years. We can find his Sun Sign, Karmic Path, and story of his later life in his given name, while the title he left this world carrying denotes more of the same along with the incredible ill-fate that became him. In both the birth name and the changed title, we have 14 letters from the alphabet containing 4 vowels that completely stick to telling the tale of his life story.

### MICHAEL LUTHER KING

- A REAL TRUE EARTHEN MAN IN A GREAT HEART
- HE CAME A CHARMING NUMERICAL "MAGICIAN"
- KARMA GRANT HIM A TIE TO KARMIC HEALING
- HE IMAGINE THE HUMAN HEART HEALING THE HATE
- HE CAME IN A REAL THINKER TRAIL

- HE CAN TEACH THEM IN MICHIGAN
- HE CAN TEACH THE HUMAN HEART A GREAT THING
- HE CAN CHANGE THE AMERICAN HUMAN RIGHT
- HE CAME IN A MIRACLE HUMAN RIGHT TRAIL
- HE CAME IN A CHALLENGE, HE CAN ILLUMINATE MAN
- HE CAN LECTURE IN THE LIMELIGHT RECITING
- A GREAT THING, REACHING A MAGNETIC LENGTH
- HE CAN CREATE INTRIGUE IN THE HUMAN HEART
- HE TAUGHT THE HUMAN RACE TIME A MITE THING
- A KILLER'(S) TRAGIC HATE HIT HIM IN ILL-TIMING

## DR. MARTIN LUTHER KING, JR.

- HE TAKE A DARING NAME CHANGE IN THE "KARMIC EIGHT"
- A REAL TRUE MAN IN A GREAT HEART
- HE "HAD A DREAM," A DARING UNITING DREAM
- HE GET DUE TIME IN JAIL
- A GREAT TALKER IN A DARING MAGNITUDE
- A REAL LEADER IN THE HUMAN RIGHT AND THE HUMAN NATURE
- HE URGED IN HEALING THE HATE IN THE HUMAN HEART
- A TAME MAN IN TUNE, A REAL MEDITATING "GURU"
- HE IMAGINED THE ULTIMATE HUMAN ALIGNMENT
- HE TRAINED MEN IN RETHINKING THEIR HEART
- HE INITIATED A GREAT GAIN IN THE HUMAN RIGHT
- IN THE END, KILLED/MURDERED IN A MAD RAGE IN A DARK INHUMANE HATE IN THE END

❂

## DIANA FRANCES SPENCER
Birth Name Expression: 16/7 *The Shattered Citadel*
### PRINCESS DIANA
Second Name Expression: 6 *The Romantic*
DOB: 01 July 1961
Sun Sign: Cancer
Karmic Path: 1 *The Initiator*
Lifepath: 34/7 *Discrimination–Analysis*

*"I don't want expensive gifts; I don't want to be bought. I have everything I want. I just want someone to be there for me, to make me feel safe and secure."*—PRINCESS DIANA

Princess Diana is a complete star secrets marvel, and another example that indeed is undeniably uncanny from her Lexigram revelations that denote the indication of her short life. Her birth Name Expression set up the energy by which her eventual famed and celebrity life brought her, as the Chaldeans so noted the 16 to warn "of a strange fatality, also of danger of accidents and the defeat of one's plans. If the name equals the Compound number 16, it would obviously be wise to change the spelling of the name to avoid this vibration. To find happiness in ways other than leadership at the top (the Tower and the Crown)—to renounce fame and celebrity—is another way of decreasing the negative aspect of the 16."[8]

In as much as Princess Diana increasingly became the apple of the public eye once married to Prince Charles, her life was far from perfect. The 16 energy also requests of the soul to adhere to "the Single number 7's obligation and responsibility to listen to the voice within, which will always warn of danger through dreams or the intuition in time to avoid it. The inner voice must not be ignored."[9] We also see that Diana was following the 34/7 Lifepath of *Discrimination–Analysis*, which equally requested her to not deny the inherent responsibility to the 7's singular energy.

Yet with the combination of a Cancer Sun with the Karmic Path 1, her identity and character were driven to become the protective mother figure to the world that she was. The role of *The Initiator* was equally strong within her, as she not only began multitudes of charities to care over things in need, but the Sun's influence granted her the time on stage in the spotlight of the press. Here is yet another soul who left tremendous gifts to the world, but eventually sacrificed her own life to bring them to the earthen plane.

Diana's Name Expression changed once she married. No doubt the singular energy of the 6 through the guidance of Venus was part of the natural grace and harmony that we always saw her portraying to the world. The 6's energy of *The Romantic* came through loud and clear in all of the initiations her Cancer 1 Karmic Path urged her to create, as Diana represented the perfectly balanced, poised and charming Princess. At least that was what we were all led to believe at the beginning of Charles and Di's "fairy tale."

Any soul on a 7 Lifepath tends to lead a very private life, and equally Cancer souls keep many things about themselves concealed from others the best they can. There was so much going on behind the scenes in Diana's marriage that she never showed to the world, and, ultimately, only since her death have we learned how sad, lonely, and isolated she truly was during her marriage to Charles. As shocking as it was to the world of royalty that they would divorce, one should not be surprised it was a Cancer 1 soul that yearned for her freedom and that her personal security be returned to her.

We can readily see in Diana's Lexigrams eerie revelations from the birth name, which, oddly enough, fatalistically carried right into her changed name. In as much as her Name Expression of the 6 brought her a more balanced energy, it was indeed the adherence to the 16's advice from the birth name in this example that may have changed her fate. Her Sun Sign is noted, as this example utilizes 10 letters from the alphabet containing 3 vowels, to accurately tell her tale from the name.

### DIANA FRANCES SPENCER

- ◎ DIANA IS A FINE SINCERE AND A NICE CANCER
- ◎ DIANA CARRIES A DEAR PRESENCE IN A RADIANCE
- ◎ DIANA NEEDS A FREE SENSE AND AN INNER PEACE
- ◎ DIANA NEEDS A SAFE SPACE, ESCAPES AND NICE SCENERIES
- ◎ A PRINCE SERENADES DIANA
- ◎ DIANA DENIES AN INNER PRIDE AS PRINCESS DIANA
- ◎ DIANA REPRESSES AND CARRIED AN INNER NEED IN FEAR
- ◎ IN A FANCINESS DIANA IS IN FEARS AS A PRINCESS
- ◎ DIANA IS SEEN AND RIDES IN CAR PARADES
- ◎ DIANA RESIDES IN NICE RESIDENCES
- ◎ DIANA SEES DANCES AS A PRINCESS IN FINE DRESSES
- ◎ DIANA RAISES AND FINDS FINANCES IN AIDS CARES NEEDS
- ◎ DIANA DENIES AN AIDS FEAR, DENIES AN AFRAID AIR
- ◎ DIANA IS FIERCE AS DIANA SPREAD AND INCREASED AIDS CARES

- ◉ DIANA REFRAINED A FIERCENESS AIR
- ◉ IN FEAR IN A CRISIS END DIANA DIES IN A CAR IN PARIS, FRANCE

## PRINCESS DIANA

- ◉ IS DIANA SPENCER
- ◉ DIANA SPANS AND SPINS IN RADIANCES
- ◉ DIANA IS A SINCERE AND A NICE CANCER
- ◉ DIANA IS SEEN AND RIDES IN PARADES
- ◉ DIANA RAISES AND INSPIRES AIDS CARES
- ◉ DIANA IS SEEN IN "PARADISE"
- ◉ INSIDE DIANA DENIES INNER NEEDS AND DISCERNS
- ◉ INSIDE DIANA IS SCARED AND IN PANIC DESPAIRS AS A PRINCESS
- ◉ DIANA ASPIRES AND ASCENDS A SACRED ESCAPE
- ◉ DIANA IS PRAISED AS A PRINCE'S PRIDE IS SINNED
- ◉ DIANA DIES IN A CAR IN PARIS

◉

WILLIAM JEFFERSON CLINTON
Birth Name Expression: 46/10/1 *The Wheel of Fortune*
BILL CLINTON
Second Name Expression: 10/1 *The Wheel of Fortune*
DOB: 19 August 1946
Sun Sign: Leo
Karmic Path: 19 *The Prince of Heaven*
Lifepath: 38/11/2 *Grace Under Pressure*

*"If you live long enough, you'll make mistakes. But if you learn from them, you'll be a better person. It's how you handle adversity, not how it affects you. The main thing is never quit, never quit, never quit."*
—BILL CLINTON

Bill Clinton is no stranger to shining upon any stage. No matter where one may look in his star secrets, he also has the guidance of the singular 1's influence of the Sun. The birth and secondary Name Expressions both are in the 10/1 vibrations. The Chaldeans noted the 10's *The Wheel of Fortune* to be beneficial, yet one influenced by this compound number must remember that, "the power for manifesting creative concepts into reality is inherent, but must be used with wisdom, since the power for absolute creation contains the polarity power for absolute destruction. Self-discipline and infinite compassion must accompany the gift of the former to avoid the tragedy of the latter. Discipline must precede Dominion."[10]

Thus, we have seen Bill Clinton in both arenas of being disciplined and receiving his dominion, and equally there are cases throughout his life where circumstances presented themselves to him that created obvious destruction to occur. Perhaps it is the intense guidance of the Sun in this case that he couldn't resist the time to play a little, thinking just like the royal lion that he was the king of the forest and could get away with whatever he wanted. It is rare with the guidance of the 10 that one can ever stray from the Chaldeans' understanding that discipline and only discipline will allow dominion in the life to prevail.

Bill Clinton's Sun influence doesn't stop at his names. The intensity of the Sun presides over both his Sun Sign of Leo and his Karmic Path of the 19/1. (It is also interesting to note the name William alone is also a 19 vibration.) In as much as he has seen his fair share of "incidences," it is the 19's protection of *The Prince of Heaven* over the warnings within his *Grace Under Pressure* 38/11/2

Lifepath, which the Chaldeans held to be the most favored compound number, that always grants Bill his "bounce back" in life. The Sun's energy that graces his soul undeniably makes one of his innate gifts to be the able deliverer of those eloquent and riveting speeches. It is without question Bill easily can attract attention from the masses; whether in good or seemingly bad circumstances, he is unsurpassed.

Take all of Clinton's 1 influences of the Sun and place them upon his 38/11/2 Lifepath, and Bill Clinton is further graced to gravitate to leadership. As we saw during his terms in office, there were many elements of duality that led him to the decisions he made not only for the nation, but in his personal affairs as well. The 38, which carries the same meaning as the 29, warns that "the life is filled with uncertainties, treachery and deceptions from others, unreliable friends, unexpected dangers—and considerable grief and anxiety caused by members of the opposite sex. It's a number of grave warnings in every area of the personal life and career."[11] Even further within the underlying Master Number 11, this 2 Moon guided path grants the soul with emotional and pressurized circumstances to overcome throughout the life. The more charitable the soul is along the 38/11/2 Lifepath, the greater the ease of the situations bringing on pressure are to surface in the life. Bill's established foundation and recent book *Giving* are the perfect antidotes for this kind of energy.

Bill's birth name further concludes the uncanny accuracy that is his life story. Here we can see the findings of his Name Expression, Sun Sign, Karmic Path, and Lifepath. With 13 letters from the alphabet containing 4 vowels, Bill's soul was not afraid to come to the name that was to readily display the life story told from it.

## WILLIAM JEFFERSON CLINTON

- SENT AS A REAL LEO LION NINETEEN, IN A MASTER TWO LIFELINE
- WILLIAM'S NAMES ARE IN TEN TO ONE
- WILLIAM'S FIRST NAME IS ALSO IN A NINETEEN TO ONE
- WILLIAM IS A WISE TALL MAN, WRITES LEFTIE
- WILLIAM EARNS IN A MAIN LAW CAREER
- WILLIAM IS MEANT TO EARN MILLIONS IN LIFE, A REAL MILLIONAIRE HE IS
- WILLIAM IS SEEN TO CRAFT NOTES & TONES
- WILLIAM IS MEANT TO EARN TWO NOMINATIONS IN A MAIN NATIONAL OFFICE
- WILLIAM'S TEAM MATE IS AL, AN ARIES MAN
- WILLIAM WINS TWICE; SEES NO MAJOR WARS IN OFFICE FOR TWO TERMS
- SEEN SAME AS LINCOLN AS WILLIAM "SORT OF" FREES A NATION OVER A NINETEEN-NINETIES ERA
- SEEN IN AFFAIRS IN WOMEN: JENNIFER/MONICA
- A REAL ROMANTIC, WILLIAM TELLS ALL WOMEN NOT TO TELL
- AFFAIRS ARE SEEN IN NEWS AS A MAJOR SCANDAL
- WILLIAM IS NOT MEANT TO SEE TIME IN JAIL
- WILLIAM CAN STILL SMILE AFTER ALL SORROW AS WILLIAM IS IN A MAJOR 'ONE' FAME
- WILLIAM IS SET TO FREE ALL INNER FEARS LATER
- WILLIAM IS SET TO WRITE TWO MAIN NATIONAL SELLERS:

- ONE OF LIFE MEMOIRS, ONE OF EFFORTS TO RAISE MONIES FOR MORAL MENTIONS
- WILLIAM'S WIFE ALSO EARNS TWO TERMS IN AN EASTERN STATE SENATOR OFFICE
- WILLIAM'S WIFE IS NOT MEANT TO WIN A NATIONAL OFFICE, IT'S MEANT FOR ANOTHER LEO MAN—A SENATOR FROM THE STATE OF ILLINOIS
- WILLIAM'S WIFE CAN EARN ON A NATIONAL STATE SECRETARIAL SEAT
- WILLIAM IS SENT TO SEE AN ASTRONOMICAL LIFE

⊚

## ALBERT ARNOLD GORE, JR.
Birth Name Expression: 26/8 *Partnerships*
AL GORE
Second Name Expression: 12 *The Sacrifice–The Victim*
DOB: 31 March 1948
Sun Sign: Aries
Karmic Path: 31 *The Recluse–The Hermit*
Lifepath: 29/11/2 *Grace Under Pressure*

*"No matter how hard the loss, defeat might serve as well as victory to shake the soul and let the glory out."*—AL GORE

While it may not have been Al Gore's true path to serve as the President of the United States, his star secrets certainly reveal his ability to be able to receive one of the world's highest honors, that of the Nobel Peace Prize. This pioneering Aries needs to adhere to his 31/4's Karmic Path of *The Recluse–The Hermit* request to spend time in solitude to be able to express to the world their ingenious innovations and original ideas for humanity. Gore's continued research and analysis brings us the facts about the global environmental crisis that faces us, as the 4's energy grants him the prophecy to see into the future.

Born to the Birth Name Expression of 26/8 Chaldean understanding of *Partnerships*, Saturn's governing here is key in understanding why Gore had so much trouble trying to make it to the very top of politics. It is often seen in the 26 that the person is innately able to help others, but not always the self. Al Gore has the infamous 4 and 8 energies surrounding him—being born to the 31/4 Karmic Path and Birth Name Expression of the 26/8—and he has certainly seen his fair share of the known combination of the 4 and 8 to be none other than the 12's *Sacrifice and The Victim*.

Even choosing the Second Name Expression of Al Gore alone brought this energy directly to him. The Chaldeans acknowledged the 12 energy as, "One will periodically be sacrificed for the plans or intrigues of others. The number 12 warns of the necessity to be alert to every situation, to beware of false flattery from those who use it to gain their own ends. Be suspicious of those who offer a high position, and carefully analyze the motive. 12 represents the educational process on all levels, the submission of the will required and the sacrifices necessary to achieve knowledge and wisdom, on both the spiritual and the intellectual levels. When the intellect is sacrificed to the feelings, the mind will be illuminated with the answers it seeks. Look within for the solution. Attention paid to the requirements of education will end suffering and bring success."[12]

With that being said, there's no surprise really why Gore didn't seem to be just as happy to return to his seclusion after losing the Presidency. He was far better off going back to his passion and innate ability to see far into the future about the environmental crisis at hand, fulfilling that 12 requirement of education. It is rare to see the 31/4 energy really want the public spotlight, unless particular aspects in the charts denote otherwise. Within the Chaldean understanding of the 31, "Quite often, genius is present, or at least high intelligence. At some unexpected time in the life, the glittering promises of the world will be suddenly rejected for the peace and quiet of Nature, or, if response to the 31 is not quite that pronounced, there will nevertheless eventually be a degree of retreat from society in some manner."[13] No exception to this numerical advice, Gore seems to be very much at his best when he takes the time alone to let those brilliant ideas streamline in, and then devise his next Aries pioneering plan to tell everyone about it.

One has to congratulate Gore on innately honing in on his personal energy and choosing the focus of the singular 4's request to relate a needed humanitarian cause for the greater good, rather than continue to come up against obstacles in the political playground. Apparently the *Academy Awards* were the first indication that Gore was on the right track with his timely message, as he received the Oscar for his film, *An Inconvenient Truth*, as Best Documentary Feature in 2007.

What also is in Al Gore's favor under his 29/11/2 *Grace Under Pressure* Lifepath is that the more charitable and giving he is, just like his Leo pal Bill, the less those situations of ultimate disappointment show themselves. Gore has also seen some pretty pressurized situations throughout the life, especially in relation to the family, but like a true Karmic Path 31/4, he took them on as challenges and rarely allowed them to remain obstacles. That's the beauty of the Aries 4 combination—relentless and courageous tolerance.

Al Gore is no exception to the mysteries of Lexigrams, as the name he was given at birth also sheds further insight to the real path he is here to lead. With 11 letters from the alphabet containing 3 vowels, the tale from his name yet again shows us the truth that has been right in front of us all along:

### ALBERT ARNOLD GORE, JR.

- ⊘ ON A RETROGRADE DATE AL TO EARN A NOTABLE NOBEL LABEL
- ⊘ AL A REAL ABLE LEARNER
- ⊘ AL TO LEARN A JOURNAL ART
- ⊘ ALBERT TO EARN NEAR A REAL REGAL BOLD "LEO ONE" (Bill Clinton, "Leo One" 8/19)
- ⊘ AL ABLE TO BEAR A LARGE LOAD AND ORDEAL
- ⊘ AL ABLE TO BE A GREAT LEADER NEAR NO EGO
- ⊘ AL TO LEAD A GOLDEN ERA LATER ON
- ⊘ AL ABLE TO GET TO A GREATER LEADER GOAL
- ⊘ AL GET BOLDER AND GREATER LATER ON
- ⊘ AL TO EARN NEAR A GREAT BOLD ART, TO RENDER A GREAT ART
- ⊘ ALBERT ABLE TO GO TO THE LORD AND GOD A LOT
- ⊘ AL ABLE TO TARGET A GRAND NEED
- ⊘ AL ABLE TO RELATE A REAL GREAT READABLE ELABORATE LAND TALE
- ⊘ AL DARE TO NARRATE A REAL "LAND NEAR DANGER" TALE
- ⊘ AL TO TELL ALL A LAND TALE ALL NEED TO LEARN
- ⊘ LABELED A BLAND BORE, GORE GOT TO REDO TO BROADEN

- LATER ON GORE GET A REAL LEADER ROLE NOT TO BORE
- LATER ON AL GOT TO GO ON ALL ALONE
- AL BELONG TO A GREATER ROLE TO LEAD A REGENERATOR AGE

Certainly it can be said that there's something valuable to be learned from the analysis of the energy within our names we are given in life. Along with the other connections made through Astrology and Numerology, one cannot question that these notable examples from history have told us how much weight and substance there is to absorb from a name. So, where to next? Now that we've covered some ground that undeniably displays that Lexigrams may just have a slight bit of relevance in our lives, let's allow the following chapters to allude to further evidence. As you continue onward, the Lexigrams of names and titles will become even more specific, indicating that right within the letters in front of you, there is a tale that awaits to be told.

# Chapter 5

## PEOPLE IN MUSIC

*"Words mean more than what is set down on paper. It takes the human voice to infuse them with deeper meaning."* —MAYA ANGELOU

It has been said numerous times that music makes the world go round. What has become more than music to my own ears is seeing how the talents of the very people that create the music our world knows and loves so well are hardly exempt from the Lexigram formula of telling the tale from within the name. It seems that no matter what area of life a person came down to excel in, there is no doubt they were meant to be born to the name that is able to spiral into the story that undeniably matches the unfolding of the personal life. We'll also add another layer of analysis here in places—that of the Personal Year Cycle. This is how you or any soul evolves year to year along your Lifepath. Each birthday, a number from 1 to 9 guides that year's cycle, allowing us to flow in 9-year periods. We will also dive into specific birth chart references, as, sometimes, it just cannot be resisted to dive deeper into the Universe's wisdom by all planetary measures. So, off we go again, for more captivating examples that tell us exactly how our world of music indeed has gone round.

Remember how the planet of NEPTUNE contains the very word TUNE in it? But of course you will find many Pisces and even those 7 Karmic Path souls who have graced the music business since the origins of music. Even dating back to the late 1700's, we find Neptune-guided souls that also were given names that would assure that their talents not go to waste. Perhaps you've heard at some point along your life a familiar classical piece called Sonata No. 14, or *Moonlight Sonata,* which was composed for a woman named GIULIETTA. It surely seems logical that a Neptune-influenced person would be able to create such a HAUNTING yet ENLIVENED TUNE. That would be the 16 December 1770 soul's urge of LUDWIG VAN BEETHOVEN, who was born in a historic town called Bonn, which now is in modern-day Germany. Not only did Beethoven follow the 16 Karmic Path of the 16/7, but he walked the Lifepath as well of the 25/7, and carried a Name Expression of the 52/7. Talk about swirling in the seas of Neptune! Group all of this mystical and seeker energy with that of being the Sun Sign of a Sagittarius, and it is clear to see how the musical aims of this intense communicator have never stopped shooting their mighty arrows everywhere around the world.

Most people know that Beethoven composed the majority of his music without the full use of his ears, for he began to lose his hearing at the young age of 25, when he was in a 5 Current Personal Year, one that denotes permanent changes to occur in the life. Those born to the Karmic Path of *The Shattered Citadel* are wise to remember the Chaldeans' understanding of the potential that the 16 can bring: "It warns of a strange fatality, also of danger of accidents the defeat of one's plans. To find happiness in ways other than leadership at the top (the Tower and the Crown)—to renounce fame and celebrity—is another way of decreasing the negative aspect of the 16."[14]

Just as Beethoven was gaining his popularity and name in the world, tinnitus brought on the reason why his ears eventually stopped doing their work. He found music to be challenging and especially the act of conversing with others, yet, what he did do from the depths of his Neptune-guided soul was also the other sound advice the Chaldeans said to do when one is living under the delicacy of the 16: "The 16 brings with it the Single number 7's obligation and responsibility to listen to the voice within, which will always warn of danger through dreams or the intuition in time to avoid it. The inner voice must not be ignored."[15]

It wasn't just the inner voice of Neptune and the contagious optimism of his Sagittarian Sun that contributed to his immortal talents. We should not be surprised that the world is, to this very day and for many more to come, amazed, touched, and deeply influenced by:

## LUDWIG VAN BEETHOVEN

- ⊚ LUDWIG THE EVEN ONE NEED TO BE OBEDIENT AND TUNED-IN TO THE WHITE LIGHT TO NOT LIVE IN THE NEGATIVE
- ⊚ LUDWIG TO ANOINT IT IN A BIG GAIN IN ALL NOTE AND TONE BEAT
- ⊚ LUDWIG BELIEVED AND VALUED ALL TUNE ALONG AN EVOLVING LINE
- ⊚ LUDWIG LIVED IN BOTH BONN AND VIENNA

- LUDWIG HAD AN OBLIGATED ENLIGHTENED NOTABLE TUNE TO LET OUT
- LUDWIG BEHELD IN LOVE IN A BELOVED GIULIETTA
- LUDWIG UNABLE TO HAVE A LONG ALIGNED LOVE
- LUDWIG LEAVE ENLIVENED HAUNTING ELEVATION WE VALUE ON AND ON
- LUDWIG INVENTED THE LENGTHENED TONABLE TUNE
- LUDWIG LEAVE BEHIND A BENEVOLENT ELEGANT TANGIBLE TUNE THAT LONG OUTLIVE IN A VALUED WEIGH GUIDE THAT GO ON IN TIME

One of the most well-known American jazz musicians and band leaders in the swing era was Mr. GLENN MILLER, another Pisces born over 200 years after Beethoven on 01 March 1904. On the Sun-guided 1 Karmic Path, aside from possessing the ability to light up all around him from any stage, he led the pack as one of the bestselling recording artists from 1939 to 1942 that started to be known as the "big bands." True to *The Initiator* energy of the 1, Miller founded his own band, still known to this day as the Glenn Miller Orchestra. Aside from his capabilities through the 1 Karmic Path, his leadership abilities equally flowed as he followed the Mars-guided 18/9 Lifepath of *Spiritual—Material Conflict.* The 18 is so very often seen, whether as a Karmic Path or Lifepath influence, to bring a soul to the heights of fame and celebrity. Miller was without a doubt a pioneer of the jazz/swing age, and created multitudes of signature sounds that have been left as timeless classics still cherished today. As the Name Expression of GLENN MILLER rings to the 17's *The Star of the Magi* eternalized energies, we can be sure his work will live on for eons to come.

Of interest to note is Miller's passing. While as a Major in the Army en route to Paris, France from the United Kingdom, his plane mysteriously disappeared over the English Channel and was never to be found. Second to Scorpio, our Pisces do love a good mystery, and in as much as theories have abounded, Miller's is one that still remains unsolved. More clues as to how Miller took the communications within his Piscean 1 soul to the masses lie of course within the tale from his 19 *The Prince of Heaven* birth Name Expression:

### ALTON GLENN MILLER

- GLENN A GENTLEMAN IN A REAL RELIANT EAR
- GLENN IN A REAL GAIN IN A NINETEEN NAME
- GLENN REAL GREAT AT A MAIN NOTE & TONE ART
- GLENN MEANT TO MENTOR A GREAT GENERATION
- GLENN MEANT TO TRAIN MEN IN A REAL GREAT EAR TO LEARN
- GLENN ENROLL IN NAMING AN ELEGANT NOTE & TONE ERA
- GLENN TO ORIENT A GREAT NOTE & TONE ETERNAL LINE AGE
- A GLENN MILLER NAME TO REMAIN ON & ON IN A GAIN
- MAN NOT MEANT TO GET TO MILLER LATER ON IN TIME
- A MEAN REGIME NATION GOT A MAIN MILLER ENGINE
- AN AIR ENGINE TALE MEANT TO REMAIN AN ENIGMA IN TIME

One should not find it odd that NAT KING COLE, which GET NAT A TON O' GIANT GAIN IN A NICE LINE, a melodic Piscean soul born on 17 March 1919, wrote the song "Unforgettable." Born to the 17/8 Karmic Path, just like Glenn Miller's second Name Expression, what is done in the lifetime is meant to be known for all eternity, as the Chaldeans claim: "17 is 'the number of Immortality,' and indicates that the person's (or entity's) name will live after him."[16] Here, too, is the strength of Saturn that, through the singular 8, gave this Fish a work ethic that was unsurpassed. With a 31/4 Lifepath, the incredible talents of this singer and jazz pianist had Uranus's inventive energies all along the way to lay down the structure and foundation for all he was to leave forever as his gifts to humanity.

Under the Name Expression of NAT KING COLE, undoubtedly the 20's *The Awakening* energies channeled a welcomed sensitivity to Cole that brings endless comfort to any ear with the Moon's guidance over the singular 2. Also in alignment with Miller's energies, our Nat was born to the full Name Expression of the 18's *Spiritual–Material Conflict,* wherein he took himself to those Universal 9's! Equally, we see this name is the true teller of some of the story that history was to unfold for him:

## NATHANIEL ADAMS COLES

- ๏ HE IS A HANDSOME MAN
- ๏ HE IS SET TO ASTONISH AS A SENSATION
- ๏ HIS NOTES AND TONES SEE ESCALATIONS
- ๏ HIS NOTES AND TONES CALM ALL MEN
- ๏ HE IS SEEN AS A MILESTONE
- ๏ HIS NOTE AND TONE SELECTIONS ARE MEANT TO LAST

- ◉  "MONA LISA" IS ONE, SO IS "SMILE"
- ◉  HIS NAME IS SET TO LAST EONS ON
- ◉  HIS NOTES AND TONES CHANNEL A TIMELESS
  MOOD

From one king to another, let's check out the man who immortalized himself as the pioneer of rock and roll, Mr. ELVIS PRESLEY, who had that undeniable talent of shaking his LIVELY PELVIS. One might stop and wonder, what exactly was it that made Elvis the phenomenon that he was? Why does he carry an everlasting affect to this very day? You can bet there are some revelations within all of Elvis's star secrets that can help us answer these questions!

For Elvis, born 08 January 1935 to a 27 Lifepath, this was a highly fortunate and blessed number as far as the Chaldeans understood the mysteries of numbers to be. His 27 Lifepath of *The Sceptre* denotes, "This is an excellent, harmonious and fortunate number of courage and power, with a touch of enchantment. It blesses the person or entity it represents with a promise of authority and command. It guarantees that great rewards will come from the productive labors, the intellect, and the imagination. All of these creative faculties have sown good seeds, which are to reap a rich harvest."[17]

Planet Mars rules the 27 as it reduces to a singular 9 vibration, which tells us in this case of a Lifepath influence (and as we just saw in Miller's 18/9 Lifepath and Cole's 18 Name Expression), that the soul ultimately has the potential to be a pioneer of sorts—having a widespread affect upon the masses and possibly achieve fame and celebrity in the lifetime. Hmmmm....now that, oddly enough, does sound like the 'King" doesn't it? Couple Elvis's 27 Lifepath with his 8 Karmic Path, ruled by none other than fatherly and disciplined Saturn, and we start to see the reason why Elvis worked at the levels he did while reaping incredible material rewards in his short lifetime. Saturn also rules his native Sun Sign of Capricorn, the steadfast and equally laborious Goat.

One's numerical Karmic Path directly interrelates with the personality and innate abilities of the Sun Sign. So, Elvis's character was indeed influenced by "Super Saturn," resulting in an extraordinary and rare list of achievements. He couldn't help himself but to work. Once in the understanding of the material rewards that came his way from the fruits of his labors, Elvis not only got hooked on drugs, he was first addicted to work. Those go-getter Goats are well-known in the Zodiac to become so ambitious, especially in the career, that there is not equal attention paid to other important areas of the life, which tend to suffer as a direct result.

Anyone who knows anything about Elvis knows that, despite all of his amazing talents, there was something ultimately out of balance outside of his exceptional career. Money could buy him anything he ever materially wanted. By any planetary take, even though Elvis had multitudes of possessions in the world, these were the very last things that could help him most.

What is also interesting to note is the Name Expression of ELVIS PRESLEY, another Mars 9 vibration, granting him that extra drive and bound him to fame, celebrity, and influence upon the masses within the career. Yet this vibration of the 9 is the 18, which represents the Chaldean understanding of *Spiritual–Material Conflict*. The 18 "symbolizes materialism striving to destroy the spiritual side of the nature. It often associates the person or entity represented by it with bitter quarrels within the family circle—with wars, social upheaval, and revolution. If the name has this vibration, it should be negated immediately by changing the spelling to equal a more fortunate Compound number. In this way one may be more victorious, in both the spiritual and material worlds, over the restrictions of the 18."[18] Even the first name of ELVIS alone rings to the 18/9.

Yet another hmmm.... Undoubtedly, Elvis had a pretty hard spiritual and material conflict going on within his area of career. He always kept the influence of God in the realms of his music, as we have plenty of Gospel recordings from Elvis that live on to this day. Yet, we will see that those other indulgences and material toying were awaiting Elvis to make the responsible choice about them. It seems the one thing that he did not use his Saturn wisdom about was that of his own health. In the usual revelations of Lexigrams, it is once again the name at birth that tells the mighty tale of the man that is forever coined, plain and simple, "The King." Uncannily enough, the truth to be told that history has already proven lies right within his name:

## ELVIS AARON PRESLEY

- ALL SEE ELVIS IN A PERSONAL LOVELINESS
- AS ELVIS PLEASES ALL, EVERYONE LOVES ELVIS
- OVERSEAS ELVIS SEALS A LOVE IN PRISCILLA
- ELVIS IS NO PASSIVE PERSON, ELVIS ASPIRES
- ELVIS IS SEEN IN A REAL PASSION, AS ELVIS LIVES IN A REAL LOVER PERSONA
- ELVIS LIVES IN A REAL PASSION AS ELVIS EARNS IN SEVERAL AREAS
- ELVIS IS A VERSES PRAISER, "IN A VALLEY"
- ELVIS PRAISES A SAVIOR IN A REAL PRAYER

- ELVIS SEES A LIVELY SALARY
- ELVIS PLAYS AS A SAILOR AS ELVIS EARNS
- ALL PRESS SELLS ELVIS IN A LIVELY PELVIS
- ELVIS SIRES LISA AS ELVIS SPOILS LISA IN LOVE
- ELVIS SEES A REPRESSION IN EVIL PILLS
- YES ELVIS SEVERELY LIVES ON PAIN RELIEVERS
- ELVIS REVELS IN REAL SEVERE NOSE EVILS
- ELVIS LIVES IN A REAL PASSION IN PILLS AS PILLS ARE PRESLEY'S PRISON
- YES ELVIS LIVES ON SLEEPY PILLS AS ELVIS LIVES IN A LONELIER LIE
- ELVIS IS A REAL RARE PIONEER PERSON
- YES ALL SEE ELVIS LEAVE EARLY ON
- ELVIS'S LOVELINESS LIVES ON AS ELVIS IS SEEN ALL OVER EONS ON

Whether Elvis is still actually alive as some do truly believe, it was The King himself who did once say: "Reincarnation has gotta be real—it explains a lot about why people are the way they are." I'm just going to put my money down that Elvis may be thinking, at the very least, that he's about ready now to come on back down and go for it all again. Maybe next time, it'll be in a shyer Virgo incarnation, so he can take better care of himself, and be sure to live in a fuller lifetime to let his spirit evolve once more.

Speaking of Virgos, here is another musical icon that recently departed this great earth, whom Madonna cited soon after his death with the words "Long live the King." Here we also find one more soul who left an incredible legacy behind, and equally did not take care of his body, but surely knew a lot about love. MICHAEL JACKSON: CAN CLAIM HEALS EONS ON, once said: "If you enter this world knowing you are loved and you leave this world knowing the same, then everything that happens in between can be dealt with."

Whether you like or dislike Michael Jackson, one cannot be in any denial of the significant impact he brought to this world, in multitudes of ways beyond the legacy of his music he has now left behind. Certainly one could write a book alone about how the Universe affected the life of the "King of Pop." But we only have limited room within this chapter for now, and by the planets' take, this other legendary King was not cast into the easiest of Karmic Paths to achieve his success upon. Yet accomplish it he most surely did, born 29 August 1958. This made him an at service to the world Sun Sign Virgo, a 29 Karmic Path walking along a 42/6 Lifepath.

Jackson was not exempt from the emotional turmoil that can be seen living out a Karmic Path of the 29's *Grace Under Pressure*: "The 29 is a number of perhaps the heaviest Karma of all. It tests the person or entity it represents for spiritual strength, through trial and tribulations echoing the Old Testament story of Job. The life is filled with uncertainties, treachery and deceptions from others, unreliable friends, unexpected dangers—and considerable grief and anxiety caused by members of the opposite sex. It's a number of grave warnings in every area of the personal life and career."[19]

Sound like anything Mr. Jackson had to endure in his now seemingly short lifetime? From the very beginning, when we saw Michael emerge as a member of The Jackson 5, he was subjected to abuse as a child. Here is where the duality of the 29—with the underlying 11's energy—first showed itself to Michael, as the world saw him as the brilliant child star that he was, but on the flip side, he was a scared, beaten child that no one had any clue this was happening to. As the Moon directly governed over Michael, those emotions were never far away, which made him very sensitive and parental like a Cancer Sun Sign. Many 29 Karmic Paths, no matter what Sun Sign they are born to, have trauma and circumstances of misfortune that place emotional scars upon the soul very early in the life.

We all know the life that Jackson led, the high level of popularity his music became through his brilliant and innovative ways of entertaining us all. Yet, even with all of his Virgo service-oriented deeds to the world, his 29 Karmic Path attracted those troubles with the opposite sex, failed marriages, and the accusations that came his way of child molestation, which he was never found guilty of in a court of law. The 29 specifically asks a soul living out this Karmic Path to gravitate to charitable causes as one way to alleviate the possible burdens that the 29 can bring to the soul. The response of grace, as the title denotes, also works marvelously when those situations of pressure show up in the life. As the Chaldeans advised: "Remember that the development of absolute faith in goodness and the power of the self... the constant and energetic cultivation of optimism... will act as a miraculous medicine for the problems of the number 29."[20]

Aided by his 42 Lifepath of *Love—Money— Creativity,* certainly there was much ease brought to Jackson's life. No doubt, along his life he did heed the karmic mystery behind the 42, which asks a soul influenced by it to utilize their creativity, apply it with the intention of love and witness the money "magically" come their way. Money, however, in the end, couldn't solve the emotional turmoil that Jackson suffered from the roots of his life. Yet love was the medicine that Michael continuously did extend to the people who were a part of his life, and to the masses that he also brought comfort to with the money he generated in his lifetime.

The conversation could endlessly go on about the marvels and opposing trails of Michaels' life, but let's allow the revelations of Lexigrams to finish the story that we already know to be true. Once again, those very letters that compose a given name are eager to share another uncanny tale that verifies their validity. As we close, we suppose it was no coincidence Jackson's funeral was not only held on a Full Moon, but on a Lunar Eclipse as well.

### MICHAEL JOSEPH JACKSON

- MICHAEL CAME IN A MOON EMPHASIS
- HE ENCOMPASS A SPECIAL COMPASSION
- MICHAEL IS A HOPE CHAMPION
- MICHAEL IS IN ACCLAIMS AS HE COMPOSES
- MICHAEL IS A PEPSI SPOKESMAN ONCE
- MICHAEL HELPS ILL, HOMELESS PERSONS
- MICHAEL HEALS IN A COMPLIANCE
- MICHAEL CAN ACCOMPLISH, AS HE PLEASES AS A MESSIAH
- HE HAS A PALACE HE CAN ESCAPE IN AS HIS HOME
- MICHAEL HAS A PALENESS ILL
- HIS NOSE IS SEEN AS A CHAMELEON IN SHAPES
- SOME PEOPLE COMPLAIN MICHAEL IS A MEAN ONE IN SMALL MALE MISHAPS
- HE IS NO MANIAC, NO NEMESIS AS HE IS SEEN AS

- ⊚ MICHAEL IS IN SOLACE, A CALMNESS AS HE IS ALONE
- ⊚ MICHAEL'S NAME IS A CLASSIC ICON EONS ON
- ⊚ ON A MAIN MOON ECLIPSE ALL CONSOLE IN SILENCE AS MICHAEL IS SOMEPLACE ELSE

I'm still not sure why a Neptune-ruled musical soul has yet to claim the official kingly title, but I'll leave that up to the Universe to unveil when it's ready. Perhaps the pioneering group that our next musician was a part of could be considered "The King of all Bands." Okay, now we are going back into those Piscean realms for sure. If GEORGE HARRISON, whose SONGS EASE EONS ON, chose not to pursue music, one could definitely say music as we know it today would not be exactly what it is. Born 25 February 1943, Neptune's influence over both his Pisces Sun Sign and 25 Karmic Path granted Harrison the innate ability to channel the music which has now become eternal. Take a Pisces and place their Sun in the 5th house of creativity within a natal birth chart like George's, and a most insatiable desire to manifest artistic creation from within is bound to happen.

And so it did happen for George, starting with the Beatles. Within a Masterful 33/6 Personal Year at the young age of 16—while working as an apprentice electrician (an equally fitting way for him to utilize his soul's talent for accessing details)—he left school and began the journey that would take him to celebrity status when the Beatles were still known as the Quarrymen. By 1963, in Harrison's 28/1 Personal Year of initiations and the start of a brand new 9-year cycle, the Beatles had achieved success and the infamous Beatlemania had begun.

Pisces are always known as the fish that keep on swimming (just think of the Ellen Degeneris voice-over as the blue fish in *Finding Nemo*—this is a Pisces!), and in Harrison's case with being a 25 Karmic Path, this is especially so. Not only was he known as the quiet Beatle, there was the quality within him that enjoyed his solitude and surely sought life beyond the fame and celebrity that touring with a band involved. In a 9 Personal Month, on 04 January 1970, Harrison recorded his last session as a Beatle. 1970 marked one of Harrison's 8 Personal Years of recognition, gains, and harvest. This was not to be received as part of the struggles he had always felt as a Beatle. His release of the album *All Things Must Pass* undoubtedly proved he was meant to shine in his own spotlight, especially when it reached Platinum status in the U.S.A. alone. By the following 27/9 Personal Year of momentous occasions, finalizations and endings, Harrison organized a charity event. The Concert for Bangladesh, attracted over 40,000 people for two sold-out shows at Madison Square Garden.

Harrison's years to follow were equally filled with all kinds of artistic adventures, including Neptune's love of film and cinema. He created his own film production and distribution company, Handmade Films, in 1978, a 34/7 Personal Year. Yet it wasn't until his next 37/1 Personal Year, 1981, that the company started it's first film, *Time Bandits*. If a Piscean 25 soul follows a 26/8 Lifepath, one that requests wisdom, responsibility, stability and learning from experience, it surely explains why this spiritually driven Pisces gravitated to Hinduism and sought to spread its message to others through his work.

The world came together in incredible sadness on 29 November 2001, when George Harrison passed away at the young age of 58 from lung cancer. It is unfortunate to know Harrison was a heavy smoker, for his Saturn in Gemini, the sign which directly rules the lungs, highly warned him to protect this part of his body. His Lexigrams as well tell the tale of his eternal gifts now left to us, and eerily reveal that this Beatle wasn't actually meant to age at all.

## GEORGE HARRISON

- GEORGE GOES EONS ON IN NO EGO
- GEORGE HAS AN HONOR
- GEORGE EARNS IN HONORS AS A SINGER
- HIS SONGS ERGO EONS ON
- EARS HEAR HIS SONGS IN EASE
- HIS SONGS SEE GAINS AS HONORARIES
- GEORGE IS A SEER IN A RANGE O' GAINS
- GEORGE SHARES IN RINGO'S SONGS
- EARS HEAR HIS SONGS IN AN AGREEING REASON
- GEORGE HONES IN ON A GANESH SHRINE
- GEORGE HONES IN ON A HARE KRISHNA AIR
- GEORGE IS A SHARING ONE
- HE HAS NO AGING
- GEORGE IS A SOARING HERO
- GEORGE'S SONGS SHINE EONS ON AS GENRES

Okay, okay, I do believe with all of the swimming we've already done in Neptune's vast seas in this chapter, we ought to come up for a little air. Since we are in the Beatles mood, 18 June 2006 marks the Gemini date of another legendary singer/songwriter and musician extraordinaire, PAUL MCCARTNEY. Here, again, the 18/9 influence brings a soul into the limelight of fame and celebrity on a Universal level. In his song "The End," Paul wrote, "And in the end, the love you take/is equal to the love you make." Well-attuned Geminis can bring this kind of statement to life with the active duality their minds. Because Paul's Gemini Sun sits in the 3rd house in his natal birth chart—which is the area of life in the chart ruled by Gemini—the one side of him surely relates all too well with the other.

In a 1 Personal Year cycle in 1957 when he was only 15, Paul became a Beatle and began what the world now knows to be the most influential band in rock music to date. For the next 13 years, he teamed up with the "Fab Four" and forever changed the face of music, each within their own individual ways. During this era, he was blessed to have met Linda Eastman, a photographer with whom he shared a 30-year relationship. In a 3 Personal Year of expansion in March 1969, he and Linda were married in his Venus-ruled 6 Personal Month—a month most auspicious for marriage. Paul was not only the last Beatle to tie the knot, but he also enjoyed the success of a marriage that did not end in divorce.

It was with deep sadness in the very last month of McCartney's 5 Personal Year of permanent changes, on 17 April 1998, that he lost Linda to breast cancer. December 1970 marked a previous 5 Personal Year for Paul when the world was shocked and dismayed that the beloved Beatles were officially disbanding. Number 5 Personal Years mark tremendous movement for any individual who is in one every 9 years, and by McCartney's cycles at this particular point in time, we were never to see the Beatles together again. However, Paul was fortunate and in his own masterful ways, launched his solo career. After all, an 18/9 Karmic Path is meant to do things all on their own.

Paul's Lifepath is a 31/4, lending to his extreme humanitarian values, where he has a tolerance for all brotherhood and sisterhood. He has been an advocate for the masses, animals, and the environment. We find his birth Name Expression, along with his new title, SIR PAUL MCCARTNEY, to be none other that the 15's *The Magician*. I think it's perfectly clear the magic Paul has enchanted on just about anything he touches. While PAUL MCCARTNEY alone vibes to the 10's *Wheel of Fortune*, the cycles of death and rebirth have occurred numerous times for him. For further validation on the marvels of Sir Paul, on with the Lexigrams from the name he began it all under.

### JAMES PAUL MCCARTNEY

- YES PAUL CAME AS A SUPREME STAR
- YES PAUL A REAL EARNEST MAN
- PAUL CAPTURES ERAS AS PAUL CREATES
- LASTS AS AN ETERNAL STAR
- YES A REAL CLEAR ACCURATE EAR
- A NATURAL MASTER, PAUL CAN PLAY ALL TUNES
- PAUL CREATES A MASTERY ART AS A PLAYER
- MANY, MANY CAMERAMEN SEE PAUL
- PAUL CAN SEE AN ETERNAL SACRAMENT AS HE MEETS L. EASTMAN
- PAUL LASTS YEARS LATER PAST STAR PALS

I would keep going on this whole Beatles rockin' vibe, but I'll let you ponder John and Ringo. Since I have been sworn to be a good teacher, I'm sorry I cannot give you all the answers! Nevertheless, let's continue with our musician journey and keep up the rockin' tunes for sure, but let's stick to what the combination of The Twins, 9, 31, and Paul's seem to create. You know there is a man totally responsible for the electric guitar that allows our musicians to play their rock n' roll. You have to just leave it up to another great Gemini mind to invent such things as LES PAUL did. Born on 09 June 1915, this innovator on more than two levels changed the entire music scene as we had known it from Beethoven's time. What do you get when you cross a guitar with electricity? Certainly it was LESTER WILLIAM POLSFUSS's job to pioneer REAL AMPLIFIER PLEASURES.

Les Paul, who also follows a 31/4 Lifepath, cannot help to pass along a great invention to the world, one that has long-term affects and reaches humanity on a significant level. Combined with the cleverness of a Gemini mind and the ability to pioneer through his 9 Karmic Path, there was a great deal LES PAUL found himself laying down structure and foundation for in a masterful way. Even his name change brought him to a finer name energy of the "get it all started" that's never been started before 1, as his Name Expression became the most fortunate and blessed 19, *The Prince of Heaven*. The Chaldeans were surely right in how we saw LES PAUL's life as it unfolded, as they understood the 19: "This number promises happiness and fulfillment—success in all ventures as well as in the personal life."[21]

While on the heavenly journey of the *Prince* for his career, Les Paul was not exempt from the unexpected while going along on his 31/4 Lifepath. It is always said those guided by Uranus in life will see disturbances along the way, yet they have a built-in kind of tolerance that always will get them over the hurdles they need to jump over to keep going in the race. While amidst the potentials of a conflicting and aggressive 9 Personal Year in 1948, Paul came close to death in a serious car accident, wherein he damaged his Gemini-ruled right arm and elbow. Doctors had thought his arm would never return to fluid movement, but as Les Paul even took on the doctor role, he told them to set it in the natural position he used to play the guitar. By the time he entered his 2 Personal Year by 1949, he had full mobility. This is how a pioneering Gemini 9 walking a 4 Lifepath overcomes his supposed obstacles, for there wasn't one here in Les Paul's mind, even in a seemingly worst-case scenario.

There seems to be a bit of a debate on the actual spelling of Lester's original last name, but as far as we determined how the varying name expressions thus calculate, the correct spelling is POLSFUSS. This combination, with his first and middle names, arrives at the 28's Name Expression, which through the singular 1's energy puts him right on the center stage of life as *The Initiator,* and one who needs to be in control of his own career, rather than depend upon others. Makes perfect sense, right? Long before kicking his 28 birth Name Expression up to the smoother path of the 19—as his LES PAUL name came to be—Lester was engaged fully in this kind of energy in his career. When you've got Mercury, Mars, Uranus, and the Sun grouped together in the soul's primary influence, it is no wonder at all how much Les Paul accomplished in his lifetime, as the tale can be told.

### LESTER WILLIAM POLSFUSS

- ❂ LESTER IS A<u>N</u> AIR MARS SOUL O<u>N</u> A FOUR PLATFORM
- ❂ LESTER IS A REAL TRUE MASTER EAR

- EARNS A LES PAUL RENAME, SET TO SURPASS ALL ELSE
- LES PAUL IS TO SEE A TRUE MASTER LIFE OF EASE
- LES PAUL IS TO SEE MULTIPLES OF STAR FORMULAS
- LES PAUL SELLS REAL AMPLIFIER PLEASURES TO ALL MASSES
- LES PAUL IS A SUPER PURE SPIRITUAL POWER
- LES PAUL SURE IMPRESSES US ALL AS LES PAUL ALTERS A FORMULA
- A LES PAUL IS A SURE TIMELESS POWER
- LES PAUL IS A STAR SET TO A LIFE OF FAME

While I think he primarily played a Fender and not a Les Paul, let's keep on breathing in that air and take a look at A GREAT GUITARIST, such as the Libra 3 STEVIE RAY VAUGHAN. Here's where we will see how Lexigrams equally can manifest what one desires from the name you may choose to utilize as your Name Expression, verses the promise of the birth name alone.

Born 03 October 1954 to STEPHEN RAY VAUGHAN, we see this expansive and Libra leader to be born to an equally mutable 23/5 Lifepath of *The Royal Star of the Lion*. While NEPTUNE may think he's the only planet to truly carry a TUNE, you can't forget the gifts of Venus when it comes to a Libra. Throw in some of Jupiter's natural understanding of things in threes, and music will undoubtedly follow. Speaking of things happily ruled by Jupiter, did you also just realize SAGITTARIUS, oddly enough, spells GUITARS? Whether it is a Sagittarius or a Three, more often than not, you're going to find these Jupiter people innately understand rhythm. Yet, if they don't get a rein on all that mutable fire energy that can see them in no limits, they will not be around to understand anything.

STEPHEN RAY VAUGHAN did just this through his 3 Karmic Path as well as the birth Name Expression of the 21/3, *The Crown of the Magi,* as a true leader of helping us all jam-out to the blues. He did spin into the realms of drugs, yet sobered up and remained so for the last 4 years of his life. Even though he had passed 10 years earlier, on 22 February 2000, marked his induction into the *Blues Hall of Fame.* Had Stevie been physically present, this would have been a 5 Personal Year for him, one bringing him more to the masses along with all of the movement and stir occurring. Even after any soul has departed this earth, if their work is to live on, we do see this is still in timing with their birth information, as if they were still living. I'll bet that in 2000, after his induction, Stevie Ray Vaughan album sales (there are 18 to choose from) jumped slightly.

STEVIE RAY VAUGHAN's Name Expression ticks to the 19's *The Prince of Heaven.* Not a bad choice to have the most fortunate compound number to accompany a natal 3 Karmic Path. This certainly gave Stevie a bit more fixed energy through the singular 1 to attract people to him while he shined upon stage after stage. By 1984, just as his first Saturn Return was completing, he received in his 9 Personal Year of harvest, recognition, and REWARD, a W. C. Handy AWARD for Entertainer of the Year and Instrumentalist of the Year, of which he would see many more, even more after his passing. Although he was born to STEPHEN RAY VAUGHAN (I'd love to tell you my findings here, but remember I have to leave some things for you to start to figure out on your own when you are ready), it is his amended Name Expression wherein we see more of the gifts that this talented Libra 3 has left to us all as:

## STEVIE RAY VAUGHAN

- YES STEVIE IS HERE AS A TRUE AIR THREE STAR
- STEVIE IS SENT AS A VERY GREAT GUITARIST
- STEVIE IS IN A SURE GREAT VARIETY AS STEVIE TUNE-IN EVERYTHING
- STEVIE HAS A VERY VERY VERY GREAT EAR HE HEARS IN
- STEVIE INVENTS TRUE GREAT STRING TUNES
- STEVIE REST IN A VERY GREAT HARVEST AS HE INVEST IN HIS GUITAR
- IT IS A GUARANTEE STEVIE IS A RISEN SIGNATURE STAR
- STEVIE IS SEEN IN NAUGHTIER AREAS AS HIS HUNGERS RAGE IN A SEVERITY
- STEVIE IS IN A GREAT HERITAGE
- YES STEVIE IS SEEN AS A VINTAGE VIRTUE AS HE SEE HIS GRAVE
- STEVIE'S TUNES ARE IN REVIVES AS STEVIE'S TUNES STAY HERE

Let's move on from air and play with some fire ambers. There's no better choice to do so than taking a star peek at the stellar firecracker of a Sagittarius, CHRISTINA AGUILERA, who was undoubtedly SENT AS A REAL TRUE SINGER. She is, as the stars can verify, all fire, baby! Born on 18 December 1980 to a 30/3 Lifepath, this gal is exactly as she's always presented herself—one independent flame that burns endlessly. You shouldn't be too surprised with all the fire influence here, as when you combine the energy of both Mars and Jupiter, it is best to watch out for what will be ignited! (You may need to keep water handy, trust me.)

When her debut album *Christina Aguilera* hit the pop scene on 24 August 1999, Aguilera was soon to close an expansive and sprouting 3 Personal Year. That August marked her birth of sorts, when she came out to the world fighting for her voice to be heard. No one seemed to be afraid of it. Next came *Stripped*, released in a balancing 6 Personal Year on 29 October 2002. After 13 million copies, even through Christina's 18 *Spiritual–Material Conflict* energy brought her some along the way, she had proven by her 8 Personal Year, in 2004, that she was to be recognized for her masterful singing talents.

She was equally destined to hit it again as *Back to Basics* was released 15 August 2006. In her 1 Personal Year cycle of the ever-fortunate 19, she was at the start of a brand new 9-year era in her evolution. August marked her 9 Personal Month of universal energy coupled with fame and celebrity, a most auspicious time for her to yet again reach the masses. This album's release date's Lifepath was none other than the Masterful 22. (That's the simplicity of adding this calendar dates numbers all together to arrive at a total.) But of course, *Back to Basics* jumped right out of the gate at number one, and with Uranus guiding its 22/4 Lifepath, it is sure to display many reinventions of Christina's undeniable talent. Intuitively, Christina chose a title that also grants it the energy to reach the masses easily.

*Back to Basics* numerically vibrates to the 23, the *Royal Star of the Lion*. Mercury's influence over the singular 5 energy here surely will allow this masterpiece to communicate quickly and handsomely to the world at large. Now some 4 million copies later, I think it spoke quite well. Here's a fun example of how, as always, the clues within the uncanny Lexigrams lend more insight to their fate, as we must remember, it's not only names but also the titles we can choose, too, that are so important in the stories they can tell: BACK TO BASICS: IT STICKS COAST TO COAST; IT TICKS, IT TOCKS; ITS TASK IS TO COST; IT BOASTS A BIT AS IT ACTS; IT IS CAST TO ACCOST. I know, I know Stars, sometimes I stretch your minds a bit with these, but that is how we all learn more in life, isn't it?

Our Star Christina has some tricky numbers like the late Michael Jackson dealt with when it comes to her Name Expressions. Born to CHRISTINA MARIA AGUILERA, once again we see the 38's (same meaning as the 29) *Grace Under Pressure* energies. While the 18 Karmic Path alone can present aggression and challenge to the soul, this really intensifies the emotions when they do. As Christina's life most certainly has seen, she did not have the closest relationship to her own father growing up, nor as an adult, as one can learn about in her lyrics. Yet the 18 denotes she is of a universal energy, with the singular 9 granting her the ability to affect masses of people in her lifetime. With the Lifepath of the 30's *Loner—Meditation*, Jupiter requests she expands us all as she does so, but she must spend her time in solitude to be able to handle the mighty task.

What is more interesting to note is her current Name Expression of CHRISTINA AGUILERA also rings to the other number that represents *Grace Under Pressure*, the 29. Although it is for certain Christina has matured with age, as long as she gravitates to charitable acts as her career keeps reaping her rewards, she'll smooth out any emotional attachments this number loves to bring on. Let the Lexigrams finally conclude the birthright of Christina's true path in this lifetime:

## CHRISTINA MARIA AGUILERA

- ◉ SHE IS SENT A SAGITTARIUS EIGHTEEN STAR AS SHE AIMS A THREE TRAIL
- ◉ CHRISTINA IS SENT AS A REAL TRUE MASTER SINGER
- ◉ CHRISTINA IS HERE AS A TRUE SIGNATURE SINGER
- ◉ CHRISTINA LEARNS EARLIER MEN CAN CLAIM A MEAN ANGER
- ◉ THIS GENIUS GIRL CAN SING REAL HIGH IN GREAT TUNE
- ◉ SHE SEES A START IN THE LATIN MUSIC SCENE, THEN IN USA/AMERICA SHE INTRIGUES US AS A NAUGHTIER GIRL
- ◉ SHE IS A GREAT STAGE MUSICAL STAR, A NATURAL TALENT, A TRUE TREASURE
- ◉ IT IS CERTAIN SHE SEES THE MAIN CHART HITS AGAIN & AGAIN
- ◉ AS CHRISTINA RISES IN A REAL TRUE STAR LIGHT, SHE CAN LAST AS AN ETERNAL STAR
- ◉ HER RESULTS ARE RICH GAINS AS SHE EARNS
- ◉ SHE IS A REAL STAR TREASURE THAT CAN LAST

It is interesting to note that Christina, at the time of this book going to press, seems to have found herself back in some not so happier ambers of her own in the soul's process. So I'll stop playing with the fire now before we get too hot. Are your ears ringing alive with the harmonious messages from within the music world? Now that we've got you even further in-tune, I suggest we don't stop now, and keep going, for there are far too many other areas of life we need to keep our spiraling wings awake for, so let's turn down the volume just a bit. We'll be journeying into the likes of other notable stars and celebrities who grace our stages, so if you need your glasses to see the big screen, put them on.

# Chapter 6

## PEOPLE IN TV / FILM

*"Seeing the awesome power of the word, we must understand what power comes out of our mouths."*
—Don Miguel Ruiz

So we've seen some pretty circumstantial evidence thus far in how Lexigrams work for some of our historical figures and people who have captured our ears with the likes of music. We'll continue on now with some other kinds of STARS that shine in the ARTS of TV and Film, who were cast into their roles that their names decided to play out in the tales that can be told. What you'll soon discover here is, whether it is from the original birth name or the stage name they chose to utilize, it will no longer be a secret to investigate that the fame was surely meant to find the people who have made their mark as they became celebrities and public icons.

A most notable example of how Lexigrams are a star secret not to be taken lightly is our dearly beloved JUDY GARLAND. We all know her from the timeless story of *The Wizard of Oz*, and her brilliant career that followed afterward. She was a star that for certain left us too soon. Judy Garland became her stage name, but it is through the energy of her original name, FRANCES ETHEL GUMM, that we see the real story of how she became known as the legendary

ETERNAL STAR that she will forever remain. Born to a Gemini Sun on 10 June 1922, living out a life through the Twins influence more often than not leads one to live a life of duality, which she did embrace. Under the 10 Karmic Path, it can now be said that Judy saw the turning of the *The Wheel of Fortune,* as the Chaldeans so deeply understood this compound number to mean, that it goes faster when dominion is not practiced in the life to ordain a peaceful existence.

Ms. Gumm was sent to *The Crown of the Magi* 21 Lifepath, that of the Optimist. Jupiter's expansion over this 3 Lifepath promises luck and fortune, while the 21 claims the soul's testing is over—yet her other influence of the 3 is found through the 12, as her birth Name Expression requests that she always remain the "kneeling, submissive student" so as not to fall to *The Sacrifice–The Victim* scenarios that potentially follow this number. As Judy Garland, she changed her entire Name Expression to the pure 4, which does grant individuality and invention, but highly warns of obstacles and the unexpected to occur. And so it was as Judy got swept up into the MGM spotlight, the uncertainties celebrity life brings began to knock at her door, thanks to MGM's regulation of her weight. It's all here from the letters composing:

### FRANCES ETHEL GUMM

- FRANCES CAME AS A REAL "GEM"
- SENT AS A MASTERFUL MEGA MGM STAR AS A TEENAGER
- EMERGES AS A REAL MASTER STAR AS A TEEN, SHE HAS A GRACE & AN ELEGANCE
- AS SHE ACTS SHE CREATES A GARLAN<u>D</u> NAME CHANGE

- SHE CAN ACT, A REAL NATURAL EARNS MEGA AT MGM
- THEN SHE SEE A REAL SLAUGHTER AS MGM REGULATES HER
- SEEN IN REAL MGM SCREEN FEATURES AND HUGE STAGES
- SHE HAS AN UNSAFE CAREER AS HER HEART RACES
- SHE HURTS HERSELF AS SHE GETS LEAN AS SHE HAS TEARFUL MATCHES NEAR MEN
- SHE HAS MEGA FANS
- SHE CAN LAST AS AN ETERNAL STAR
- SHE HAS A REAL TRUE GRATEFUL GENTLE HEART

Although the world has yet to truly see another star that imitates the Gemini likes of the clever Judy Garland, one modern-day master talent is seen embracing Cancer's leadership in the actress category. Born 22 June 1949, stellar film and stage actress MERYL STREEP started her last 9 Personal Year off in 2006 with the blessed 36/9, and wasted no time getting to the momentous part that increases her fame and celebrity all the more with June 30's anticipated release of the film *The Devil Wears Prada*. Our Cancer-ruled Master Number 22 actress again surely saw many praises from that latest finely crafted performance. With a Venus-ruled 6 Lifepath, Meryl is meant to find her way in life through the arts, and possesses the ability to reap handsome financial rewards along the way.

Streep's formal education began at Vassar and led her to the Yale School of Drama. By 1977, just as she was approaching her 1st Saturn return in a Neptune-ruled 7 Personal Year, she dove deep into character to portray her first film role in *Julia*. She was listed as one of twelve

Promising New Actors of 1977 in John Willis's *Screen World* (vol. 29). By 1978, she was granted her first Oscar nomination for *The Deer Hunter*, and she was well on her way to reaping the harvest of a 9-year cycle. She went on to gain total recognition later on as she won her first Oscar for *Kramer vs. Kramer* in 1979, wherein in a 9 Personal Year, fame and celebrity had totally found her.

Still going strong almost thirty years later, 2006/07's 9 Personal Year for Streep was no exception, when again she was back in the limelight. She continues to expand within the 21/3 *Crown of the Magi's* gifts at the time this book goes to press from 2009's Personal Year cycle. While *IT'S COMPLICATED* did indeed carry Streep TO A DIPLOMATIC OPTIMIST PLACE, her 2006 runaway hit awarded her another *Golden Globe* in 2007, as it was written:

### THE DEVIL WEARS PRADA

- IT ASPIRE AS IT TRAVELS AS A WIDESPREAD HIT
- ITS STAR IS STREEP IN HER VERSATILE LEADERSHIP WEALTH
- IT IS HIP, A HIT LIST LEADER
- IT IS SET AS STREEP IS A REAL REWARD REAPER LATER

The stars and planets above back up the innate talent we already know MERYL STREEP has. With a Name Expression of the 15's *Magician*, it is easy to see how she casts those spells of hers as she works. It's always been about achieving a real balance either way with the repeated energy of Venus through the singular 6, which is also displayed in her birth name. With a birth Name Expression of the 24's *Love Money Creativity (*which in a nutshell means:

do what you love through your creativity and the money is sure to follow, just don't abuse it!), we see this adds to the story that is able to tell its Lexigram tale from within, which further indicates this masterful life is gracing her with an easeful path to stardom.

### MARY LOUISE STREEP

- SET TO SEE A PRIME MASTER STAR TRAIL
- A REAL TREASURE, A PLEASURE TO SEE
- SET TO USE A 'MERYL' ALIAS AS A TRUE STAR
- MERYL STIMULATES US TO LET OUT OUR EMOTES AS TEARS
- MERYL IS A REAL MYSTERIOUS SOUL SET TO IMPRESS US
- YES MERYL IS TO SEE LOTS OF PRAISES
- MERYL IS A REAL SUPREME STAR SET TO LAST
- MERYL IS SET TO PLAY SOME REAL SUPERIOR ROLES
- YES MERYL IS TO SEE SOME MATURE, SERIOUS PARTS
- MERYL SURE IS SET TO SEE ROYALTIES AS A PRIME STREAM

While Meryl makes us look within on film and the stage, there are times when real life stuns us and makes us wish we were watching just a make-believe movie. A star was born in Perth, Australia on 04 April 1979 to the name HEATHCLIFF ANDREW LEDGER that did just this, as we witnessed another budding Hollywood talent's life be taken far too soon, back in January of 2008. Ledger's 4 Karmic Path had an extra punch of Uranus's originality and invention with this Aries Sun placement. Leadership positions suited Ledger and he undeniably brought his pioneering spirit to all of his courageous acts along his 34/7 Lifepath of *Discrimination–Analysis*, which gave him a keen eye for details and the ability to absorb information, which is then spun out in another fashion after deeply depicting it.

Neptune guided Ledger along his 7 Lifepath, wherein his gravitation to the screen and acting arts is of no surprise. His knack of being able to create the kind of character anyone could relate to was marked by his 4 Karmic Path with intense human understanding. The ability to succeed in the cinema arts was the innate path Ledger yearned to follow. Unfortunately with a 7 Lifepath so is the potential of the tendency to fall to delusion through the intake of drugs and substance abuse.

Ledger was deeply affected by the well-known Chaldean Numerical understanding of the mysteries surrounding the combination of the 4 and 8 energies. Beyond his 4 Karmic Path and 13 degrees Aries Sun, he also saw other influences of these vibrations. Ledger's natal Mercury is at 26 degrees Pisces, Saturn at 8 degrees Virgo, North Node at 17 degrees Virgo, South Node at 17 degrees Pisces, and Pluto at 17 degrees Libra. The Chaldeans always note that the combination of these numbers causes certain types of hardship, or lessons to be learned in life, some much harder to accept than others. Ledger was also, oddly enough, finishing his 17/8 Personal Year, and he was reaping in his harvest of the previous 7, receiving tremendous recognition and gains. He passed on 22 January, on the 4th floor, apartment 4, a space of 4,400 square feet. January represented his 9 Personal Month, and a 4 Personal Day for him. Uranus's guidance through the 4 not only brings individualism, but when one is not careful, the gate is wide open for the unexpected to occur.

As Astrology will also indicate, Ledger was at the beginning stages of his first Saturn Return, with the planet of karma and fatherly influence returning to where it exactly was when Ledger was born. With his 8-degree Saturn in Virgo placement, the then current Saturn in Virgo had just conjuncted his natal Saturn while passing directly over it during this Retrograde passage. The Saturn Return can be one of the more challenging periods in any soul's life. It is times such as these that being aware of one's star secrets can be key to handling and understanding the influences surrounding any soul.

When Saturn entered Virgo in September 2007, it was right away that Ledger saw the energies begin of his Return, as he parted from Michelle Williams. This separation deeply affected him, as well as the distance that came between him and his young daughter Matilda. Williams, a native Virgo Sun was also currently experiencing her 1st Saturn Return, and it is extremely overwhelming when both one's Sun and Saturn are conjunct within the natal chart when such a planetary passage as the Saturn Return occurs. Their daughter Matilda is also a Scorpio, who more often than not sees death and rebirth occur throughout the lifetime like no other sign in the Zodiac.

As Ledger passed on within a 17/8 Personal Year, we yet again see the eternal energies of *The Star of the Magi*. This number's karmic mystery is deeply understood to be the number of eternity, where those upon the earth influenced by it will be remembered long after they are gone. And so will it be with Health Ledger. His star will undoubtedly shine on as one of the great acting talents of his time who left us far too soon.

As we conclude with the usual evidence of Lexigrams, make no mistake that each and every soul has the power of choice to not allow the negative derivations to manifest. One should also never predict through Lexigrams a living entity's death. Yet, when the event has transpired, it is an eerie finding that we hope, for all souls, can be a learning tool that it is essential what you name anything in life. Not only does Ledger's name capture his story—both Michelle Williams and his daughter Matilda have the energy within their names that equally tells the tale that the world sadly saw unfold upon 22 January 2008.

## HEATHCLIFF ANDREW LEDGER

- HEATH HERE IN A GREAT CARING HEART
- HEATH HERE IN A FINE GRAND LIFE
- HEATH A REAL LEARNER
- HEATH HERE IN A REAL GRACE
- HEATH A REAL LEAD TALENT, HE FIND HE CAN ACT WELL
- HEATH REACH A GRAND DREAM FEW FIND IN AN ACTING CAREER
- HEATH FIND HE A LEADING MAN IN AN ACTING ART
- HEATH FIND A REAL ACTING GIFT
- HEATH A REAL LARGE GAIN WHEN HE ACT
- HEATH A GREAT EARNER IN AN ACTING AREA
- HEATH THEN CREATE A REAL CAREFREE LIFE
- HEATH IN DANGER WHEN HE DRIFT IN A HIGH
- HEATH IN A REAL INNER HEAD HINDER
- HEATH NEED A REAL HEALTHIER INTERNAL LIFE
- HEATH HAD A HIDDEN FRAGILE HEALTH DANGER
- HEATH WANDERED WHEN HE FLEW HIGH

- IN A HEADLINER IN WINTER WE LEARN HEATH DIED IN A FATAL END
- IN A FATED END HEATH REACHED A CHALLENGED TRAGIC DEATH
- HEATH FLED AN EARTHEN LIFE THEN LIFTED IN AN ETHEREAL LIGHT
- HEATH HERE IN A REAL ETERNAL LEGEND

We see, too, the people closest to him have similar clues to reveal and validate what became Ledger's ill-fate:

## MATILDA ROSE LEDGER

- EARLIER MATILDA IS SET TO LOSE A DEAR DAD TO A REAL SAD DOSE
- MATILDA DOES SEE A STAR DAD DIE EARLIER
- MATILDA IS STILL SET TO SEE DREAMS ARISE
- MATILDA IS SET TO SEE A MASTER ERA LATER

## MICHELLE INGRID WILLIAMS

- IS SEEN IN MAIN NEWS AS HER DEAR LEDGER DIES
- MICHELLE WILL SEE A SAD LEDGER HEADLINE
- MICHELLE WILL HEAL IN A MIRACLE
- MICHELLE IS IN GRAND HEALINGS

Okay, it's definitely time to lighten things up a bit and put our Kleenex away. How about some LAUGHTER? We all need to HEAL THE GREAT HEART, GATHER A REAL LAUGH, and GET THE REAL HEAL. One can definitely do this if they turn on the good 'ole TV and take in some of the hilarious Sagittarian talents of JON STEWART, the STAR host behind Comedy Central's smash HOT HIT, *The Daily Show*. This Archer is no stranger to aiming in some big ideas.

Born on 28 November 1962, his Karmic Path of the 28's *The Trusting Lamb* grants him the ability to magically bring initiations to life coupled by the expansiveness that his strong Jupiter-ruled Sagittarian persona is constantly shooting for. Jupiter's also seen governing over his Lifepath of the 39/12/3, so it is no wonder at all how Mr. Stewart has landed in the role of the comedic philosopher, actor and writer, all while spreading around that underlying wisdom which streams through just about everything he touches. This man follows his 39/12 Lifepath advice to a tee: he constantly educates himself. With his natal Sun, Moon, and Mercury all in the jovial Archer sign, one can readily see how not only education but comedy comes so easily to Jon. The energy of Jupiter is how he forms his identity, deals with his emotions, and develops his mentality. Sagittarian energy can be known to be brutally honest and quite blunt at times, a quality seen often as Jon expresses his ingenious jesting of the daily news, yet there is always a brutally honest truth behind the irony he reveals to us.

Jon entered a second Personal Year in 2006. As this current 9-year cycle evolved, no doubt we continued to witness the creative originality of Jon's style to grow and expand to new levels. As his birthday fell in 2005, a 1 Personal Year began for Jon, marking the beginning of his now current 9-year cycle. The spin-off of *The Colbert Report* certainly indicated the furthering of Jon's clever talents as a producer, along with some prestigious recognition of his hosting talents when he was granted the role at the Academy Awards ceremony that year.

However you want to look at Jon's names, he is the master at what he does. The name JON STEWART expresses itself as the 11, and it surely seems he has found a way to avoid the turmoil that can surround the Chaldeans understanding of *A Lion Muzzled–A Clenched Fist*. Maybe it is because he cut his entire value in half from his birth Name Expression of JONATHAN STUART LEIBOWITZ, which is the 22's *Submission and Caution*. I think Jon has it all figured out, as the Chaldeans also said of this master number: "The karmic obligation here is to be more alert, to curb 'spiritual laziness,' and develop more spiritual aggressiveness—to realize your own power to change things, to prevent failure by simply ordaining success."[22] I think when it comes to the spirit behind seeking the truth as all good Sagittarian souls do, those arrows of Jon's are more than aggressive. Congratulations on the mastery, Jon.

## JONATHAN STUART LEIBOWITZ

- JON IS SENT TO LEARN AS A REAL WISE HONORABLE "ONE"
- JON IS SENT TO EARTH TO BE IN SHOW BIZ, HE IS BEST AT A REAL TRUE JEST
- JON IS A TRUE NATURAL STAR TALENT
- HE SURE IS SET TO BE A USA NATIONAL STAR HOST IN A REAL ZEAL
- WE ALSO SEE HE SURE IS SET TO BE THE BEST NEWS HOST AT NITE
- IT IS AN ABSOLUTE THAT JON RETAINS OUR ATTENTION
- JON STARTS AS AN INSTANT HIT, A STAR WRITER
- HE HAS THE BEST JEST OF THE WORST NEWS ON HIS STAR SHOW

- IN NO HESITATION WITH BRUTAL HONESTIES JON IS SET TO TRANSLATE THE NEWS
- HE IS SET TO SHOW US TO A REAL JOURNALIST TRUTH
- JON IS A REAL HILARIOUS LABORIOUS ONE
- JON RELATES HIS STAR SHOW TO ALL ON A NORTHEAST SET
- AS A STAR WRITER JON WRITES A HILARIOUS USA HISTORIAN BEST SELLER TO RISE ON THE HIT LIST
- JON IS TO SIRE A SON NATHAN LATER ON
- SOONER THAN LATER HE IS SET TO HOST THE BEST IN SHOW BIZ
- JON IS NOT THAT INTO "THE RULES" AS HE LEARNS TO USE HIS OWN TRUTH
- JON IS INTO A WIL SHORTZ ROUTINE AS HE USES HIS BRAIN
- JON IS SURE SET TO LAST AS AN ETERNAL STAR TALENT

We've witnessed Jon commenting on his shows about "star and planet things" such as a Mercury Retrograde period. That makes it absolutely certain our expansive Sagittarian has an open mind to the esoteric and the mighty planets above, more to back up that spiritual aggressiveness that is required! No doubt he keeps his optimist channel tuned in properly, as he also seems to know how to pick the right names for his projects:

**THE JON STEWART SHOW**

- TO SHOW THE NEWS AS A JEST
- SET AS A HOT SHOW
- OOH WEE, JON'S THE HOT HOST

## THE DAILY SHOW

- ⟲ YES! IT IS A HIT SET TO LAST WIDELY
- ⟲ WE HAIL THE SHOW AS A DAILY "LAW"
- ⟲ WE SEE IT LATE DAY TO DAY
- ⟲ OH YES ITS HOST IS A HOT HIT

## THE COLBERT REPORT

- ⟲ THE OTHER TOP HOT "HOOT"
- ⟲ HERE TO HELP COHERE THE BETTER CHEER
- ⟲ THE OTHER BLOOPER AND BLEEPER HERO

While Jon has become a modern-day truth-telling kind of hero, there is another soul who embraces a different kind of HERO IN A FINE HOPE role though her work. Inventive and individualistic, Aquarian OPRAH WINFREY surely knows how to bring forth her water bearing energy to reap handsome rewards. Born 29 January 1954 to an 8-degree Aquarian Sun in her second house of earning power, she is innate at understanding that hard work and responsibility are the roots which will manifest an amazing harvest. Winfrey has displayed her ruling planet Uranus's love of humanity countless times over in her amazing career. With a Karmic Path of the 29's *Grace Under Pressure*, the key in this lifetime is to react to pressurized situations with the opposing energy of complete and utter optimism. Coupled with a 29-degree Sagittarian rising, it is no wonder Winfrey took on the challenges her early life presented to her and reacted with the grace and enthusiasm her Karmic Path demands, and being charitable under this vibration greatly dilutes any negative affect to come to the life. Since a very young age, she has risen above the circumstances of a broken home, rape, and the mystery of who her biological father truly is.

Winfrey's Lifepath also places her under Uranus's rule with the 31/4, one that gravitates her to obstacles in life, yet her soul intuitively understands these are only to be stepping stones to lessons needing to be learned. Winfrey knew from a very young age she would earn her dollars through the means of nurturing humanity, which began at a tender 2 years old when she mesmerized the members of her church by translating and conveying a passage from the Bible. Drawing upon her 19-degree Mercury in Aquarius in the 2nd house, her gift to acquire riches through her innate gift of communication was already set in stone. This blessed *The Prince of Heaven* degree of Mercury denotes she has the power to lift and bring the masses to a more beneficial place.

By the age of 31, in an 8 Personal Year of recognitions and gains nearing the close of her then-current 9-year cycle, Winfrey began the *The Oprah Winfrey Show*. A year later in 1986, she established HARPO PRODUCTIONS. (There is no surprise here either that Winfrey must have a clue about those Lexigrams... OPRAH is HARPO!) This capped off the 9 Personal Year, a major transitory year that allowed her to enter into another 9-year cycle of life, starting in 1987, which she evolved handsomely through. Twenty-three years later, within another 5 Personal Year in 2009, she made the decision to set the goal to make a permanent change to end her talk show on 09 September 2011. This will occur in a 7 Personal Year for Oprah, one where she will be urged to spend time in solitude to regroup. Just wait and see what she'll reinvent and ultimately harvest in her 8 Personal Year by 2012.

The world has seen Winfrey lovingly bring only joy to countless lives over the years that have followed since her hit shows' inception, and our Aquarian wonder has been recognized time and time again with one award and achievement after another. By 2003, yet again one of those 8 Personal Years of recognitions and gains, at the ripe age of 49, she was completely established as a self-made billionaire over her vast entertainment empire. From the theatre, TV shows, literature clubs, and the instant success of *O Magazine,* Winfrey continues year to year to bring her charitable and optimistic soul to the needs of the humanitarian cause. We needn't worry just because her show is ending that she'll stop bringing new life to things.

OPRAH alone is graced with the 23's *The Royal Star of the Lions* blessings of communication to the masses. OPRAH WINFREY vibes to the pure 6, wherein Venus surely requests she bring balance to all she touches. Once again we see a birth Name Expression that also is guided by the ever-powerful messenger Mercury, as OPRAH GAIL WINFREY carries the 14's *Movement and Challenge* magnetic communication understanding. To affirm the complete tale, we gain more insight into the life of this remarkable woman by seeing how her birth name shows her story to unfolding. We couldn't help but also include the titles she has chosen to bring her healing light and hope to the world in her more than graceful ways.

### OPRAH GAIL WINFREY

- ◉ OPRAH HAIL HER LIFE IN A REAL HOPE
- ◉ OPRAH WILL GAIN A FINE HEALING POWER
- ◉ EARLY ON IN LIFE OPRAH PROFILE A POWER IN RELIGION
- ◉ IN ONE RAINY YEAR OPRAH IN PAIN IN A HORRIFYING RAPE

- OPRAH REPAIR IN A REAL PRAYER
- OPRAH LEARN NO FEAR OR NO WORRY WILL WIN IN ANY LIFE
- OPRAH RARELY IN AN ANGRY WAY IN LIFE
- OPRAH LEARN ONE A GONER IN AN EGO
- OPRAH HONE IN ON A REAL POWER WAY
- OPRAH EARN IN HER OWN LARGE FLOWING WAY
- OPRAH REAP A REAL FINE POWER IN HER LIFE
- OPRAH EARN A FLOWERING YEARLY HONOR
- OPRAH PLAY A GROWING HELPING ROLE IN LIFE
- OPRAH AN ORIGINAL HERO IN AN OPEN GLORY

## THE OPRAH WINFREY SHOW

- YES IT IS A HIT FOR YEARS
- IT IS SET AS A PROFITEER OPERATION FOR YEARS
- ITS HOST OPRAH IS HERE TO HEAL OTHERS
- WE SEE TONS OF FRESH, FINE, FREE HOPE
- OPRAH SHOW THE HATE HAS NO WAY TO SHINE
- WOW, IT HAS THE POWER TO EARN TONS
- OPRAH OPENS THE HEART'S WINDOW TO THE EARTH
- IT IS SET IN A FINE WAY TO SHINE ON
- IT IS SET TO HONOR TOP HONORARIES
- IT IS A THERAPY TO TRANSPIRE WISHES
- IT IS SET TO REFASHION AS IT OPERATES
- WE SEE OPRAH IS A TOP PIONEER IN A NEW FRONTIER

## HARPO PRODUCTIONS

- IT IS A TIP TOP AND PROUD PRO "CHAT" ART CO.
- IT IS IN NO RAINS, NO PAINS OR SIN
- IT ADOPTS SHARP PRODUCTS

- ◉  IT CAN DO NO CORRUPTION
- ◉  THIS IS IN A TOP SAINTHOOD IN OPTIONS
- ◉  IT CAN COUNT ITS DURATION AS IT IS IN TONS O' CHARITIES
- ◉  THIS CAN UPSTAND TO TOP UTOPIAN HONORS
- ◉  IT IS NOT TO STOP IN ITS SUPPORT TO PATRONS
- ◉  IT IS TO NOURISH US ON AND ON
- ◉  IT IS TO TOUCH TONS IN SUPPORT

While Oprah was destined to be placed on earth to be seen on the realms of stage and TV, another soul was sent down to nurture us through his star gifts in broadcasting. The man who said, "I knew that God put me on this earth to be on the radio," was none other than the late ED BRADLEY. How wonderful it was that Ed Bradley so deeply listened to his inner voice back in 1963. In the 1st year of a 9-year cycle, Ed found himself working for hardly any money at WDAS in Philadelphia, yet this is the pivotal moment where his dream began to unfold. The 1 Personal Year is when we find ourselves at a new beginning in the life, planting seeds that will manifest to greatness over the course of time. Ed Bradley is a star that no doubt listened to his secrets within, and the beautiful garden that was to handsomely blossom became one of the most influential and successful careers in TV journalism.

Born to a master number Karmic Path on 22 June 1941, Bradley was blessed with the Cancer energy of the nurturer and a most charitable personality. 22's possess an extreme humanitarian nature, while keen in the ability to bring foundation and perfection to everything in life. With a 7 Lifepath of *The Seeker,* he led his life with sensitivity, mystery, and sympathy, and certainly spirituality was seen in his every move throughout his long and incredible career. With a Moon in Gemini, Bradley loved anything intellectual, but especially apparent was his love of jazz music, for it soothed his emotions greatly.

While under the name ED BRADLEY, we find a Name Expression of the 18/9's *Spiritual–Material Conflict,* of which Ed surely embraced the spiritual side more often than he indulged in the energy of greed, which materialism can sometimes bring along with a career of fame and celebrity. Funny how we can derive YEARLY ED A REAL REBEL as he carried this 9 energy, which through the influence of Mars always denotes some daring and bold moves along the way. Yet, as we look to his birth name of EDWARD RUDOLPH BRADLEY, JR., we see his original Name Expression is the 42's *Love Money Creativity,* which carries the same karmic mystery as the 24 that we just saw in Meryl Streep's numerological analysis. Just one more example of how a soul can reap such balance along their career by honoring their soul's innate requests.

The 24/42 refers to the weaving of a tapestry filled with the entire color spectrum all along the life that keeps returning a bountiful harvest when diligence is applied. Ed Bradley was once quoted as saying, "My formula for success has three elements: the talent you're given, the hard work you do to get better at whatever it is that you do, and a certain amount of luck. And I always found that the harder I worked, the better my luck was, because I was prepared for that." So many of the details in Bradley's birth chart and numerical energy points to why he could make such a statement: he listened to his inner voice, got good at what he was talented at, and worked hard. The luck he manifested was only from the roots of his intense labors that he loved doing so much.

With Venus guiding his 42/6 birth Name Expression, which also admired the beauty of the infamous Lena Horne, we also shouldn't be too surprised Ed was on *60 Minutes* for a total of 26 years. As always, the tale once again of a life that was superbly led is right in front of us waiting to be told:

### EDWARD RUDOLPH BRADLEY, JR.

- AN EARLY PRELUDE, ED HAD A HARDER ROAD
- ED BEHOLD A REORDER AND HE EYE AHEAD
- ED A REAL LEARNER AND AN ABLE DURABLE LABORER
- ED A READY PROBER, HE A REALLY DEEP LAD
- ED A READY PEOPLE HELPER
- ED A REAL WORDLY LEADER
- HE REAPED A REAL WORLDY JOB
- HE HEAR ALL A WORLD WORRY
- HE WORE A REAL DAPPER WARDROBE
- HE PROUDLY WORE A BEARD AND A REBEL EARR(ing)
- YEARLY HE A REAL BROAD LEADER
- HE HAD A PURE PEOPLE POWER
- HE DRAW YOU <u>IN</u> REAL DEEP, HE ALLOW A REAL AWARE
- ED'<u>S</u> "REAL" REWARD: A LENA HORNE READ
- ED A REAL DEAR LEADER, ED REWARDED YEARLY A REAL RARE AWARD
- HE AWARDED A PEABODY AWARD
- HE HERALD A REAL HERO ROLE

Whether you watch the news on CBS or not, you'll find another TV journalist that was by all means meant to grace the airways as he EARNS BIG ON ABC: CHARLES GIBSON. It seems our water signs most definitely have a way that they sooth us with their sensitive delivery of telling us the bad news we probably do not want to hear the majority of the time. Another water sign coupled with innate leadership energy, Gibson was born to swim as a Pisces Fish on 09 March 1943. With his pure courageous motivation of his Mars-ruled 9 Karmic Path, this broadcaster's career spanned 44 years before he retired in his 5 Personal Year of major movement and change in 2009. While we may no longer have Charlie greeting us in the early hours of the morning or empathetically reporting the world news to us every evening, we doubt he truly has stopped working.

While following his 29 Lifepath of *Grace Under Pressure,* CHARLES DEWOLF GIBSON for sure understood how to combat the natural forces this number can present. He was fortunate enough to be raised with an exceptional education at the Sidwell Friends School in his early years, before attending Princeton, where he first began finding leadership roles in radio. With his birth Name Expression of the 58/13/4, we can most certainly see how he brought his own true sense of the 13's *Regeneration–Change,* as he reported on the doings of humanity through his lengthy career, which saw more than its fair share of it.

Through the Name Expression of CHARLES GIBSON, we find the 25's *Discrimination—Analysis* that allowed his Piscean soul to dive deeper into the current events or topic at hand. Anyone with a 9 Karmic Path is known to tell it pretty much like it is in life, but as Charlie did for us so many times, it was accompanied by his Neptune influence of being able to deliver it in a smooth and syrupy fashion. There was a wise yet extremely calm way Gibson carried himself on the air.

From his star secret energies, his life at Sidwell, and all the way to ABC's *World News Tonight with Charles Gibson*, it all was just awaiting to unfold in this lifetime from the name Charlie chose to come back to and make it all manifest from:

## CHARLES DEWOLF GIBSON

- ⊙ CHARLES IS HERE AGAIN AS A REAL WISE FISHES LEADER ON A GRACE LIFELINE
- ⊙ HE HAS AN ALIAS AS HE IS CALLED "CHARLIE"
- ⊙ HE LEARNS IN A SIDWELL FRIENDS SCHOOL EARLIER ON FOR COLLEGE
- ⊙ HE LEARNS HOW RADIO IS AN AREA HE WILL SOON GO FOR
- ⊙ AS HE GOES ON HE LEARNS HE HAS A DEAR NEWS ANCHOR ROLE HE FILLS WELL
- ⊙ HE IS SEEN AS HE EARNS ON ABC NEWS SHOWS IN HIS LONG GOLDEN CAREER
- ⊙ HE HAS A BIG FOLLOWING AS ALL HEAR HIS NEWS
- ⊙ CHARLIE HAS A REAL FEELING WE SEE AS HE IS HEARD RECALLING NEWS
- ⊙ CHARLIE HAS A NO-FEAR FEEL AS HE IS WISE AS HE SHARES ALL NEWS
- ⊙ HE SHOWS HOW CHALLENGES CAN GO IN A REAL BIG WORLD
- ⊙ HE HAS A WHOLENESS AS HE RECALLS ALL NEWS DEALINGS

- HE LEADS HIS SEARCHINGS FOR NEWS IN A REAL CLEAR FRIENDLINESS
- HE HAS SAID AGAIN AND AGAIN, "GOOD MORNING AMERICA"
- HE IS HERE TO RECALL ALL WORLD NEWS ONCE AGAIN
- CHARLES IS SEEN AS A LEGEND IN REAL BIG ABC NEWS

Speaking of big, there is one last but certainly not least example of a soul who came into his own celebrity spotlight long before saying *"You're fired"* on his reality TV show *The Apprentice*. DONALD TRUMP certainly believes, "As long as you are going to think anyway, think big." What a fascinating statement to have come from the lips of a Gemini 14, but are we really all that surprised at this point in our star understanding that Trump would utter these very words? Big is definitely what is always on Trump's clever and ever-moving mind. From selling buildings, authoring books, and capturing the socialite spotlight to teaching others how to be savvy in business on TV, there isn't much Trump chooses to do on a small scale. So we decided to take a more detailed look as we examine how this particular celebrity gets it all accomplished and then some.

Coming back down in his big way upon 14 June 1946, Trump was not meant to be shy by any means, as his Karmic Path requests of him, which is all about the 14's Chaldean understanding of *Movement–Challenge*. Oddly enough, Trump has time and time again seen the flux this particular Karmic Path is said to bring as the Chaldeans noted: "Magnetic communication with the public through writing, publishing, and all media-related matters is associated with the 14. Periodic changes in business and partnerships of all kinds are usually beneficial. Dealing with speculative matters brings luck, likewise movement and travel associated with combinations of people and nations can be fortunate. However, both gains and losses are sometimes temporary, due to the strong currents of change, which are ever-present."[23]

With a 31/4 Lifepath, Mr. Trump is no stranger to receiving those unexpected Uranus obstacles in life. He is built from the inside out within his masterful 22-degree Gemini soul to innately know how to get around them, and he wastes no time in doing so. All the sooner he can get back to laying down those foundations the 4 energies drive him to invent. A mutable Gemini is known to do everything fast, and with Mr. Trump's Karmic Path of the singular 5 also being ruled by our messenger Mercury, this combination grants Trump with an innate mental sharpness that makes most people's heads spin. Even when dealing with his large-scale problems, he keeps on moving and finding another path to reap success upon.

What is an important observation is how Trump is blessed with a 17-degree Leo rising, one of the more commanding ascendants to be born to within the zodiac. His rising sign degree is the 17's promise of legacy and eternity, so there is no doubt how our "king" of real estate has evolved as he has, not to forget his showmanship on *The Apprentice*. With his Mars in Leo in his 1st house, this is a man who can hardly stop working, especially with Mars at a Saturn-ruled 26 degrees of Leo, granting the ability to reap intense financial gains. Donald, however, is warned, just as he is through his 14 Karmic Path, of those he chooses to partnership with, as he truly does know best how to do it all on his own.

Governed by an expansive Sagittarian Moon at 20 degrees in the 5th house, the house that urges our creative nature to unfold (and with Sagittarius in this area of life for Trump, even his love affairs can be seen to be under this mutability as well), Trump has another ace in his pocket of taking command in life. It is clear why Trump can have the confidence to also have stated, "In an argument, you have to learn to control your emotions. The other person is the revolver, but you are the trigger. The revolver won't hurt you as long as the trigger isn't pulled." With the karmic mystery of the 20's Awakening, this is certainly something Trump learned early in life and mastered to achieve the magnificent results we have seen. Talk about cool under pressure.

2005 saw Trump just finishing up and evolving through a 9-year period in life, and things definitely shifted for him in 2006 as he entered a blessed 19/1 Personal Year, embarking on a brand new 9-year cycle in his life. His second Saturn return finished in July 2005, where since the summer of 2003 the energies of the karmic adjustor planet signified a critical time of needed change in his life. Could it be possible that Donald has finally worked out the right marriage partnership with the second round of Saturn around his chart in his lifetime? So far it seems to be working in his favor. He started his 1 Personal Year of new beginnings at age 60. The Chinese Zodiac is in equal agreement that our greatest wisdom shows up at this time, as we align in the same elemental year as the animal under which we were born, just after concluding the second Saturn Return. Yes, my Dear Stars, it can take that long to really figure some things out as we are ironing out those kinds of kinks in our lives.

While Donald (as this book goes to press) is certainly making sure President Obama has all his birth facts logically straight, his Lexigrams lend more conclusive evidence to how the famous path of this real estate guru (and beyond) was meant to unfold here on earth this time around. Following Trump's recent interest in the road to the White House in 2012, one is not in any doubt that his Leo Rising sure can roar.

### DONALD JOHN TRUMP

- DONALD NOT A NORMAL MORTAL MAN
- DONALD A TOP PRO DUAL MAN
- DONALD NOT A DORMANT MAN
- DONALD A LOUD MOUTH
- DONALD NOT A POOR MAN AT ALL, DONALD LOAD UP ON "LOOT" A LOT
- DONALD ON A TOP PRO HONOR PATH NOT TO PART OR DROP OUT
- DONALD TO HOLD A MAJOR AMOUNT O' LAND
- ADULTHOOD DONALD UPHOLD A MAJOR TON O'LAND
- A TOTAL PRO MODULATOR, DONALD JUMP TO LAND ON TOP
- DONALD A PRONTO "JUMP-TO" MAN, TO OUTDO ALL
- DONALD'S MOON JUMP AND JOLT DONALD TO AN ULTRA OUTDO MOOD
- DONALD AN ALL-AROUND MAN TO HONOR
- DONALD A HUMAN AUTHOR TO ADORN

- DONALD ADOPT AND ADAPT TO ALL THAT DO NOT LAND ON TOP
- DONALD NOT TO JUMP TO A MAD DRUM OR DOOM DO A "DAMN OR DARN" TURN UP
- DONALD TO MOLD A TOP TUDOR POOL THAT OUT A MORON THAT MOAN ON
- DONALD AN ULTRA PROUD PROMO MAN
- DONALD AN ALL-AROUND MAN TO HONOR, OR NOT?

Well, that sure is a mouthful about our people of fame and fortune that fill our movie and TV screens. How amazing is it that the very names we either know them as, or that they are born to, make all the tales of their lives happen as we witness it? So, between music and notable celebrities, what could possibly be next? Oh, we have a few more mesmerizing chapters ahead that further our claim that whatever you really want to know about is always right in front of you. I'll share with you now just how funny it has become to just keep on reading in my personal life, for words are now forever speaking to me in a such a different way that I am sure, by now, you too may have already have had this very same thing begin to happen to you. But do keep on reading, as there are plenty more mysteries about life and people that have been awaiting to delight your spiraling mind as it is in the midst of shifting to a whole new awareness as we continue.

# Chapter 7

## ARTISTS / WRITERS

*"Words without thoughts never to heaven go."*
—WILLIAM SHAKESPEARE

As we've just heard some true Lexigram music to our ears, let's shift to the marvels that we can take in through our eyes. Art has always been a part of humanity since the beginning, and it has remained as an important and necessary need in our culture, no matter where you may be living in the world. This is a real simple one but THE ARTS: REST AS A STAR HEART SET, so no matter how famous anyone's may ever become, indulging in the beauty is something the Venus in all of us requests. Remember how the TAURUS energies always RUST ART AT US. That's a weird spiral I know. But think a little further on this, and you'll realize Taurus is the energy that fixes and keeps our material gains—as well as any art form—in proper order. What is old and preserved is something Taurus innately knows how to protect. Yet there are plenty other planets that will manifest great art in souls. So without further adieu, I hope you are ready to take a little tour de art, both in the material and written forms, from around the world.

When you combine the energy of Neptune with the beauty of the Venus-ruled 6, the end result may be none other than exceptional artistic talent (either that or a really good lawyer!). Take a soul following a Saturn 26/8 guided Lifepath, and perfection in the arts is where we can find out how MICHELANGELO, IN AN ANGELIC HEALING LINEAGE CLAIM, made his mark upon history. Born 06 March 1475, this Italian Renaissance painter and sculptor also used his ability to display his creativity through architecture, poetry, and engineering. Oh, to be a Pisces swimming in the seas of possibilities! Coupled with his ability to capture the vivid imagination he possessed as a Fish, his 6 Karmic Path innately knew how to bring balance and enhancement to just about anything he touched through his artistic communication of the human spirit.

One should not be surprised that Michelangelo remains the most renowned artist from the sixteenth century, for his ambition carried him far along his 8 Lifepath, which knew innately how to work and manifest achievement after achievement. To this very day, his art is the most preserved over that of any other artist from his time. While his true Pisces 6 gifts brought him to communicate through the realms of his multiple forms of art and the various ways he expressed balance in life, the leadership and stability of his 8 Lifepath allowed his mutable soul to take a true direction to manifest it all in the material, which can still be admired nearly 500 years later. Just leave it to an 8 Lifepath to keep living up to tradition.

MICHELANGELO's Name Expression rings to the *The Sceptre's* 45/9, and it is plain to see how amazingly high he held his torch through his career, and the continued Universal fame he will never stop receiving. How any artist chooses to spell their name will undoubtedly show the energy of that numerical vibration unfolding in their career as they are known. While his full birth Name Expression granted the delicacy of the 29's *Grace Under Pressure,* he certainly gravitated to allowing the underlying 11/2's masterful talents to emerge. This Pisces 6 was quite the open soul in how his full name at birth undoubtedly tells the tale of his life. While we know a book alone could be written on his story from the many letters within his name, the ones within have uncannily manifested and attributed to his legacy that has remained for centuries:

## MICHELANGELO DI LODOVICO BUONARROTI SIMONI

- MICHELANGELO IS SENT AS A MAIN ITALIAN RENAISSANCE ARTIST AS A VENUS SOUL
- MICHELANGELO'S MASTER ART IS SET TO BE ETERNAL AND LAST OVER ALL TIME
- HE IS SENT TO RECEIVE A MAIN ACCLAIM IN ALL ART AREAS HE TRIES IN
- HE IS SENT TO LAST ON THE EARTH AS AN ARTISTIC GENIUS
- MICHELANGELO'S ART IS SET IN STONE IN THE SISTINE
- HIS ART ON THE CEILING IS ABOUT THE *CREATION OF ADAM, ADAM AND EVE IN THE GARDEN OF EDEN, ISAIAH, THE ANCESTORS OF CHRIST*
- MICHELANGELO'S *DAVID* IS SET TO BE ETERNAL
- MICHELANGO'S DOME DESIGN IS ON *THE BASILICA* IN THE *VATICAN*
- AS A TRUE CREATIVE SOUL HE SHINED IN HUMAN ETHEREAL ART

⊙  MICHELANGELO RELATED LOVE TO ALL HUMANS
IN HIS ART; HE HAD A REAL RIVAL IN LEONARDO
DA VINCI; HIS ART IS VALUED IN THE MILLIONS
AS A HISTORICAL ETERNAL TREASURE EONS AND
EONS ON

From Italy to the Netherlands, another historical artist made his mark that was born to promote his leadership during the Dutch Golden Age, and we think you've
probably heard of him too, as he BE NAMED AN ART
BRAND TREND, REMBRANDT? Yet again we see
how another water sign as the Cancer soul, born 15 July
1606, brought an innate receptivity to the work he created through another vibration of the Venus-ruled 6, the
Karmic Path of the 15's *Magician*. In true alignment with
what the Chaldeans understood the 15's influence to be:
"It's extremely lucky and carries the essence of enchantment
with it. 15 is associated with "good talkers," eloquence
of speech, and the gifts of music, art, and the drama."[24]
Aside from the artistic mastery of Rembrandt, he was
always highly accredited for how his works told their own
story so vividly without the use of words at all. We also
find that, like Michelangelo, Rembrandt also followed the
very same Lifepath of the 26/8. Two water signs, both with
Venus-ruled 15 and 6 Karmic Paths, creating art that was
to remain eternal along their 26/8 Lifepaths of manifesting their master materials. Nope, our star secrets make no
sense at all now, do they?

A little interesting fact about REMBRANDT is that
he wasn't born with the D in his first name at birth. Again
like his predecessor Michelangelo, he adapted to utilizing the signature of only his first name, versus his initials,

as he completed his works. While Rembrandt's full birth Name Expression calculates to the 25, REMBRANT also has the Name Expression of the 25/7, and it surely casts him into the Neptunian waters of being able to explore all the details and observations that the karmic mystery of *Discrimination–Analysis* means here. But in 1633, he chose to add the D to make REMBRANDT and, thus, changed his Name Expression to the 29's *Grace under Pressure*. (I'm actually beginning to wonder if Rembrandt was indeed Michelangelo reincarnated!) It is of interest to note that in the years to follow after making this choice, he definitely saw those situations of pressure appear in his life. Known to overspend, he placed himself in many situations that brought on more than their fair share of hardship, among all that his imagination continued to create on canvas. The key here for him would have been to deeply understand the need with the 29 Name Expression that requested him to be charitable, which would have given him more than he could have ever expected in return.

While we all may look to artists or historical figures and place them on pedestals, we must understand in the end that they, too, are just human beings like any of you who are reading this book right now. No one comes here to live a life that doesn't present challenges. Yet, in the end, being wise about our choices as we live out any of our incarnations reflects within our personal results. Had I been around for Rembrandt to ask, I would have told him to leave out that D. He already had everything going for him with the name he originally chose:

## REMBRANT HARMENSZOON VAN RIJN

- REMBRANT IS SENT AS ONE IN A HARMONIZE VIBE
- HE IS SENT AS A MASTER INVENTOR TO SHINE IN THE ARTS
- HE HAS ART BRAINSTORMS THAT HARVEST EONS ON
- HE AMAZES AS HE ANIMATES HIS ART OVER HIS ERA
- HIS ART IS MEANT TO SOOTH AS IT AJOINS AS IT IS IN SMOOTH HARMONIES
- HIS MASTER ARTS ARE AS NARRATIVES IN THEIR AMAZEMENT
- AS HIS NAME RESTART, HE THEN SEE RESTRAIN IN MONIES
- AS REMBRANT HARVEST, HE SEE NO MONIES TO INVEST
- REMBRANT REMAIN AN ART MASTER SEEN IN HONORARIES
- HIS ART IS TO REMAIN EONS ON IN MAINSTREAM ART MENTIONS
- HIS VETERAN ART IS SEEN AS IT MOVES ON THE EARTH EONS ON

*Est-ce que tu parle français?* Let's head south to France and see what was happening around the turn of the twentieth century, when HENRI MATISSE, another MASTER AT THE ARTS, was making his creations. Born 31 December 1869, we'll begin to see some differences in the work that came from this Capricorn innovator. While our previous two examples of sensitive water sign artists under the influence of the 6 brought us all that was pretty and in balance from their times in history, this example shows the individualism that art was heading toward during the Modernism and Fauvism movement. When you have a 31/4 Karmic Path soul, who is also following a 31/4 Lifepath, you can be sure the originality of Uranus will be bringing you something quite unexpected. But as the 31's *The Hermit–The Recluse* energy requests, one must take their solitude to do so.

During a 5 Personal Year in 1889, Matisse came down with appendicitis while he was enrolled in law school. This unexpected occurrence brought on a permanent change that Matisse was not to anticipate and would forever alter his Uranus 31/4 Lifepath. Thanks to his mother, who bought him some art supplies to entertain him while recovering, Matisse then discovered his true talent and passion that was just waiting to be awakened within him.

He went on to study for a number of years until 1896, and within a 3 Personal Year of expansion and growth, Matisse sold two out of the first five paintings he ever exhibited in the known French salons. These humble beginnings saw Matisse utilizing the traditional Flemish style, as his Capricorn soul felt safe here at first, but as his first Saturn Return was approaching, true to his 31/4 influence, all was about to originate in a new life of art for Matisse, which was completely alive and well with color. It was different, and the world, as with most 4 innovators, just didn't quite understand its significance at first.

True to the life of many artists, but especially to one with the karmic influence of Capricorn (for whom art is sure nice to look at, but it doesn't make for stability), Matisse saw his fair share of struggles along the way. Intensified by the unexpected twists and turns his 31/4 energies brought forth, it took Matisse some time to establish his innate right to be considered a master in the arts. Later on in his career, he did go back to a simpler and reserved means of his paintings, after letting out the Fauvism stage of his career, of which he was considered the leader at that time. HENRI MATISSE, as well as the name MATISSE alone, carries the Name Expression of the 12's *The Sacrifice–The Victim,* and he saw more than his fair share of learning some lessons over again. Not your usual Capricorn. I cannot help but wonder, though, just what kind of lawyer he would have made?

Matisse was known to be well dressed, groomed, and did not carry the look of an artist, though he worked extremely hard as an artist. No surprise here, either, coming from an old Goat. Although it would have been long, I would have recommended he sign his paintings in his full original name, which granted him the Name Expression of the karmic blessings of *The Sceptre,* through the Universal 27/9. Another name choice that is even better is BENOÎT alone, which vibes to the 24/6, *Love Money Creativity.* Yet, can we even imagine saying, "Oh, did you see the BENOÎT?" (However, it would BE IN TONE EON ON.) While his original name assured he would attain fame within the art world, by choosing to use the shorter version, the energy of the 12 brought to his present-day experiences the situations of sacrifice he was to face.

### HENRI-ÉMILE-BENOÎT MATISSE

- ⊙ HENRI IS SENT ON STAR LINES TO 'THE HERMIT THREE-ONE' THAT ALTER ALL THE TIME
- ⊙ HE HAS BEEN SENT AS A REAL MASTER AT ART HE LEARNS LATER
- ⊙ HENRI IS ALMOST TO BE IN A TAMER LINE TO EARN IN
- ⊙ IT IS HIS MOTHER THAT BE THE ONE TO LET HIS MASTER ART BE SEEN

- HENRI LEARNS HE HAS A BEST TALENT TO BE ABLE TO RELATE REAL ART
- HENRI LETS HIS NOBLE STABLE AIR BE HIS REASON AS HE IS RESILIENT ON HIS MISSION
- HE STARTS IN A SENSIBLE ART THEN HE ENTERS A LIBERATION ERA IN NO LIMITATION
- THESE ARE TIMELESS AT BEST AS ALL SMILE AT THEM
- THESE ARE SET TO RISE MORE LATER ON IN A REAL INTEREST
- SOMETIMES HE IS SEEN TO MISS HIS RENTS AS HE EARNS IN TRANSITIONS
- HIS ART IS A SENSATION THAT IS MEANT TO BE SEEN MILES ON THIS EARTH
- HENRI IN HIS ENTIRETIES IS SEEN AS AN ETERNAL MASTER ART MAN

Let's touch down back in the United States to one of our most recognized artists that captured the majority of the Hollywood and Broadway scenes on paper during his impressive reign. ALBERT HIRSCHFELD, who HIT IT AS A REAL STAR ARTIST, was born under a grand Gemini Sun on 21 June 1903. Known for over an incredible 80-year career of capturing the life and times of celebrities throughout the twentieth century with the simplicity of ink on paper, there is no question how Hirschfeld became appropriately titled "The Line King."

Albert Hirschfeld was gifted right from the start. Even though Al was distinctly known through his caricatures, he did begin his art enthusiasm through the mediums of painting and sculpture, alongside the obvious knack of his intimacy with the line in his drawings. Before a lifelong artistic career while residing in New York City, Hirschfeld studied in Paris. Like many extremely talented souls who achieve greatness in their field, Al possesses an auspicious astrological aspect called the grand trine within his natal birth chart. Grand trine? You might be saying: What on earth does that mean? Umm...do I have one of those?

Within Al's personal photograph of the universe (his natal birth chart), we can easily determine a distinct connection between three of his planets: Mercury, Mars, and Saturn—representing his thinking/mentality, drive, and self-reliance, respectively. For Al, these planets sit in the three air signs, as trine essentially means things of the same element, with a different task at hand. With his Mercury at 8 degrees Gemini, Mars at 7 degrees Libra, and Saturn at 9 degrees Aquarius, mathematically, these planets relate and connect to one another in the birth chart in a very friendly, easeful and relaxed manner. Perfected forms of expression, more often than not, occurs from this mathematical influence from the heavens. Thus, a grand trine is formed in any birth chart when the degrees of any three planets form an equilateral triangle. Whenever an astrologer sees this shape, they ought to know an innate talent is never far off. In this example, Gemini, Libra and Aquarius make up the Zodiac's air signs, those that stimulate the intellect, linear thinking, and relating to others.

Couple Al's grand trine influence with a Master Number 22 Lifepath and it becomes even more evident he was to reach the status that he did. With any 22 influence, it is Uranus's urging through the singular 4 that allows the soul's originality and unique way of acting prevail along the journey, promising to manifest equal masterful rewards.

And so it was with Al. Further granting Hirschfeld creative reign was his 21 Karmic Path, *The Crown of the Magi*. Jupiter's guidance over the singular 3 here had no trouble reaping the benefits from these creative juices. 3 energies are known to accelerate at the arts on some level, since their communicative need for expression and freedom are key. Once tapped into, these abilities flowed like a river throughout Al's steady and fruitful career.

By 1945, as Al entered one of his many 1 Personal Years, he witnessed, true to the new beginnings, energy that marked that year's cycle and some momentous starts. First, he became the father of a daughter named Nina. On a "fluke," he hid her name within a drawing to commemorate the occasion. This infectiously caught on as a game of sorts that would never end; from that moment on, Hirschfeld fans everywhere wanted to find more and more NINAs in his dazzling lines. Thus, here the well-known Hirschfeld signature began, wherein the number listed after his name indicated the number of NINAs one could find.

It is sad to open a Sunday *New York Times* "Arts and Leisure" section and not be able to find those wondrous lines on paper that intimately, and yet so simply, relate the subject matter at hand. Al worked consistently until his passing on 20 January 2003. His grand trine in the air signs undoubtedly aided in his clarity that lasted throughout his 99 years, as these energies are known to retain their mental capacities, while Gemini is a great influence to retain youth.

The Name Expression of AL HIRSCHFELD ticks to the Neptune-ruled 7. No question why Al obviously gravitated throughout the course of his career to all the Neptune theatre and film actors that made up the core of his art. Born to the name ALBERT HIRSCHFELD, whose Name Expression is the pure 6, it was a truly balanced and harmonious journey for Al, as Venus blessed his way. The mysteries found within his Lexigrams strike yet another fascinating chord. Here, again, is the conclusive evidence that alongside our astrological and numerological wisdom, there is one more piece of a soul's story to be told. So Al, it really was no "fluke" after all.

## ALBERT HIRSCHFELD

- AL IS THE REAL "THREE STAR" DEAL
- LET IT BE, AL IS A CHILD ARTIST
- AL HIT IT AS A REAL STAR ARTIST LATER
- AL FEELS BEST AS AL IS FREE AT THE THEATER
- HE RE-CREATES THE STARS AS HIS ART
- AL'S CLEAR ART IS A REAL HIT, IT CREATES A LIFT
- AL'S ART HAS A FRESH FREE FEEL
- AL'S ART HAS THE REAL THEATER FEEL
- AL'S HEART IS AT THE THEATER
- HE LIBERATED THE THEATER AS HIS ART RISE
- AS A THRILL, AL HIDES HIS CHILD'S "ID"
- AS AL'S ART HIDES HER "ID," THIS IS A REAL FAB HIT
- AL'S ART IS SET AS IT IS CHERISHED
- ALL FEEL AL'S ART IS THE BEST!

Before we move on to art in the written form, there is one last ART IN A GREAT HEART artist, the late KEITH HARING, from whose name, at first glance, you may not think you would be able to derive much of a story. We couldn't resist finding a TAURUS example as well to demonstrate a soul's true urge to create in the ARTS. Born on

04 May 1958, Haring, like Henri Matisse, was governed by a practical earthen Sun Sign, yet had the originality and innovation of his 4 Karmic Path backed by Uranus to break him out of any normal Bull mode. What Haring also has, in close proximity to our "Line King" Al, is a close grand trine in his natal birth chart. Though not as exact as Al's, undoubtedly when one has a 20-degree Mercury in Aries, 29-degree Pluto in Leo, and 25-degree Saturn in Sagittarius, it is fairly certain something pretty powerful will manifest from the mind, on which one will need to be self-reliant.

What made Haring's art a fast success with the masses was the influence of the 32/5 Lifepath of *Communication* he walked along during his seemingly short life. After moving to New York to study at the *School for Visual Arts,* his Uranus 4 Karmic Path side got very excited by graffiti art, and he began to do public pieces right in the subway. Guess who showed up to view them? The masses of humanity, who soon knew exactly how cool and accepting Haring was of everyone getting along in a sense of brotherhood and sisterhood, like a 4 soul wants. In a 1 Personal Year of new beginnings in 1981, he started filling his lines (which where a bit thicker that Al's) with his courageous colors and created chalk drawings on paper, as well as human figure installations for galleries and beyond. Whether he knew it at that time or not, he would have only 9 years left for his 32/5 Lifepath to spread his work further to the public with Mercury's quick pace, before passing during a 9 Personal Year in February of 1990.

KEITH HARING never shortened or changed his name, so he was always guided only by the 16's *Shattered Citadel* Name Expression, which more than blessed him with the

7's sympathy and compassion for humanity. Having the 16's need to remain in the eye of the storm Name Expression in combination with the unexpected events of the 4's Karmic Path, it is not too hard to see why Haring came to leave his incredible legacy. Sadly his soul left us far too soon, when he was only 31 years of age. Another interesting point to mention here is the individual Name Expressions of KEITH and HARING, which both carry a vibration of the 17's *The Star of the Magi*. The Chaldeans stated of the 17: "This is a highly spiritual number, as the 17 is "the number of Immortality," and indicates that the person's (or entity's) name will live after him."[25] And so it is written in the stars that this earth and people's hearts will not soon forget the wonders of:

### KEITH HARING

- KEITH AN EARTHEN THINKER
- KEITH IN A GIANT HEART, HE THE ART GENII
- KEITH THINK IN GRANITE IN THE GREAT ART
- KEITH GATHER ART IN A GREAT HEART
- KEITH RETHINK ART TAKING IT IN HEART
- KEITH GATHER THE KIN IN A GREAT GAIN
- KEITH INHERIT A HIGHER ART GAIN
- THE GREAT ART IN HEART HE HEAR IN AN INERTIA
- KEITH REIGN IN THE GREAT IGNITER IN ART IN AN EARTH RANGE
- KEITH THINK THE HEART, THE EARTH IN A GREAT RIGHT
- THE EARTH INHERIT THE ART KEITH THE GREAT GATHER
- THE HEART RETAIN THE ART KEITH IGNITE

Like our notable artists, those who take pen to paper as their artistic form have existed right alongside them. WRITERS, if they are savvy, will have you glued to their story or prose as they try to catch a RISE and WISE WIT within their words. Whether you are a modern-day fan of his timeless works, one WISE SPEAKER who left us with plenty to keep reading was WILLIAM SHAKESPEARE. Thought it best to keep the Taurus theme going here, along with Mercury's help with further understanding about how the 5 can have an influence hundreds of years after a soul has passed. Shakespeare's Taurus Sun rose on 23 April 1564.

When one is born to the 23 Karmic Path of *The Royal Star of the Lion*, it is easy to understand why Shakespeare's works continue to this day to be an endless source of entertainment all over the globe. The Chaldeans' stated that the 23 "bestows, not only a promise of success in personal and career endeavors, it guarantees help from superiors and protection from those in high places. It's a most fortunate number, and greatly blesses with abundant grace the person or entity represented by it."[26] Messenger Mercury guides the 23's singular 5—ensuring that the person has all the potential to reach the masses—as all forms of communication and versatility mark the expression of their outward persona. Deeply influenced by Venus who watches over any Bull, the arts, harmony, and beauty are of major significance to any Taurus. Shakespeare left us countless artistic examples through his ornamental words.

Shakespeare's 25/7 Lifepath of *Discrimination and Analysis* granted the keen ability to dive deep into the psychological realms that were displayed in his characters. The seeking energy behind Neptune's influence over this

7 vibration was strong, as Shakespeare followed the path of solitude to produce communication all of his life. The 25/7 along with the 23/5 equally are able to exhibit the innate talents of writing and detailed analysis. The vast collection of Shakespeare's poetry and plays grace us through their intense prose and verse, provoking the inner psyche. Shakespeare even left the earthly realm with his own auspicious ending. His Sun set upon the very day it rose, 23 April 1616, now known as *St. George's Day*. Only 52 when he died, it is interesting to note this age reduces to a 7 vibration, and is the reverse number of his 25 Lifepath. This date (4+2+3+1+6+1+6) coincidently not only adds up to his 23/5 Karmic Path, but also to the Personal Year energy he was about to enter, one of permanent and dramatic change. A mysterious exit by the numbers indeed.

More conclusive evidence on the reason why WILLIAM SHAKESPEARE has remained eternal lies within the very name in front of us, as once again history always seems to prove itself. It is evidently clear why the world has never forgotten his gifts, as they are still seen, heard, and read around the globe almost 400 years later.

### WILLIAM SHAKESPEARE

- ◉ SHAKESPEARE'S SKILLS AIM HIM AS A REAL LAWLESS SEEKER
- ◉ AS HE ARISES HE HEALS, HE ASPIRES ALL EARS IN HIS PHRASES
- ◉ EARS HEAR HIS PHRASES AS IMPERIAL HALLMARKS
- ◉ HE SEES PRAISE AS ALL HIS SPEAKERS SPARKLE
- ◉ A REAL KEEPER, HE WILL HELP SHAPE ALL ERAS
- ◉ HIS SPEAKERS WHISPER SIMPLE WISHES

- ◉ HIS SPEAKERS SEE MISERIES, SPELLS, SPILLS, LAPSES, ARMIES, SPARKS, SMILES, SHRIEKS, SHAME, MASKS, & KILLERS
- ◉ HIS RELEASES ARE SWEEPERS, ALL ARE REAL PLEASERS
- ◉ HIS SERIALS ARE SHAKERS, ALL ERA SELLERS
- ◉ WE WILL RESHAPE AS WE REMAKE HIS PILLARS AS WE IMPRESS

Where there is earth, there will surely be water close by. Our next writer guided by the fluid element of receptivity, ERNEST HEMINGWAY, who WAS SENT AS A WRITER IN GREAT GAINS, was a MASTER at telling tales of THE SEA, among many others. This Cancer native, born 21 July 1899, would have been foolish to follow anyone else's lead in life, for he was surely star designed to take the lead in multitudes of ways. Aside from the cardinal energies guiding his Sun Sign, he walked the Lifepath of the 37/10, the one that requests whatever it is you do in life, you best be the one initiating it. By the young age of 25, in an 8 Personal Year of harvest and recognition, his first novel *The Sun Also Rises* was born.

Hemingway was true to his Karmic Path energy of the 21's *The Crown of the Magi,* as he had no problem expressing his innate talent through this creative and expansive guidance. Yet, like many Jupiter 3 Karmic Paths, if he felt restricted in areas of love in any way, he would move on to someone new who might respect his need for freedom. A 3 will have this no other way. Married 4 times, it seems his last two wives, Martha and Mary, had genuine karmic ties with him. Another thing about 3 Karmic Paths: they typically love foreign travel and animals, more often than not coming to their rescue in some way.

Yet, in 1952, after the release of *The Old Man and the Sea,* during another 8 Personal Year of reward and honor (the book won a Pulitzer prize in May 1952), as he celebrated his birthday that year, Hemingway found himself to be in a blessed 27/9 Personal Year. It would be the last novel he would ever write, though his fame and celebrity continued. In addition to the Pulitzer, the book was featured on the cover of *Life* magazine (01 September 1952) and sold more than 5 million copies in 2 days. Now that's fortune! To receive such blessings in a 9 Personal Year, one must not turn to conflict or aggression. Hemingway went, on a safari to Africa. Ooopps, he was meant to save the animals, not kill them! This choice resulted in the manifestation of the plane crash that practically ended his life, and in turn, created health issues he would deal with for the remainder of his life—which, he was to see an additional 9 years of— until he took it just before his birthday in 1961. I recently visited his infamous house in Key West, and witnessed one of his safari trophies upon his writing room wall. I couldn't help but wonder, with all of his kindness to cats, why not extend it to all the rest of the furry creatures?

Born to the Name Expression of what the Chaldeans heralded as the best one you can get, the 19's *The Prince of Heaven,* I would also have told Hemingway to keep that middle name on all of his titles. Not that having the Name Expression under ERNEST HEMINGWAY ringing to the 10's *Wheel of Fortune* is all that bad. It surely caused many cycles to come and go for Hemingway, as he surely saw in his marriages. While he did gain a place that ordained him as a brilliant writer, his need to extend generosity to the animal kingdom beyond cats may have altered his entire path. The 10 carries this sound advice: "The power for manifesting creative concepts into reality is inherent, but must be used with wisdom, since the power for absolute creation contains the polarity power for absolute destruction. Self-discipline and infinite compassion must accompany the gift of the former to avoid the tragedy of the latter. *Discipline must proceed Dominion.*"[27] But history has been made from the letters within this Cancer 21's birth name of:

### ERNEST MILLER HEMINGWAY

- ERNEST IS SENT AS A WATER SIGN "THREE" IN A STARTER LINE
- ERNEST LEARNS HE IS A MASTER AT THE WRITING ART
- HE IS INNATE AT A REAL TALE THAT RELATES A MAN IN THE SEA
- ERNEST IS INNATE AS HE RELATE ANY TALE IN AN EASY WAY
- HE IS A REAL WRITING MASTER THAT TELLS A REAL EASY TALE
- AS HE WRITES, ERNEST EARNS WINNINGS THAT HE IS THIS MASTER AT IT
- ERNEST SEE A REAL WEALTHIER TIME AS A MASTER WRITER
- ERNEST HAS A IN A WATERY WEST ISLE
- ERNEST IS SET IN MANY MARRIAGES
- MARTHA IS HIS THREE MARRIAGE
- MARY IS HIS LAST MATE IN MARRIAGE

- HE HAS AN ILL HARM AS HE GET AWAY AS HE WENT GAMING IN AN ANIMALS ELIMINATE
- HE IS ILL ALL HIS REMAINING YEARS AS HE WENT GAMING
- ERNEST TERMINATES HIS STAR LINE AS HE IS IMMENSELY ILL
- ERNEST IS SEEN IN A HERITAGE AS A REAL GREAT MASTER WRITER IN HIS ERA

Speaking of heritage, our next shining example surely knows all about taking her words to the masses and then reaping some of her own. J. K. ROWLING created quite the GROWING LINK with her HARRY POTTER series that we all know took a sure HOP TO REAP A TOP PRO RATE at this time in our literature history. Born on 31 July 1965, this Leo author has taken center stage in her writing career along her 32 Lifepath of *Communication* worldwide, which ensures it can be done through the art of writing. Coupled with the 31's Karmic Path of *The Hermit–The Recluse,* it's no wonder how this Lioness has taken plenty of this energy's required time necessary to be in solitude all of her life since she was a child to manifest her creative genius, which unfolded the fantasy tale of the boy who is more than a superb wizard.

Rowling is a fine example of how a name change can do absolute magic in one's life when one adheres to the advice of the compound numbers understanding. She was born to the name JOANNE ROWLING, which carries the expression of the 15's *Magician.* Yet again, we see the gifts of this more than charming Venus-ruled vibration: "15 is a number of deep esoteric significance, the alchemy vibration through which all magic is manifested. It's extremely lucky and carries the essence of enchantment with it. 15 is associated with "good talkers," eloquent speech, and the gifts of music, art, and drama."[28] Well, it most certainly has been more than enchanting for Rowling with the success rate of our Mr. Potter's continual popularity these days, whose total copies to date have entertained and satisfied more than 400 million readers. (Please take note of the 4 theme going on here.) Yet, why the change of name when you've got it so good?

The idea that now has Rowling set for life was birthed for her in a 2 Personal Year from her 1989–90s cycle that nurtures and tends to the imagination. Her mother passed the following year, and this is one of the many times she saw those 4 obstacles thrown in her path along the journey to complete her goal. But, achieve it she did, in none other than an 8 Personal Year of recognition and harvest in 1995. When she first set out to publish the very first release of her soon to be Potter series, it was advised to not reveal she was a female writer so that the young male population would not be discouraged from "naturally" wanting to read the book. So the name J. K. ROWLING came to be, which is a combination of her first initial, the one from her Grandmother Kathleen's first name, and her last name. This Name Expression rings to the 12's *The Sacrifice–The Victim.* The 12 is known to carry the warning: "The figure 1 is the teacher (whether a person or life itself). The figure 2 is the kneeling, submissive student. Sometimes, the result of severe emotional stress and mental anguish creates amnesia, forgetfulness of lessons previously learned."[29]

It is known, as well, that for Karmic Path 4s, mental health constitutes a critical balance the soul must take note of in the life. Rowling often credits that writing the Potter series was a true form of therapy for her, as she has had her own battles with depression in life, but she has risen handsomely above it as she took the 12's sound advice to heart: "12 represents the educational process on all levels, the submission of the will required and the sacrifices necessary to achieve knowledge and wisdom, on both the spiritual and the intellectual levels. When the intellect is sacrificed to the feelings, the mind will be illuminated with the answers it seeks. Look within for the solution."[30]

The 31 agrees: "Quite often, genius is present, or at least high intelligence. At some unexpected time in the life, the glittering promises of the world will be suddenly rejected for the peace and quiet of Nature, or, if response to the 31 is not quite that pronounced, there will nevertheless eventually be a degree of retreat from society in some manner."[31] Rowling has definitely been doing her soul's homework, as she has spent many years composing 7 books, and although she does not plan on an 8th, I don't think her countless fans would mind. But, if she does choose to now retreat from the world and enjoy life with her new husband and family, at least now you can't be mad. She's just listening to that voice within. (And isn't is such a joy not to see a Leo native basking in the realms of the ego anyway?) Taking a trickier Name Expression energy such as the 12 and reaping Jupiter's good fortune here to limitlessly aim her Potter arrow, Rowling has achieved a true phenomenon status. But then again, any 4 Karmic Path is truly known as an enigma, as their inner worlds, when properly guided, more often than not change our outer world like no other number individually can.

By all legal standards now, Rowling has remarried and taken the new Name Expression of JOANNE MURRAY, since 26 December 2001, all while in a 5 Personal Year of movement and permanent change, in an 8 Personal Month of karmic connections and reward. It was also in 2001 that she relocated and purchased an estate in Scotland and got that nature thing fully going, which her soul needs to be able to take those retreats, and maybe sometime in the future she may just write that 8th sequel. But with her present Name Expression of the 13's *Regeneration–Change*, with as wise as we've seen Rowling/Murray to follow her star secrets, she may just not choose to embrace any more author power in this way. "*13* is a number of upheaval, so that new ground may be broken. It's associated with power, which, if used for selfish purposes, will bring destruction upon itself. There is a warning of the unknown and the unexpected."[32] So, we'll all just have to wait and see what this Leo genius will do. Whatever is next, 2010–11 marks another 5 Personal Year for her, and there will be plenty of different things that will alter her course, which may just be choosing another alias to write under. There's a lot this renowned author likes to keep private about herself, but still, a little Lexigram magic works in telling us bits and pieces of this first ever known billionaire author.

### JOANNE ROWLING

- JOANNE A REGAL LEO LION LONER IN A REAL LEARNING LINE
- JOANNE A REAL AGILE LINEAR ONE
- JOANNE IN A GROWING GAIN IN A LEARNING LINE
- JOANNE GO ON LONG IN NO EGO

- JOANNE NO IGNORE AN JOIN IN AN INNER ANGLE
- JOANNE NEAR A REAL LARGE EARNING
- JOANNE A REAL WINNER IN A NEW LEARNING EARNING
- JOANNE REIGN ON IN A RENOWN LINE
- JOANNE JOIN A GALORE OWNER OWNING LINE
- JOANNE GAIN IN A NEW GLOW, A NEW REALIGN IN O'ONE
- JOANNE NOW IN A REAL WINNER LINE IN A REAL GLOW

## J. K. ROWLING

- J.K. IN NO JOKING WIN
- J.K. IN A GROWING WIN
- J.K. IN A WORKING WIN
- J.K. RING IN A GROWING WORKING WIN
- J.K. WIN ON LONG IN A GROWING WIN
- J.K. A WORKING LION GROWN, NOW WON

While there are all the other different sub-titles attached to HARRY POTTER, this name alone expresses itself as the 14's *Movement–Challenge*. Are we at all surprised that a 5 Mercury-ruled vibration is responsible for being the messenger behind the name of the boy who used much more than wizardry and spells to capture over 400 million fans? Maybe you've even seen them—those who dress up and line up for hours out in front of every book store imaginable whenever a new book in the series was released; it's a party every time. Those Chaldeans surely knew what they were talking about: "Magnetic communication with the public through writing, publishing and all media-related matters is associated with the 14."[33] I'll say. Funny, too, the

5 is Rowling's Lifepath. Wow, look what happens when you stay on the right numerical road in life.

## HARRY POTTER

- TO HOP TO A TOP PRO REAP PATH
- OPT TO A TOP HOT PRO PARTY, YEP, HARRY A TOP HERO
- A THERAPY TO PORTRAY A TERROR THEORY
- TO ROAR TO A TOP HEARTY REPORT
- TO REAP A RARE TOP PRO TROPHY PAY YEAR TO YEAR
- YEAR TO YEAR, A PRETTY PAY PRAYER REAP ON
- THE EARTH'S HEART'S HOPE TO REAP A HARRY PARTY YEAR TO YEAR
- TO REAP A TOP PRO PAY YEAR TO YEAR

There's one more sort of phenomena book before we close this chapter, which also derives the same phrase, TO REAP A TOP PRO PAY YEAR TO YEAR. One of my favorite 2007 holiday gifts was the treasured book *EAT PRAY LOVE* by ELIZABETH GILBERT. An instant *New York Times* bestseller when it released in 2006, this true tale of the author's soul-searching adventures gained within a quick and continuous momentum. Gilbert's splendid spiritual story moved on to remain at the top spot of the *New York Times* bestseller list for 187 weeks. The movie has now been made, and the actor who played the lead role of Gilbert is JULIA ROBERTS. (Who, wouldn't you know, IS SURE TO BE A BEST STAR, regardless of whether you agree that she was the perfect choice for the role.)

By the time I finished the energetic and satisfying mystical journey of *Eat Pray Love*, I was yearning to dive into what was behind the star secrets of this talented writer. Gilbert notes in the book that she is a Cancer Sun Sign— but of course that's about as telling as the daily horoscope— which only urged me to know all of Gilbert's other "star stats" specifics. As it always is with the exploration of one's Lexigrams, both Gilbert's name and book title are eerily on target in their own tales from the letters contained within their names.

It wasn't surprising at all to learn Gilbert's Cancer Sun was born 18 July 1969. The Chaldean Karmic Mystery of the 18 is *Spiritual–Material Conflict* and is exactly where our star writer found herself at 31 years of age, in a finalizing 9 Personal Year—in a material marriage bound for divorce as her soul was indeed screaming from within to "get spiritual." Hence the premise of where she was at the beginning of *Eat Pray Love*. The key to anyone born on the 18th of any given month is to gravitate to the Chaldeans profound understanding that this Karmic Path requests, "the only way to dilute or diminish its effect on the life is by spiritual means, by unfailingly and repeatedly meeting deception and hatred from others with generosity, love, and forgiveness, by "turning the other cheek," and returning good for evil, kindness for cruelty, honesty for dishonesty, honor for dishonor. In this way, the vibration 18 may be used for great success in illumination and enlightenment."[34] With Mars guiding this singular 9 vibration, it is the utilization of courage over conflict that will always allow successful outcomes to prevail.

My heart felt more for Gilbert when I discovered her Name Expression of the 35/8 of *Partnerships*. Now, there is nothing negative about this energy, yet when a soul represented by this particular influence of Saturn through the singular 8 falls to materialism—ignoring the spiritual within their intimate relationships—chaos is bound to occur. Toss in an 18 Karmic Path with this name energy and certainly one can be very challenged when they are unaware of these forces guiding them from the Universe. I said I wouldn't give away any part of the story, so unless you've seen the movie you'll have to read the book to have this make a little more sense to the life of Gilbert.

Gilbert did marry before her first Saturn Return and first Numerical Period Cycle were finished, which in this day and age typically results in the union not being able to endure the lifelong commitment. When such an important decision is made before the soul's true self-discovery and exploration period is complete, often the life choices made will not fit into the path that the soul is meant to continue upon. Once our first Saturn Return is complete and our second Period Cycle numerically has begun, we are all the more in tune with our sense of true self like never before. Gilbert is undeniably vulnerable as she shares her truth of this deep experience and the courageous healing process that followed within the book.

Gilbert mentions some details of her astrological birth chart; she doesn't quite fit the typical Cancer description and was once told she actually has major placements in "unstable" Gemini, which explains the disconnection with her Cancer character. Immediately, without any research, I attributed this to her brilliant writing ability, as Mercurial Gemini excels at communications; yet upon finishing the book and acquiring her full natal information, my thorough calculations noted she only has one planet in

Gemini—Venus. Upon learning that her Moon is in Virgo and that Gilbert follows a numerical 41/5 Lifepath, more factual information fell into place about the true source of her supposedly unstable Mercury energy.

With both her Moon and Venus in the two Mercury-ruled communication signs, coupled with her Mercury-guided 41/5 Lifepath—which the Chaldeans also coin as *Communication*—my "Sherlock Holming" made far more sense. No wonder Gilbert is a teller of exceptional tales and beyond eager to see the world at large! Mercury's got quite the strong influence over her emotions, values and follow-up in life. The life is constantly about movement and change (many 5 Lifepaths are seen to divorce, one of those inevitable changes they see along the way), granting her an impeccable ability with the 41's (which carries the same meaning as the number 32) blessings to possess "the magical power to sway masses of people—the complexities of advertising, writing, publishing, radio, television are not always, but usually are an open book."[35] While Gilbert may not need the ultimate solitude that Rowling does to express her 5 Lifepath energy, do you see an amazing parallel of energy here?

Gilbert intuitively titled *Eat Pray Love* to a Neptune-ruled 7 Name Expression, representing spirituality, solitude and natural healing—topics that you'll find within this clever travel memoir. It's funny that Gilbert doesn't find herself very Cancer-like, but there is no other sign more well-attuned to writing about the past, and especially their own emotional experiences, than our sensitive Crabs—and it's Gilbert who undeniably excels at the task. Already known for her communication successes through writing about travel and the like, it truly was this book's spiritual accounts that took her 18 Karmic Path's energy right to the Universal Nines! By now it also has been translated into more than twenty languages and, oh yes, we already mentioned the movie you may have seen.

There's an overload of astrological and numerical forecasting that coincide with Gilbert's time travels throughout Italy, India, and Indonesia over that year. But I would think it unfair to give away any of this precious story in case you haven't had the chance to pick up a copy of this gem of a book yet. (By the way, when you do, it's that kind of "hook book" that you'll be ever thirsty for more after it's over.) As the numbers are so divinely able to tell us, Gilbert's 23/5 *The Royal Star of the Lion's* Personal Year cycle in 2005–06 brought her "to the masses" and blossomed what has been transpiring for her since 2001. It was 13 May 2006, on a 5 Personal Day in a 1 Personal Month of new beginnings in her 5 year of permanent change, when *Eat Pray Love* hit the *New York Times* bestseller list in hardcover and spread to the masses like wildfire ever since.

Born with the added initial *M* to pop up her current Name Expression to the 39/12/3, yet again we see the influence of the Chaldeans understanding of *The Sacrifice–The Victim*. Without the *M*, Gilbert has figured out what to do about those partnerships, but she will always be requested (as she shares with us in the novel that truly along her life, dramatically changed everything) to adhere to the educational process as a permanent student.

Without further hesitation, I conclude with the normal on-target Lexigram revelations, which won't give anything away expect to verify just how much this author's name tells her tale and how the title *Eat Pray Love* uncannily, like Rowling's choice, lends its own wise advice, and why it remains—and will always remain—in the hearts of the public.

### ELIZABETH M. GILBERT

- LIZ A REAL RELIABLE BRIGHT LITERATE GIRL
- LIZ A REAL GREAT LEGITIMATE TALE TELLER
- THE ABLE TALE TELLER, LIZ HIT IT REAL BIG A LITTLE LATER
- LIZ GET A BIG GREAT TILLAGE LATER, LIZ HIT A "MEGAHERTZ"
- LIZ A REAL ABLE GREAT GAL MEANT IN THE LIMELIGHT
- LIZ REAL GREAT AT A HERMIT MILEAGE TALE ART
- LIZ A REAL RELATER IN A GREAT MIGHT
- LIZ EMERGE A REAL LIBERAL GIRL IN A GREAT MERIT
- LIZ HEAL HER BITTER HEART, HER RAGE, HER HATE, HER BATTLE
- LIZ LET A LIMIT HEAL HER MATERIAL REALM
- HER GREAT HEART GET BETTER: LIZ LIBERATE IT
- LIZ LET IN THE BREATH THAT HEAL HER HEART
- LIZ A REAL ABLE HEALER, LIZ ABLE AT THE TRIBAL HEAL THAT GATHER ALL
- LIZ A REAL ALERT, EAGER, AGILE GIRL
- ITALIA, A TREE, BALI: THE BREATH ALL HEAL LIZ BETTER
- LIZ REALIZE IT BE A BRAZIL MATE, A BRAZIL HEART THAT HEAL LIZ
- LIZ BEAR A BIG GREAT HEART THAT LET IT ALL BE
- ALL HAIL LIZ A REAL GREAT ETHEREAL TALE TELLER

## EAT PRAY LOVE

- TO LEAP TO A TOP PRO VOTE
- TO REAP A TOP VOTE EARLY
- TO REAP A TOP PRO PAY RATE TO REVEAL A REAL YEAR TRAVEL TALE
- TO LET A TRAVEL PALATE REVEL
- TO REPLAY, TO REPEAT, TO RELATE A REAL POETRY TALE
- A TALE TO REVEAL LOVE A REAL RELY
- A TOP ART TO PROVE REAL LOVE PLAY A REAL PART
- TO REAP A VERY REAL VALOR
- EVERY YEAR TO YEAR TO REAP A TOP PAY
- A VOTE TO REPEAT TO PRAY, TO LOVE, TO EAT
- EAT PRAY LOVE A REAL TOP ROYAL PEARL

Okay, that covers some artistic ground with a few examples of some of our most endeared writers, and remember the next time you look at a famous painting, why not see what the artist's name reveals? Don't forget your pen and paper, or at least have your Blackberry or iPhone turned off when in those kinds of public places to jot down your spirals. Trust me, you won't want to be interrupted anyway. So now, we've explored historical figures, saw some Hollywood true marks of fame, tuned-in to some stellar music, checked out art, and read why our beloved writers just do those witty things they do. I don't know about you, but I gotta get up and move around a little, and do a little stretching. It's time to play some games and get out there to tackle some sports. Our LEXIGRAM MEGA MAGIC GAME is about to get really competitive.

# Chapter 8

## PEOPLE IN SPORTS

*"The word is not just a sound or a written symbol. The word is a force; it is the power you have to express and communicate, to think, and thereby create the events in your life."* —DON MIGUEL RUIZ

When I first began my journey that now has become a lifelong one of Lexigrams, I must admit I didn't gravitate into SPORTS right away. But, once I opened up this spiraling spectacle, there was more conclusive evidence that told me whatever game these TOP PROS OPT TO TOP SPOTS souls are playing, here was another area in life that gave me even more mental goals to arrive at in my head. I soon discovered I had another endless source of, *Are you kidding me? No way can you spell that in that athlete's name! Oh wow... the team's name spells that??? I can NOT believe this!* But, within the TON of notable players and sports talk to follow, rest assured that we all can believe in the magic of Lexigrams if we want to verify this area of life. (Interesting, isn't it, about the word TON? You either have too much or NOT!) What we'll also find is there is an equal parallel within the numerological energies surrounding our star athletes and the like that casts more intrigue into how it all plays out, as there especially seems to be plenty of competition between those 1, 3, and 9 energies for some preliminary rounds, and the 7 comes in to wrap up it all up with agility. So let's have some fun and get warmed up to exercise our minds within the world of sports.

Early on in my own Lexigram "career," starting back in 2001, I was living completely full-time in the greatest city in the world and of course chose to be mindful of what THE NEW YORK YANKEES were up to, as they certainly were showing their KEEN SWEET WORTHY KEY STAR EASTERN RANK abilities. To date, this franchise holds the record for capturing most championship titles out of any US Sports team, baseball and all other games included. What else does this 37/10/1 Name Expression that has found themselves in the center of the winner's circle tell us?

## THE NEW YORK YANKEES

- ⊚ SENT TO SEE KEY OWNERS KNOWN TO OWN THOSE SWEET WINS
- ⊚ THEY RESONATE AS A 'ONE' AS THEY ARE RENOWN HEROES EONS ON
- ⊚ THEY KNOW HOW TO SEE ANYWHERE AS THEY THROW
- ⊚ SEEN ON THE NEWS NETWORKS AS THEY EARN NEAR A WORTH
- ⊚ YEAR TO YEAR, THEY ARE TO EARN SWEET THRONES
- ⊚ NEW YORKERS HEARTS ARE THESE YANKEES

There is a wealth of history behind this team, starting with the obvious talents of LOU GEHRIG, A HUGE HERO, born on 19 June 1903, to the 29's Lifepath of *Grace Under Pressure*. Born to the benefits of the 19's *The Prince of Heaven* Karmic Path, he tapped into his initiating abilities: being known as a major hitter, one of the greatest 1st baseman, thus acquiring the nickname of "The Iron Horse." Those situations of pressure—and typically emotional ones that the 29 Lifepath he walked on can present—brought him to be the first person known with what is now called Lou Gehrig's disease (amyotrophic lateral sclerosis, or ALS). It was within a 2 Personal Year in 1938–39 that he was diagnosed with this at the time unknown and fatal neurological disturbance in the body. As a Gemini, Lou's part of the body to monitor for health issues, aside from his lungs, was his nervous system.

Born to the name HENRY LOUIS GEHRIG, we find that the energy of the 12's *The Sacrifice—The Victim* was Lou's Name Expression. We'll be finding many more of the 3 vibrations within our athletes to come, but here is an example of how the 12 manifested itself in such a way that Lou was unable to live a full life once diagnosed, as the disease took over, and his sacrifice was to cease playing baseball. Known to all as LOU GEHRIG, this Name Expression was the pure 8, and Saturn seemed to step in here as well to add to whatever karmic pressure Gehrig was to see in his short but stunning lifetime of achievement. There's a whole other numerical karmic mystery behind the combination of the numbers 8 and 4, which was Gehrig's team number, now permanently retired. Add 8 + 4, and then go back to the 12's understanding. The whole 4 and 8 continual mystery is one, which if you spend some more time investigating on your own, will provide endless insight into how karma works out in life. But for now, let's get back to how names start to turn on their own level of competition as we explore the tales within the names that make up our world of sports.

### HENRY LOUIS GEHRIG

- LOU'S <u>A</u> GENEROUS ONE IN <u>A</u> YOUNG HURRYING LINE
- LOU GREGARIOUSLY REIGNS <u>AS</u> <u>AN</u> "IRON HORSE"
- LOU SURELY SHINE ON IN A SLUGGER HERO ROLE EONS ON
- LOU SURE SEEN IN <u>A</u> ROUSING RINGER ROLE
- LOU GINGERLY REIGNS IN <u>A</u> HERO ROLE IN GLORY
- IN <u>AN</u> IRONY, LOU SEE <u>A</u> ROUGH GRUELING HEINOUS ILL <u>A</u>S HE <u>A</u> YOUNGER SOUL
- LOU'S SOUL GOES ON YOUNG, <u>AS</u> HIS HERO ROLE LINGERS EONS ON IN GLORIES

Another Yankees player forever held in all-star fame is MICKEY MANTLE, who MAKE IT IN AN ELITE YANKEE TEAM, born 20 October 1931. We've moved out to center field with this switch hitter who has yet to have any present player break his records, such as the most home runs, RBIs, runs, walks, and extra base hits performed in a World Series. When you follow the 17's *The Star of the Magi* Lifepath, you can bet what you do in that life will be remembered for all eternity, as the Chaldeans said: "17 is "the number of Immortality," and indicates that the person's (or entity's) name will live after him."[36] The 8's energy is known to follow the soul throughout the life wherein important dates will fall on this vibration, and Mantle debuted his major league career on none other than 17 April 1951, as an era of total new beginnings was about to unfold in his life as he was in the cross-over from a 9 to a 1 Personal Year. Interesting to note here, too, is the showing of the 29's *Grace Under Pressure* again within the Name Expression of MICKEY MANTLE. While a brilliant player, Mantle definitely saw his fair share IN A MEAN TIME over the years, especially with the media, and plenty of injuries along the way. Yet, as a balanced Libra soul innately knows how to do, he seemingly found his charming side that weighed those pros and cons and didn't give in too often to his double Moon influence from his 20 Karmic Path and his known Name Expression.

Choosing to come back to the name that saw him carry out his recording-breaking career in baseball, MICKEY CHARLES MANTLE rings to the 51's karmic mystery, which the Chaldeans oddly never granted a "title" of it's own. Of the 51, they said: "This number carries a strong potency of its own. It's associated with the nature of the warrior, and promises sudden advancement in whatever one undertakes. It is especially favorable for those who need protection in military or naval life, and for leaders of any 'cause' unrelated to war."[37] Funny, even though it was from an osteomyelitic illness wherein he almost lost his entire leg while trying out his football talents, Mantle was not allowed to serve in the Korean War because of this. With his heart true to baseball, once recovered, this is where he took his Libra leadership, seeking to balance his Scales once more. Undoubtedly, as we can see, he was sure meant to be right at home with those Yankees, even if he was from Oklahoma.

## MICKEY CHARLES MANTLE

- ๏ MICKEY IS SENT IN AIRY MATERNAL CHARMS AS AN ATHLETE
- ๏ AN ILL MAKE MICKEY MISS THE MILITARY TEAM
- ๏ MICKEY IS A REAL MEAN AS A CENTER TEAM
- ๏ MICKEY IS A REAL MAINSTREAM YANKEES MAN
- ๏ MICKEY EARNS ALL MAIN SERIES TITLE MIRACLES

- ◉ MICKEY IS A REAL YANKEES TALENT ERAS IN
- ◉ MICKEY CAN REALLY HIT IT, AS HE A MAIN SLAMMER AS HE SHINE
- ◉ MICKEY HAS A RICH RETIREMENT IN THE MATERIAL
- ◉ ALL CLAIM MICKEY ETERNALLY A REAL YANKEES ALL-STAR

Jumping to some more modern-day Yankee All-Stars, I'm just going to touch briefly on a few of the players you've more than likely heard the names of, even if you aren't an avid sports fan. Born 12 March 1962, this Piscean 12 player we sure know has been seen as the greatest, but also seen to live true to his 12 Karmic Path, and as the Chaldeans always said of it, "Sometimes, the result of severe emotional stress and mental anguish creates amnesia, forgetfulness of lessons previously learned."[38] It's no mystery that this Fish swims in some pretty scary waters that have led him to have to recover more than once from his Pisces urges to fall to his addictions.

## DARRYL EUGENE STRAWBERRY

- ◉ YES, DARRYL A REAL GREAT BASEBALL STAR
- ◉ DARRYL REWARDED AWARDS AS A BASEBALL STAR
- ◉ A SAD WASTE AS DARRYL ALWAYS DARES LAWS
- ◉ ARRESTED AS A WASTED REBEL NEAR BRAWLS AT BARS
- ◉ SEES BETRAYALS AND RESTS AT REAL BARS AS LAWYERS REDEAL

With all the evidence to compile, I could devote a whole book just to sports. But before we move on to other ways to play the game, a quick take on BERNIE WILLIAMS, who

WILL SEE REAL SERIES WINS AS BERNIE SLAMS A
BASEBALL and is another Yankees player who surely has
acquired a few world series rings in his successful career. The
24 Name Expression of *Love Money Creativity* surely has
aced the meaning of this number's title, which promises that,
if the soul does what it loves through creativity, the money
flows easily. This Venus-guided 6 vibration also is the same
energy behind the 51 number that Bernie wore as a Yankee,
and undoubtedly paved the way of balance for him along
his baseball career. And did you know this not-so-shy Virgo,
born 13 September 1968 and walking the 37/10/1 Lifepath
of *The Initiator,* is also a creator of music?

## BERNABÉ FIGUEROA WILLIAMS

- BERNIE CAME AS AN ORIGINAL CALM MELLOW
  SOUL IN BIG SMILES IN A "ONE" LINE
- AS A BASEBALL SLAMMER BERNABE BE IN A BERNIE
  NAME
- BERNIE IS SEEN AS A FAMOUS BASEBALL GAME
  FIGURE
- BERNIE EARNS AS A REAL LARGE FIGURE
  MILLIONAIRE EARNER IN BASEBALL
- BERNIE IS SEEN IN RELIABLE BASEBALL WINS
- BERNIE LABORS AS BERNIE EARNS IN BIG WORLD
  SERIES WINS
- BERNIE IS ALSO A RELIABLE EARNER IN SONG ON A
  MAIN LABEL, BERNIE "WAILS"
- BERNIE IS A REASONABLE SOUL IN SURE BELIEFS OF
  WELL BEING
- BERNIE IS A LIFELONG LEARNER ALL IN GAINS
- BERNIE BEARS A FREE IMAGINABLE LIFE IN REAL
  LIBERAL ANSWERS

I could undoubtedly devote this whole chapter to the *Yankees* talents over the years, but let's switch up our game and call upon all hockey fans. GILLES GRATTON, A REAL GREAT LEO GOALIE was at the top of his game during the 70's as a goalie for various Canadian and American professional teams. This star player, born 28 July 1952, was surely in-tune with his star secrets. A Leo following the energies of a 28/10/1 Karmic Path will only want things truly managed in his own way. Gratton, whose goalie mask was that of a Lion (or as he preferred to call it, a tiger—in either case, he growled at his opponents on the ice), was a choosy player, as he wouldn't play when the moon didn't aspect Jupiter to bring forth that ultimate good luck and fortune within his natal chart. He also was firm in his beliefs of his own reincarnation. Being in tune with spirituality was due to his 34/7 Lifepath of *Discrimination–Analysis*, which we are sure granted him the agile ability on the ice, as 7 energies are also typically innately gifted at movement, dance, or any kind of performing. Equally this guidance of Neptune keeps him seeking out all of those mysteries of life in his solitude. Perhaps we should have a spiritual chat sometime, Gilles?

While you may not have heard of this name in awhile, GILLES GRATTON will forever remain eternalized for his stellar goalie talents with his Name Expression of the 17's *The Star of the Magi*. This energy, coupled with his pure Sun guidance of being a Leo 28, without a doubt intensified his ambitious side, which was to take center stage on the ice.

## GILLES GRATTON

- GILLES IS SENT AGAIN AS A REGAL LEO LION "ONE" TO GET ALL GAINS IN
- GILLES IS ON AN INTERNAL STAR LONER TRAIL TO LEARN IN
- GILLES "GETS" ALL EONS STAGGER IN ONE ALIGN
- GILLES IS SO SET AS A STELLAR GOALIE GREAT ON AN ETERNAL TRAIL
- GILLES IS SET ON A REAL STAR GOALIE STAGE AS A GREAT ONE
- GILLES IS SENT AS A REAL GREAT, STRONG, RELIANT GOALIE
- GILLES IS IN GREAT EARNINGS AS A STAR GOALIE TALENT
- GILLES IS SET TO EARN AS A TORONTO, RANGERS, & "ST. LOUIE" GOALIE
- GILLES IS A REAL LITERAL LION, SEEN AS A TIGER ON A STAR GOALIE STAGE
- ALL TAG GILLES AS STRANGE AS GILLES NOT EARN AS GILLES TRINES ARE IN NO ALIGN
- GILLES TENSION IS IN A REASON TO NOT LET REAL GOALS IN A NET
- IT IS A RARE GILLES LET A GOAL INTO GILLES LION "LAIR" NET
- GILLES SET AS A STELLAR GOALIE STAR EONS ON

He may have never been a star in the NHL, but this KEEN ONE RUN IN ICE RINK man, MIKE ERUZIONE, didn't take the offer to be one after the "Miracle on Ice," otherwise known as the 1980 U.S. Olympic hockey teams' truly unexpected claim over Russia to seize the gold medal, wherein he scored the winning goal for the U.S.

Born on 25 October 1954, this is an interesting choice for a Scorpio to make in the peak of attaining his power. Again we see the *Discrimination–Analysis* through the 25 to play an important role here, as the Chaldeans said of this keen judgment number: "25 bestows spiritual wisdom gained through careful observation of people and things, and worldly success by learning through experience."[39] Eruzione, instead, chose to use those observational skills, making a career as a commentator for the Olympics, broadcasting games for the New York Rangers and New Jersey Devils, providing endorsements, and always being available for hire as a public speaker.

Still keen in his Scorpio force and 25 wisdom, this miracle on ice would have found fame and celebrity no matter what, as he follows a 27 Lifepath of *The Sceptre*. The Chaldeans promised to one walking this path "This is an excellent, harmonious and fortunate number of courage and power, with a touch of enchantment. It blesses the person or entity it represents with a promise of authority and command."[40] Eruzione was the hero of the 1980s Olympic triumph for the U.S., as well as the captain of the team he led to victory.

As MIKE ERUZIONE, he unquestionably is meant to be known by the masses with the Name Expression of the 14's *Movement–Challenge*. Still using this name spelling, he is true to the energy behind this compound number's energy: "Magnetic communication with the public through writing, publishing and all media related matters is associated with the 14."[41] Funny, with a Scorpio 25 soul, the psychic energy that can be present is intense. Maybe Eruzione sensed if he did take that offer from the NHL, he could have been seriously injured beyond making it worth whatever magnificent salary they tried to tempt him with. He is still known today to captivate attention wherever he speaks, and that 27 Lifepath of his allows Mars to come out to motivate his audiences time and time again.

There is definitely a star secret to reveal why MICHAEL ERUZIONE chose the speaker path over the continued life of a hockey athlete. His birth Name Expression is the peaceful and balanced vibration of Venus through the masterful 33's *Love and Magic*. Similar as well to the meaning behind the 24's *Love Money Creativity*, the Chaldeans said of this very fortunate number: "Due to the double 3, people whose name equals 33 are more fortunate in every way when involved in a harmonious partnership of some kind with the opposite sex, which applies to the career as well as romantic and marital relationships."[42] Aside from being a gifted speaker, Mike is happily married to his wife and has three children. Once more, here is another miraculous story from the letters within the name:

## MICHAEL ERUZIONE

- ☉ MICHAEL CAME IN A REAL NICE CLEAR CALM NUMERICAL HARMONIC ZONE
- ☉ HE REALIZE HE CAN HARMONIZE ON REAL ICE
- ☉ MICHAEL A REAL MECHANICAL LINEAR HERCULEAN MACHINE ON ICE
- ☉ HE CAME IN AN IRONICAL 'MIRACLE ON ICE' CLAIM
- ☉ HE CAN CLAIM IN A REAL ICE MAN HERO ZONE
- ☉ HE LEARN A CHOICE IN A "NORMAL" LINE EARN HIM AN INCOME IN A REAL RELIANCE
- ☉ HE CAN LAUNCH A CAREER IN A HEALER HERO MORALE ROLE

- HE EARN A REAL HUMANE HEROIC CEREMONIAL REALM
- MICHAEL CLAIM AN ICE ENCORE IN A 'MIRACLE ON ICE' CINEMA
- MICHAEL CAN ENRICH IN A REAL ROMANCE

Let's move from the ice rink to the court, where our next athlete certainly has seen her fair share of WISE WINS as she IS IN A MAIN ARM in this lifetime as the tennis guru SERENA WILLIAMS. Born 26 September 1981, it is no doubt the leadership of both her Libra Sun Sign and 26/8 Karmic Path governed by Saturn that has allowed her to see her hard and graceful work pay off in handsome ways. 8's know how to toil, see ahead, and then watch their bountiful harvest unfold. For Serena, this goes far beyond tennis, extending into a multitude of areas including now being part owner of the Miami Dolphins. See this kind of soul walking down the famed 36/9 Lifepath that she does, and we have further understanding of why her current career as of 2011 is certainly to the Nines. Mars fuels her path to be motivated with plenty of competitive energy that is definitely in alignment with what the Chaldeans said of the 36 (which carries the same meaning as the 27): "It guarantees that great rewards will come from the productive labors, the intellect, and the imagination. All of these creative faculties have sown good seeds which are to reap a rich harvest."[43]

SERENA WILLIAMS puts all of those details and analysis into her tennis game by carrying the Name Expression of the 25's *Discrimination–Analysis*. Blessed with the ability to observe and overcome past mistakes, she makes sure she is practically flawless in her skills. I would imagine this is where a different imagination comes into play, as we have seen her wear some pretty interesting fashion as she seeks to score in Love. In a 1 Personal Year in 2009, she also began the Signature Statement, a line of jewelry and handbags primarily sold on the Home Shopping Network.

Her birth name of SERENA JAMEKA WILLIAMS grants her the Name Expression—which also enjoys the world of creating style—to aim her innate athletic talents to be properly developed through the 30's *Loner–Meditation*. Of the 30 the Chaldeans said: "This is a number of retrospection, thoughtful deduction, and mental superiority over others."[44] One cannot deny Serena's mental superiority on the court, as she more often than not captures the win, no matter who she matches herself against. Yet, when you have the Lexigram revelations that Serena does, how could she not?

### SERENA JAMEKA WILLIAMS

- SERENA AWAKENS IN AN AIR WILL IN A MARS LINE IN A NAME IN AN AIM
- AS SERENA RENAMES A SEEKER AIR RELEASES A REALNESS
- SERENA IS SEEN IN MAIN WINS AS A MEAN MAIN ARM MAKES NEWS
- EARLIER, SERENA IS SEEN IN RAW WEARS AS SERENA JAMS SLAMS
- SERENA EARNS IN A NIKE WEAR LINE, AS NEW SNEAKERS ARE SEEN
- SERENA MAKES AN ARENES LINE ALL LIKE AS ALL ARE SEEN IN WEARS
- SERENA MAKES A MAIN JEWELRIES LINE
- SERENA EARNS IN A MIAMI MAN ARENA AREA
- SERENA EARNS NEAR MASS SALARIES

- SERENA IS IN A MAIN REAL AWARENESS AS SERENA EARNS IN MASS WINS
- SERENA IS KEEN IN A REAL MEAN SLAM AS SERENA A MAIN SLAMMER
- SERENA SEES A SAME NAMESAKE AS A SIS MAKES MAIN NEWS
- SERENA IS A REAL AIMER SEEN IN MAIN SMILES

While the stars seem most certainly to SMILE upon Serena, you so know that'll go for MILES. Should you be talking about miles and sports simultaneously, you could be talking about bike racing. We'll be seeing the lengths that car racers and horses can go in their tales from their names, but first there are a few more within our different areas of sports that speak volumes about the validity of Lexigrams. To become a victor and endure those long miles, one definitely needs A REAL STRONG MASTER LEG, and you know who has one? LANCE ARMSTRONG. Born on 18 September 1971 to a brilliant "to the 9's" mathematical birthday formula, this 36/9 Lifepath is surely true to his super innate Mars guidance that gives this athlete an endurance and arousing force that was awaiting to grant him a famed life seen by the Universal masses. Not only has Lance taken center stage in the biking world, but his drive to survive and prevail over seemingly unbelievable odds off the track has spoken to the world loud and clear.

Armstrong has a numerical magical formula that is a rare one to discover in any given soul's numerological birth chart. Notice how his month, day, and year of birth all separately share the commonality of being a 9 vibration: 9th month, 18th day, $1 + 9 + 7 + 1 = 18$, wherein they individually will reduce to 9, and then all add up to his 36/9

Lifepath. These energies all determine different periods of time in his life, and deeper details are gained on other sections of time within his life from adding them together in various ways to once again arrive at the same result of 9. We did say Lance was to the 9s! This Mars presence creates the magnitude of energy he possesses, whereby, aside from his determination, his physical strength is backed by a vitality that few souls possess. (Should you be born to 09 or 27 September in the same year of 1971, you've got LANCE'S CLEAN ACE in your star secrets hand too!) While his Virgo Sun isn't always sure how to cooperate with this kind of energy, it absolutely intensifies the natural, detailed-oriented, and perfectionist ways he chooses to do things in.

One incarnated to the 18's Karmic Path of *Spiritual–Material Conflict* is not exempt from seeing the tendency toward strife to unfold at times within the life. Mars can project more aggression and penetrating energy through the 18 over any other 9 vibration. Yet, as any 9 native must remember, it is the very act of courage and ultimate kindness that will overcome any altercation that comes their way. And should you have the 9's underlying energy in every section of your numerological birth chart, get ready to be a true warrior in life. As Lance overcame a nearly fatal battle with cancer, which was diagnosed on October 2, 1996 (in a 7 Personal Year of inner work and solitude), he took no time in driving his disease to a complete remission. By 1998, while still in an 8 Personal Year of recognition and reward, January marked a 9 Personal Month of finalizations and endings, wherein he returned to the use of his strong legs by being fully engaged in planning his comeback that February. July 1999 saw Armstrong in the energies of a driving 9 Personal Year, as we saw another momentous feat of Armstrong that furthered his fame when he won the Tour de France. As he began a brand new 9-year cycle a couple months later that September, he carried his 36 *The Sceptre* Lifepath torch high as the reigning victor every year in France through 2005.

Many may not know that Armstrong is not Lance's original last name at birth, but he was born to the full name of LANCE EDWARD GUNDERSON. To this day, he has no contact with his natural father, part of that 18 Karmic Path he chose to return and fight this time around, as he carries the 9's finalizing and conclusive tone that Gunderson was never his birthright. Adopted by his Mother's second husband, TERRY KEITH ARMSTRONG, when he was only 3, he has conflict in this parental partnership as well, as a 9 will always sense when dishonesty is present in a person miles away. Hmmm... did you per chance take a spiraling peek at Terry's name? You bet Lance's intuition is right, as his second dad has the potential either way: YES OR NO TERRY IS/IS NOT IN AN HONESTY AS HE GOES. A father now himself, with 3 children from his first marriage, and post-cancer, Lance miraculously continues to overcome the odds. Presently in his fourth major romantic relationship, yet second marriage, he fathered two more souls, the last of whom arrived on 18 October 2010. OLIVIA MARIE ARMSTRONG sure is a lot like her Dad, even though she is a Scorpio. See any spiraling "predictions" here? She'll definitely do it all IN A REAL LOVE.

What is equally and utterly fascinating about Lance is whether he stayed with LANCE EDWARD GUNDERSON instead of choosing ARMSTRONG, both of these Name Expressions vibrate to the 34's (carrying the same meaning as the 25) *Discrimination–Analysis*. This totally packs an extra punch for his intuitive abilities to thrive. Apparently this number influenced him with equal might as well, as the Chaldeans said: "34 bestows spiritual wisdom gained through careful observation of people and things, and worldly success by learning through experience. Its strength comes from overcoming disappointments in the early life and possessing the rare quality of learning from past mistakes."[45] We see, too, that in there are similar and different tales each of these names have placed upon his life.

### LANCE EDWARD GUNDERSON

- LANCE CAME AS ONE SURE WONDER SOUL A WORLD SOON SEE AS A REAL LEADER
- LANCE NEEDS COURAGE AND ENDURANCE AS LANCE GOES ALONG
- LANCE NEEDS NO ANGER OR ARROGANCE AS LANCE GOES ALONG
- LANCE DECLARES A DEAD-END DAD NO ONE LANCE CAN GO NEAR
- LANCE CAN SCORE LARGE AWARDS AS A REAL GRAND RACER
- LANCE'S SLENDER LEGS ARE SURE GRAND LANCE'S "GUNS" AS A RACER
- LANCE EARNS NEAR A LONG LEG RACE SLOGAN
- LANCE SEE A CLEAR ANSWER AS LANCE WANDERS ON
- LANCE ANNOUNCES SAD ENDS AS LANCE WEDS
- LANCE SEE A CANCER DANGER LANCE USE COURAGE ON
- LANCE SEE A DANGEROUS CANCER NOW UNDONE AND CLEARED

- LANCE CAME AS AN AWARE SOUL SEEN NEAR ADORNED AWARDS
- LANCE, USE DRUGS AND A REAL DANGER WARNS A CAREER REWARD GOES UNDER

## LANCE EDWARD ARMSTRONG

- LANCE SENT TO RACE AND EARN AWARDS AS A REAL STRONG LEG
- LANCE NEEDS A TOLERANCE TO NOT LET A NATAL MARS GET NEAR ANGER
- LANCE CAME AS A GREAT MARS GENERATOR AS LANCE A MARS MAGNET
- LANCE A REAL GRAND LEADER SET TO SOAR ON AND ON
- LANCE ORNAMENTS A REAL WONDERMENT AS A RACER
- LANCE EARNS NEAR ENDOWMENTS
- LANCE GROWS AS A REAL LANDOWNER
- LANCE DOES NOT SEE REAL ROMANCE MATCHES TO LAST AS LANCE WEDS
- LANCE DOES SEE A CANCER DANGER LANCE CAN TRANSCEND TO END
- AS LANCE RENEWS AS A REAL STAR RACER NO CONTENDER CAN MATCH
- A WORLD DECLARE LANCE AS A REAL RACER LEADER AND ADORNED STAR
- LANCE SEE A DREAM CAREER END AS LANCE WENT TOWARDS A DRUG HARM LATER

During the decade preceding Lance Armstrong's birth, there was another adorned star that rose to worldly success within the realms of working hard in the boxing ring.

MUHAMMAD ALI, who DAMN, HAIL A MAUL AIM MAIM. Born 17 January 1942, there is a work ethic within Muhammad that—as we saw earlier in another Capricorn 8 energy soul, Elvis, "The King"—is a true packed punch of ambition that will knock-out goal after goal. It is interesting that even though one may not immediately note the grace and agility it takes to be any kind of star athlete, they are often as graceful as any dancer, obviously being quick on their feet. One that follows a 25/7 Lifepath, as Ali does, is known to excel in many area of the arts, especially ones where that fancy footwork is necessary. This kind of talent crosses over into an athlete's skill and CRAFT, which is, in FACT, ART! In our sports so far, the 7 has shown up multiple times aside from the dynamic fire energies. These Neptune souls equally have displayed that ability to be sharp and acute with their feet, which, just like a Pisces, the 7's energy governs over this area in the body.

The tale in the name here tells us more insight into not only how Muhammad was quick on those feet, but how his arms were the other body part that allowed him to rise to be considered the greatest heavyweight boxer the world has ever known up till now. Born to the birth name of CASSIUS MARCELLUS CLAY JR., this carries the expression of the 16's *The Shattered Citadel*. It is best not to utilize the 16 as a Name Expression, especially if you are striving for fame and celebrity.

We find, too, that the name MUHAMMAD ALI also rings to the 16's understanding the Chaldeans said of this eye of the storm number to hold: "To avoid the fatalistic tendency of the 16, one must endeavor to make all plans in advance, making certain that any possibility of failure is anticipated and circumvented by careful attention to detail. The 16 brings with it the Single number 7's obligation and responsibility to listen to the voice within, which will always warn of danger through dreams or the intuition in time to avoid it."[46] One thing he did not avoid was an arrest, owing to his persistence in not answering to his own name while serving against his true beliefs in the U.S. Armed Forces during the Vietnam War. This incident knocked him off his tower—as the 16 energy can do—as his boxing titles were taken away. Four years passed before it was properly resolved, but of course in none other than a 9 Personal Year for Ali, which in a 6 Personal Month of harmony and balance, the ongoing fight with the U.S. Supreme Court was dropped and he was allowed to completely reclaim his place in the boxing world.

Muhammad Ali is a shining example of just how a soul can make the 16 choice for a Name Expression, and with the blessings of the 17's Karmic Path of *The Star of the Magi,* quietly and patiently wait out the storms that will come their way. It is certain Ali's intuition is dead-on, as all his work here on earth goes far beyond the ring. He fights for the human right and moral outcome, which is well in tune with the 16's abilities to create compassion where there is hurt. His social activism equally has become eternalized and none of his innate gifts will anytime soon be forgotten. Once more, it is revealed within the original birth name the tale of the life he was meant to take the lead in.

## CASSIUS MARCELLUS CLAY JR.

- ◉ YES CASSIUS CAME AS A MIRACLE MUSCLE ALL MASSES SEE
- ◉ CASSIUS CARRIES A MUSICAL AIR AS CASSIUS USES MASS ARM AIM

- CASSIUS CARRIES A REAL ACCURACY AS CASSIUS AIMS
- ALL SEE A SCARE AS CASSIUS'S MUSCULAR ARMS CRUCIALLY SLAM
- AS CASSIUS RISES AS A REAL CLASSIC CASSIUS'S SARCASM SEES A JAIL CELL
- CASSIUS CARRIES A CALM AIR AS A U.S.A. CASE SEES A CLEAR
- CASSIUS RECLAIMS ALL MIRACLE MUSCULAR ARM AIMS
- CASSIUS SALARIES ARE REALLY A CLASSY SUCCESS
- CASSIUS CARRIES A REAL MIRACLE SURMISE
- CASSIUS IS A RADICALLY CALM MUSCULAR MASS ALL ACCLAIM A REAL SUCCESS

In sports, we can all be inspired by an athlete's or team's success and, in an instant, be devastated by the accidents and seemingly horrific events that can unexpectedly play out on any field we examine. The date 03 May 2008 will go down in history as the day of one of the most celebrated yet equally tragic Kentucky Derby races. This 134th race was numerically forewarned from the start that wisdom must be adhered to in all matters connected to it because of the singular 8's vibration over this year of the very combination of the 1 + 3 + 4. Couple this with a Universal day of 5-03-2008 adding to the 18's *Spiritual Material Conflict,* and one can know all *t*'s must be crossed and all *i*'s dotted; the deeper warning here is that materialism absolutely will not be tolerated.

As the triumphant BIG BROWN (with his name indicating he NOW OWN BIG WIN) made the record books, it was another Triple Crown hopeful horse who met a most unfortunate fate that granted this 134th Kentucky Derby to be filled with opposing regrets and devastation. EIGHT

BELLES, whose name at first sounds most apropos for a racehorse, was indeed given an energy through her name, which on this day in history was allowed to manifest itself in an outcome that perhaps could have been avoided. This is where Lexigrams, Numerology, and Astrology provide a significant understanding of the unseen energies swirling around human beings, as well as the very things we name and create. The names we even give our animals are no exception to the natural laws of the Universe. In this extremely sad realization, the name of the young filly had not only the very word EIGHT in it, but also its Name Expression generated a numerical vibration that, given a choice, one should not use for ultimate results unless you will honor the 12's understanding through its karmic mystery.

EIGHT BELLES's Name Expression of the 12's *The Victim–The Sacrifice* granted her through the decisions of humans to deal with the following Chaldean understanding: "One will periodically be sacrificed for the plans or intrigues of others. The number 12 warns of the necessity to be alert to every situation, to beware of false flattery from those who use it to gain their own ends."[47] And when you are a horse, what kind of fighting chance do you have against such a warning? Funny to note Eight was raced before her "run for the roses" under the number 3, in alignment with her Name Expression, and within the Derby, she was under her Karmic and Lifepath number 5—a number that represents permanent changes and movement. It was the 3rd day of the 5th month, also adding up to 8.

EIGHT BELLES was born 23 February 2005, making her a Pisces 23/5 on a 14/5 Lifepath—beauty, grace, movement, along with quick and swift changes, were part of her short life. And with the Karmic Path of the 23, she was meant to reach the masses even if under such horrific circumstances. Undoubtedly, Eight Belles will be forever cherished in the heart of genuine horse lovers for her amazing gifts. Looking further to the insight of Lexigrams, it is more than evident that our Dear Eight was never meant to be racing, at least as her name tells us so through the letters within, and unfortunately she did not race for very long. It was with deep sadness to write the truth of the matter in this case. History yet again showed us another valuable 8 lesson from Eight's incredible sacrifice, which when naming something such as a racehorse, you may prefer not to allow this potential to manifest itself.

### EIGHT BELLES

- EIGHT'S BEST LEGS SELL BIG, GET ELITE
- EIGHT'S LEGS HIT IT BIG
- EIGHT'S LEGS BITE IT
- EIGHT'S LEGS SELL IT, BITE IT BIG
- EIGHT'S LEGS GET LEGIT HIT
- EIGHT'S LEGS GET BLIGHT
- EIGHT'S LEG HIT BIG SIEGE, LEGS SEETHE
- EIGHT'S LIGHT GETS STILL
- EIGHT BEGETS THE BIG EIGHT HIT

So if you are wondering if the knowledge of Lexigrams, Numerology, and Astrology that we utilize for human analysis can equally apply to animals, that answer is a total yes! (But do hurry up and get back to this chapter while you now spiral into your own pet's name.) Our star secrets apply not only to any soul but also to any entity. Whether this is another living animal, we've demonstrated how they work equally with the titles we choose. What we name anything in life has the ability to be given a "look-see." Lexigrams are a wonderful tool to integrate into forecasting, yet one must be cautious of casting negative predictions. Remember those rules of yes and no we spoke about in chapter 2?

I can't resist going on with the horse fascination, if you don't mind. After Big Brown raced to victory in the 134th Kentucky Derby, here's a little short and sweet star peek at the following year's 135th Kentucky Derby which saw a different kind of record broken in time. What can the tales within the names tell us about who was to become the victor?

### WEST SIDE BERNIE

- SEES WINS
- IS IN BEST WINS

Yes, he had them! But then we went a bit further...

- RESIST DERBIE WIN
- TIREDNESS DENIES DERBIE WIN

### PIONEER OF THE NILE

- NOT THE ONE TO HIT THE TIP TOP
- NOT THE TOP ONE TO PIONEER IT
- OPEN TO FLOP, TO FOIL THE TOP OF THE LINE
- NOT THE TOP HONOREE

### MUSKET MAN

- MUSKET MAKES A NAME
- MUSKET MAKES A SUM
- MUSKET TAKES A SUM
- NAME MAKES "SUM" NEWS

Not too shabby! Yet it is beyond clear, in this starting gate, that it was this horse that also carried a 20 Name Expression of *The Awakening*, certainly awoke and startled them all by winning the 135th Kentucky Derby by the long shot of 50 to 1.

## MINE THAT BIRD

- HE EARN THE MAIN DERBIE BID
- HE BEAT THEM IN THE MAIN DERBIE
- HE EARN A TITAN DERBIE NAME
- IN TIME HE EARN IN A MAIN "TRINE" DREAM

The Triple Crown hasn't seen another victor since 1978. As we go to press in 2011, ANIMAL KINGDOM, even with his 14 *Movement–Challenge* to the masses Name Expression, didn't quite live up to his Lexigram possibilities: A MAIN IDOL ALIGN IN A GLAD OLD GOAL MAKING A MAIN GAIN IN A LINK. So for all of you racehorse owners out there, it's time to manifest a name for a future horse that will just spell out TRIPLE CROWN. While we are still handling the horse topic, what a cool little side note of interest to share that one rare Triple Crown winner's name from 1973 also reveals:

## SECRETARIAT

- IS A STAR RACER CRITTER
- A STARTER RACES AS SECRETARIAT CARRIES RACES
- A RACE ACE TRACES AS STAR RACE CAREER RAISES
- A RACE SETTER CAST A STAR SEAT TREAT
- AS A STAR RACER SECRETARIAT ERECTS A TIARA ESTATE
- A STAR RACER CREATES A RISE AS A RARITIES STIR

While we are talking about things that move fast, there are some awesome Lexigram finds in the speedy world of car racing. We've provided their birthdays without the analysis, giving the chance for you exercise how to tie it all in together and to see how their numbers and sign fit into their story. After all, you have to practice to get good at anything, as any athlete featured in this chapter would tell you! We'll look at just one revelation of some of the most noted NASCAR racers whose urge for speed in cars we found to be nowhere but right in their name. What else can you spiral and discover? Gentleman, please start your engines!

**RICHARD PETTY, 02 July 1937**
**RICHARD LEE PETTY**

◎ HE THE TELEPATHIC CAR RACER REPEATEDLY

**DAVID PEARSON, 22 December 1934**
**DAVID GENE PEARSON**

◎ DAVID REAPS AS DAVID EARNS AS A SPEED PIONEER

**JACKIE STEWART, 11 June 1939**
**JOHN YOUNG STEWART**

◎ SENT AS A NOTEWORTHY STAR THAT RUNS ON GAS AS HE EARNS

**RICK RAVON MEARS, 03 December 1951**
**RICK RAVON MEARS**

◎ RICK IS A MAVERICK AS RICK RACES CARS

**CALE YARBOROUGH, 27 March 1939**
**WILLIAM CALEB YARBOROUGH**

◉ HEROICALLY, CALE CLAIM A REAL REGULAR ROLE
HE CARRY WHILE HE A CAR RACER

**CARL EDWARDS, 15 August 1979**
**CARL MICHAEL EDWARDS, II**

◉ CARL CAME IN A MIRACLE CAR RACER CAREER AS
HE DECLARES REAL AWARDS

While car racing is as American as apple pie, so too
is our version of football. Or should you not be from the
US, the correct term is *le football américain*. Football is,
for most of the world, and from the European perspective,
actually, the game of soccer. But, you can't find much of a
Lexigram clue to help you out with why soccer and football don't even contain the same letters. (As we have said,
not everything has an unsolved mystery awaiting to be
unveiled.) Before we do get into America's favorite autumn
Sunday sport, would you mind if I just sneak in one more
really cool Lexigram on the man who is best known for his
football (or should your choice of term be *soccer*) talents?
Oh, thank YOU kindly, Dear Reader!

PELE, whose Name Expression is the blessed 21's *The
Crown of the Magi,* needs no introduction about his universal success. 3 energies are known to be quite cultured
and travel to all sorts of foreign lands. Born 23 October
1940, this *The Royal Star of the Lion* 23 Karmic Path can't
even help but live the life of travel and being known by the
masses, while, oh yes, his Scorpio power knows innately
how to organize his quicksilver movements that keep all
of the other players in a mystery of what he'd do next on
the field. Pele's birth name (of course carrying the Name
Expression of the 32's *Communication,* in equal energy to

intensify his 23 Karmic Path) leaves us plenty to investigate, which I'll leave you plenty to work out, as this is without question the reason he is still considered the world's greatest soccer master.

## EDISON ARANTES DO NASCIMENTO

- ☉ EDISON'S DREAM IS SET AS EDISON SENT AS A SOCCER MASTER AND MASSES STAR
- ☉ EDISON IS SEEN TO CREATE A SOCCER TRADITION AS EDISON EARNS
- ☉ EDISON IS SEEN TO SCORE TONS AND TONS AS A SOCCER SENSATION, A MAIN "SOCCER EINSTEIN"
- ☉ EDISON DEMONSTRATES A STAR TEAM STEADINESS
- ☉ EDISON IS NAMED SAME AS ONE MASTER SCIENTIST (Yes, it's true; he was named after Thomas!)

Speaking of master scientists, I think Einstein—whom we talked about earlier—logically would, being born to the same Karmic Path of the 5's energy as Pele, get a real kick out of Lexigrams. Einstein surely understood a lot about a SOUL'S POWER, and he would probably marvel at what goes on when our American football season comes to a grand close with the SUPERBOWL. Here again you'll find it's a somewhat different kind of message that evolves from this term, used since 1966, which has turned into a true American tradition to party on down while watching the last two remaining teams in the NFL entertain us in the middle of winter, and we also get to watch some of the most innovative TV advertising of the year. I can only hope Einstein would be with me here, as I just loved the revelations I found in the very word that caps off the season for *le football américain*:

## SUPERBOWL

- PURE LOSER POWER SURE LOWERS US BELOW OUR SOUL
- PURE LOSER POWER ROBS OUR SOUL
- USE "UR" SOBER SOUL POWER
- PURE SOUL POWER SURE SUPERB
- BOW, USE PURE SUPERB SOUL POWER

I am definitely into a bit of overtime here. So, I'm going to leave you with one last Lexigram spiraling scores from 2010's Superbowl. It surely was an upset at the 44th Superbowl, but the letters within these teams' titles were just awaiting to reveal the stories that we saw evidence of showing their truth in Miami on 07 February 2010.

## NEW ORLEANS SAINTS

- ARE SO SET TO WIN A SWEET NATIONAL TITLE IN TWO-O-TEN
- ARE SO SET NOT TO LOSE A NATIONAL TITLE IN TWO-O-TEN
- SET TO SEE A REAL SENSATIONAL RENEWAL IN TWO-O-TEN
- A NATION IS SET TO WITNESS A REAL SENSATIONAL WIN IN TWO-O-TEN
- ARE SEEN IN AN ETERNAL NEW LITE IN TWO-O-TEN
- ARE TO ANOINT A REAL WISE NATIONAL WIN IN TWO-O-TEN
- ARE AN ESSENTIAL NATIONAL TITLE WINNER IN TWO-O-TEN

## INDIANAPOLIS COLTS

- ⊙ IN A LOSS TO TOP, TO STOP A SAINTS PASSION
- ⊙ NOT TO TOP SAINTS IN POINTS TO PASS ON
- ⊙ NOT IN POSITION TO TOP A SAINTS PASSION
- ⊙ NOT TO TOP A SAINTS NATIONAL POSITION
- ⊙ IN NO OPTION TO TOP A SAINTS POSITION
- ⊙ NOT TO STILL SIT IN A TOP SPOT IN A SAINTS POSITION
- ⊙ IN A SPASTIC LOSS TO A SAINTS TIDAL ACTION
- ⊙ NOT TO TOP A SAINTS SOLID LOCATION SPOILS

So, if I didn't get to your favorite athlete, team, or game, guess what? That's my Lexigram gift to you for you to discover, because, it just wouldn't be right of me to tell you everything here. As any coach will also tell you, you'll never improve your innate spiraling talents if you don't start practicing. It would be so cliché as to say perfection is our ultimate destination, for the art of Lexigrams truly has nothing to do with being perfect. It has everything to do with the journey of finding out the simple truth. While we've seen just how clever Lexigrams are in telling us all about various kinds of people, let's check out their magic in some non-human entities. So, after all of the exercise we just had, take a moment to rest, perhaps have a drink of water, and prepare to turn the page to tap into more insight when it comes to the names that we are always being encouraged to buy things from. Oh, and thank you for being such a good sport during this last brain workout! Now that you are fully stretched...

# Chapter 9

## COMPANIES / PRODUCTS

*"Whatever words we utter should be chosen with care for people will hear them and be influenced by them for good or ill."* —The BUDDHA

Well, in this day and age, everything just wants to grow bigger and bigger, as making more money is the American way, right? I'll not get into an ethics lesson right now, as I do believe Lexigrams are doing this all by themselves without my input. Besides, what has been enlarged and expanded upon is from the combined eras of Pluto in Scorpio and especially in Sagittarius (the signs the planet of transformation transited through since the mid-80s, not having a care about any limitations). With Pluto now fully engaged in Capricorn for another decade and a half (this era officially began 26 November 2008, about 3 weeks after the U.S. elected President Barack Obama), when one turns to greed, they may get a harder lesson to learn than they ever thought as their reward.

Funny though, it does seem nowadays to prove to be true that the larger the COMPANIES become, the more we see the potential that their INCOME IS IN MAIN PAINS, IS IN A MAIN PANIC, MONIES COME IN SIN. The names of companies conclude with further evidence in the remainder of this chapter that even a non-human entity has this same Lexigram potential to tell the tales from the title it is granted. Some, you'll see, are quite in tune with reaping such an immense harvest, while others have taken things too far in greed, and the story of how this could have been avoided unfolds more often than not.

While definitely a large company, TARGET always seems to have their prices adjusted accordingly so we can all GET AT A GREAT RATE. You may not find actual true GREAT ART, per se, at this red dot special logo (and if you inspect it closely, it actually looks like the glyph that represents the Sun in Astrology—no wonder they attract their customers!). But the dollar value saved keeps people returning. It is another interesting point to note that the very name TARGET carries a Name Expression of the blessed 19's *The Prince of Heaven*. Equally with that "odd" choice of the red-dotted logo, which really is the glyph of the Sun, the 1's Name Expression here attracts the people to spill in the doors of TARGET all the more. As the Chaldeans so deeply understood the 19 to be the most fortunate compound number, guess we can see why TARGET is in quite an alignment of fortune indeed.

There is rarely a major populated area within the United States anymore that one can't find even better prices—but maybe not as good of quality as Target—by walking into WALMART. This name doesn't quite reveal that you can get your bargains here at a great rate, but soon we'll get to the energy behind what this company should adhere to if it is to continue building its fortunes in the long term. Aries pioneer SAMUEL MOORE WALTON was born on 29 March 1918 to a very blessed and masterful 33 Lifepath.

An Aries will surely desire to lead in the life, and with the 29's *Grace Under Pressure,* this will be done in a most maternal way. Anytime one is walking the 33's Lifepath of *Love and Magic,* they will more often than not bring a balance to whatever they come across. Certainly this is the case with Mr. Walton, who, through Venus's help along his way, brought in a mother lode of money, as well through his leadership.

### SAMUEL MOORE WALTON

- ◉ A MARS MATERNAL MASTER MAN SENT TO START A TRUE SALE STORE
- ◉ SAM SENT AS A REAL TRUE MASTER SALESMAN TO LATER RULE ALL
- ◉ SAM EARNS MOMENTOUS TONS AS ONE SALE STORES ALLURE ALL
- ◉ AS A MAESTRO SAM SELL MORE AMOUNTS TO EARN MONSTER ENORMOUS TONS
- ◉ A WALMART RENAME MUST LEARN TO SEE SMART RENEWALS TO LAST
- ◉ LATER ON WALMART ALTERS SMALLER STORES TO A LONESOME UNAWARES
- ◉ LATER WALMART STEAL ALL SMALLER STORES SALES TO SELLOUT
- ◉ EAST TO WEST, WALMARTS ROAM ON
- ◉ SOME SEE WALMART AS NOT NORMAL, NOT A TRUE NATURAL STORE
- ◉ WALMART MUST LEARN TO LAST EONS ON AS ONE

It was in the town of Rogers, Arkansas, that Walton, within a 5 Personal Year of the 32/5's *Communication* energy of going to the masses through Mercury, opened

WALMART DISCOUNT CITY, on 06 July 1962. (Walton surely was following his stars when he opened upon a 6 calendar date.) Here we find a Name Expression purely guided by the same energy of Walton's Sun Sign, the 9, through Mars. It was inevitable that this vibration would indeed take Walmart stores to Universal proportions. When Walton passed on 05 April 1992, there were 1,960 Walmart stores in existence, all around the world. Whether you agree or not with the naturalness of shopping at any given Walmart, Walton came to conquer the art of mass sales in his lifetime.

## WALMART DISCOUNT CITY

- SAM WALTON TO START A DISCOUNT TRADITION IN ANY CITY
- IT IS AN INDUSTRIAL ATTRACTION AS IT IS IN LOW LOW COSTS
- YOU CAN COUNT ON DISCOUNTS IN CARTLOADS
- IT ATTRACTS AND ATTRACTS MANY IN LOW-INCOMES
- SAM IS IN AN ULTRA ADMIRATION
- ITS DURATION IS TO LAST AS A MAINSTAY UNTIL SCRUTINY LAWS CAST WARS

Today, in this extremely complicated world, it is just the simplicity of the name WALMART that this original name has been changed to, which now carries a Name Expression of the 12's, *The Sacrifice–The Victim*. It is easy to see how Jupiter's expansive and global influence over the 3 imposes absolutely no limits on what you may find to purchase within any Walmart stores, wherever they are located within the world. There are plenty of people who don't reap in this giant's rewards, though bargains galore explode in every corner and aisle, and these are the people who are making the goods. We all know of the suffering that goes on in countries like China to produce such products at an incredibly low rate, and the conditions of these workplaces are not exactly ideal. What WALMART could more than likely deal with in the future is ALARM, AT A RAW WAR, and the LAW. Yet, if they do adhere to the Chaldean Karmic Mystery of the 12, which requests the soul or entity must adhere to education and the continual learning process, Walmart may not be taken down by the law. However far their mutable fire energy desires to burn, there is a limitation that will need to be placed upon where they have evolved. It definitely is not within its founder Sam Walton's maternal pioneering energy that deals with love and compassion.

Don't forget how, in 2004, the seemingly loving and compassionate artful creators from the MARTHA STEWART LIVING OMNIMEDIA powerhouse did indeed find themselves in a bit of a financial crisis with the law. Even though MARTHA STEWART was crowned the third most powerful woman in America in 2001, just after her second natal Saturn Return, she certainly bowed down to learn some valuable lessons by the time Saturn was transiting through her Sun Sign of Leo from 2005 to 2007. Having already served time in jail for misrepresenting stock information to her investors, it is good to see how she listened to that inner voice and paid ultimate attention as Saturn was making sure she was going to continue on in pure responsibility to make her comeback by 2006, when her company began to regain much surer footing with its first profitable return since the scandal.

One with a 26/8 Lifepath such as Martha, who was born on 03 August 1941 to the name MARTHA HELEN KOSTYRA, only knows how to work as they live out their soul's journey along the 8's path. Martha's legacy continues to ever-expand its empire to this day. But greed can never be a lasting part of the package to bring reward, and what certainly got Martha into her trouble was her Leo 3 energy that got a little too carried away with the material rewards she seemingly so easily attracted. While this combination ideally contributes to the intense drive we have seen in her nature, it is no wonder that Martha has had the goals and success we have seen. Jupiter is also associated with luck and good fortune, something that Martha seemed to have on her side for quite some time. The 3 also is seen ruling over modeling and those involved with all facets of fabricated beauty, and Martha was a well-known model in her earlier years. But how can her name and numbers tell us more about where things went wrong for her?

Martha's 26 Lifepath of *Partnerships* strongly "warns of dangers, disappointments, and failure, especially regarding the ambitions, brought about through bad advice, association with others, and unhappy partnerships of all kinds. The person is counseled to avoid partnerships and pursue the career alone, not heeding even the well-intentioned advice of others, but follow only the personal hunches and intuition—although these should be carefully examined for flaws before acting on them."[48] Martha indeed made some errors in her partnerships, and as we have seen, she placed trust in the wrong hands. With the singular influence of Saturn through the 8, Martha's Lifepath is one that she needs to proceed with caution over as she achieves and learns from experience! Saturn is also referred to as the planet of Karma, and anyone with a Saturn influence in their chart must beware of the karmic debts they will repay eventually. The 8 is a number of financial stability, caution, restriction, self discipline, and self control—so the element of greed cannot be a part of the picture in order for them to see the fruits of their labors rewarded and to reap a harvest that comes backed fully with integrity.

MARTHA HELEN KOSTYRA is a name that carries the Name Expression of the 15, known as *The Magician*, which says it is, "associated with 'good talkers,' eloquence of speech, and the gifts of music, art, and the drama. It bestows upon the person or entity represented by it a dramatic temperament and strong personal magnetism and a curiously compelling charisma."[49] With this energy ruling over her name at birth, we see that Martha in her lifetime has indeed possessed these qualities. The singular 6 through Venus rules over the feminine, needs compassion, and totally values money. Certainly these were the gifts and ideas she nurtured through her original company and the line of products that she sold before becoming a true home decor giant. As Venus rules over all that is lovely, beautiful, and appealing to the eye, so, too, were all of Martha's homemaking creations, as well as being an aid to her earlier in her life as she pursued a modeling career. Martha also saw a brief career as a stockbroker. Are we at all surprised?

## MARTHA HELEN KOSTRYA

- SENT AS A REAL SMART NEAT LEO THREE
- SEEN AS A MASTER AT THE HOME ART
- MARTHA SEEN AS THE REAL SMART MONEY MASTER NEAR ANY AREA

- ⊙ MARTHA'S KARMA HAS A MEAN STREAK
- ⊙ AS SHE RENAMES LATER ON SHE NO ERASE HER MONEY KARMA
- ⊙ MARTHA SENT HERE TO EARTH TO MAKE A LOT O' MONEY
- ⊙ THEN TO SEE THE MONEY LOST YEAR O'THREE
- ⊙ SENT TO MAKE HER MARK AS A REAL "TY"K"OON"
- ⊙ MARTHA'S KARMA SAY TO NOT LET THE MEAN MEN TAKE HER STOCK ASTRAY
- ⊙ MARTHA HAS A REAL TEST TO SEE LATER ON AS ALL HER TREATS ARE TAKEN

When we look at the name MARTHA STEWART, we also see that she did keep the 15 energy that her original birth name had. When incorporating her mega homemaking magazine of MARTHA STEWART LIVING, she gave it quite a challenging vibration of the 16's *The Shattered Citadel*. Take this vibration and couple it with her unalterable Lifepath of the 26, and throw in Saturn's current transit energy at that time, and we can see what inevitably led to her downfall. People who abuse the 16 will always be seen falling from a high place. Martha did not resist the fame and celebrity, and due to her materially driven 8 Lifepath, kept on building and building. One can only wonder: Would things have turned out different with her scandal had she chosen a different name! We will note how Martha was smart enough to adhere to one of the warnings of the singular 7 vibration, which is to avoid dark colors, especially the color black. Martha's line of products and magazine content are always in the lovely pastels and lighter shades that the 7 vibrates positively to. The 7 is also a Neptune-ruled number, with a heavy water influence, elementally. When the chips go down within a 7 vibration, they fall like the crashing waters of Niagra Falls. And as the name reveals...

## MARTHA STEWART LIVING

- ⊚ MARTHA IS A REAL MASTER IN ART
- ⊚ HER ART SEES GREAT GAINS THEN IS SET IN LIES
- ⊚ THIS NAME IS SET IN REAL ENERGIES THAT THWART IN LIES
- ⊚ THIS NAME IS IN A SIXTEEN TRAIL, A REAL EVIL WATER STREAM WHEN IN LIES
- ⊚ SHE HAS GREAT LARGE EARNINGS AS SHE EARNS IN TV
- ⊚ SHE HAS HER HEART IN A REAL MEAN REALM THAT GETS HER IN A VILE TRIAL
- ⊚ WE SEE MARTHA IS IN GREAT GAINS IN HER EIGHT TRAIL AS A REGAL THREE
- ⊚ THE LAW GIVES MARTHA A REAL WISE LEARN LATER
- ⊚ MARTHA WAS MEANT TO LISTEN TO HER HEART WITHIN AS WE SEE HER IN TEARS
- ⊚ AS SHE TAKES THE NEW NAME, HER SALES RISE THEN IN SHAME IN THE NEWS

As the success of the magazine and her growing product lines prevailed, Martha kept on going. MARTHA STEWART LIVING OMNIMEDIA vibes to the blessing of the 21's *The Crown of the Magi,* which is "pictured as "The Universe." It promises general success and guarantees advancement, honors, awards, and general elevation in the life and career. It indicates victory after a long struggle, for the "Crown of the Magi" is gained only after long initiation, much soul testing and various other tests of determination. However, the person or entity blessed with the number 21 may be certain of final victory over all odds and all opposition. It's a most fortunate vibration—a number of karmic reward."[50]

When Martha went for her stock gains, she picked a fine name, in tune with her own "three-ness." Still reaping benefits from her popular magazine, she was unknowingly in the heavy waters that the 16 brings, while she continued to established herself as the mastermind tycoon that she was, due to her Leo 3 along the 8 Lifepath of ambition. Unfortunately, such determination went against the warnings that the vibrations she was up against were bringing, and although extremely fortunate, the change to the 21 could not save her. The excesses of Jupiter under the singular 3 just came pouring out for her yet again, but as her Lifepath indicates, she placed trust in the wrong hands and Saturn came down to put a stop to all that was going on.

## MARTHA STEWART LIVING OMNIMEDIA

- MARTHA'S NEW MONIES DO NOT LAST LONG, AS SHE GOES DOWN IN THE NEWS
- IN TWO-O-O-THREE MARTHA'S WINNING MONIES GAME IS NO LONGER
- THERE ARE SOME MEAN MEN THAT LIE TO MARTHA AS SHE GOES LARGER
- HER GREAT DREAMS ARE SEEN AT AN END, AND NEED A REAL RENEW
- GREED WAS NOT MEANT TO LAST IN MARTHA'S HEART
- THE DRAMA MARTHA THRIVES ON ALSO IS NOT MEANT TO LAST

⊙ MARTHA NEEDS A GOD NOW TO WIN HER OWN
   REAL HEART

⊙ SHE HAS TO LISTEN TO THE VOICE WITHIN, AS THE
   ENERGIES WARN HER

⊙ MARTHA HAS TO SERVE TIME TO AMEND HER
   GREED

⊙ SHE HAS THE STRENGTH TO AWAKEN A NEW
   WOMAN

⊙ MARTHA HAS TO HEAL HER OWN "LEO THREE"
   HEART INSIDE IN A REAL SILENT AREA ALONE

It's wild how a name from a company can uncannily tell all, isn't it? So, how can one choose a name for something that will ensure it reaches the masses with success? Best to have Mercury as your messenger, and let him carry your mission far and wide in a 5 Name Expression. It's also not a bad idea, either, to pick one with the very word GAINS in it; then, you've probably really got a winning combination. Even though their motto is "what it means to be from Maine," it is the title of POLAND SPRING in the 23's *The Royal Star of the Lion* Name Expression that continues to bring home a hefty harvest. Mercury guides the singular 5 here, while the 23 claims: "This is a karmic reward number. 23 bestows, not only a promise of success in personal and career endeavors, it guarantees help from superiors and protection from those in high places."[51] I'll say. You don't get to be the number one bottled water company in America without help from a superior source.

Now, while we all know about the dangers of the tainted tap water out there in today's modern world, I'm still in just a little bit of wonder about what's really in the jug? I guess I may be as NAÏVE as those who may be purchasing the classier bottles of EVIAN. But don't be fooled by Poland Spring, because they are in actuality owned by NESTLE WATERS NORTH AMERICA, since 1980. I don't know about you, but I am totally "branded" by now to just think sweets and especially chocolate when I hear the word NESTLE. But Nestle was actually started around the 1860's when its founder and pharmacist, Henri Nestle, developed baby formulas for women who couldn't breast-feed. The rest is now history, as they say. One more historical fact is Poland Spring is an actual natural spring that was a world famous spa back in the day, founded in 1845. Keeping up with all things being big in companies in this day and age, let's get back to the billion-dollar-making entity of:

## POLAND SPRING

- AGO, A SPRING SPRUNG IN GAINS AND GAINS
- AN ORIGINAL GRAND SPA, LANDING IN LOADS O' DOLLARS
- ORDAINS IN LOADS O' RAPID GAINS
- A SOLID SPRING DROPPING LOADS AND LOADS
- A DARLING DRIP LANDING IN GAINS
- A SOARING GAIN IS ROLLING ON AND ON
- SLOGANS ORDAIN AND SIGNAL IN A GAIN
- LOADS O' GAINS GROSS ON AND ON AND ON
- SOARING GAINS IN NO LAPSING, IN NO SPOILS, OR NO PAINS
- IN NO LOSING GAINS IN A GRAND PAIRING
- ALIGNS IN A GRAND SPAN AS GAINS GO ON AND ON AND ON

Well, what a story from all angles there! Poland Spring (now using a newer slogan: "Just may be the best tasting water on earth!") is one of the many water companies, like S. Pellegrino, Perrier, and Deer Park, operating under the umbrella of NESTLE WATERS NORTH AMERICA, whose President and CEO just so happens to be a woman, Kim Jeffrey. This conglomerate company name expresses itself under the vibration of—guess what? The 23. The masses do nothing else now but reach for a bottled water wherever they can find one, and if you are drinking one now, take a look at your label. You are part of the mass movement that has ensured this giant's continual success. Here we are again, as the tale is told from the letters composing another 23 *The Royal Star of the Lion* name of:

**NESTLE WATERS NORTH AMERICA**

⊚ THIS NAME IS IN A "THE STAR LION" ETHEREAL TRANSLATION

⊚ SENT AS THE WEALTHIEST WATER MASTERS IN THEIR SALES

⊚ THESE ARE SEEN COAST TO COAST, EAST TO WEST IN THE EASIEST SALES

⊚ NO ONE SEEMS TO RESIST THEIR WATER CHOICES

⊚ THE MONIES SEEN SOAR ON AS A WATER TERROR SCARE IS THE SELLER

⊚ THEIR TESTAMENTS STREAMLINE THE EARTH'S HEALTHIEST STATEMENTS

⊚ THEIR SELECTION CREATIONS ARE REAL NATIONAL SALES ATTRACTIONS

⊚ THIS IS A MONSTER WATER MONARCH SET TO REACH MILESTONES

- THE WEALTHIEST CONSISTENT SALES ARE SEEN IN THE MAINE STATE
- A WOMAN CHAIRS THIS WATER ASSORTMENT ARISTOCRAT
- IS THEIR WATER REAL CLEAN OR ANOTHER REAL SCAM? TASTE IT!

So now you definitely know one more star secret. If you want your creation to go to the masses, choose a Name Expression such as the 23 and make sure the letters within that name come up with something good, and you'll reap whatever you may want with the proper intention. But, there are plenty of other fortunate numbers out there you may want to consider. Just make sure they align with your eventual long-term goals, and their tales from within reveal what you wish to manifest. Sounds so simple, doesn't it?

Even when it certainly appears that a company is competent in its earnings, as we have learned during 2007 to 2009's passage of Saturn in Virgo, if you weren't operating up to snuff, for lack of a better phrase, these large mass money-making machines saw less than better days.

One top financial player that was dealt the true auditor card when Saturn was perfecting the imperfections while transiting in Virgo was LEHMAN BROTHERS, founded in 1850. 2008 marked this company's final demise as they became the largest investment company in the history of the United Sates.

## LEHMAN BROTHERS

- SET TO EARN TONS AT THE START NEAR A REAL REASON
- THE BEST LABORERS AT STABLE LOANS

- ARE A NOTABLE MASTER TO ENABLE REASON
- ARE REAL SMART LEARNERS SET TO EARN TONS
- AS THE REAL BROTHERS REST TO THE EARTH, THE REST LEARN TO STEAL
- LATER ON THESE "SMART MASTER EARNERS" ARE NOT TO LAST
- THE TEAMS' "BAROMETER" STORM ON AS REAL ROBS, REAL RANSOMS ARE SEEN
- THE LOANS LATER ON ARE NOT REAL, NOT NOBLE, NOT STABLE
- NOT TO BE ABLE TO RELEARN AT A LOAN ART AS THESE MEN LOSE TONS
- THE MEAN MEN ENABLE A REAL TREMOR TREASON NOT TO HEAL
- THESE MEN SMOTHER AS A REAL SHAMBLE RAMBLES ON

Such a pity that people get greedy, isn't it? While the modern-day and now-former Lehman Brothers look for fairer skies, if you are still excited at all about investing, a company that still carries itself with integrity is MORGAN STANLEY, founded on 16 September 1935. Although, over the course of Saturn's adjustments while in Virgo, this company has equally seen its fair share of alterations. Yet, they are still standing, and at the time of completing this book, they have become MORGAN STANLEY SMITH BARNEY. They reaped this harvest and reward from the past 7 years work in none other than an 8 Personal Year upon 13 January 2009. This was in a 9 Personal Month of finalizations to their original name, and the 13's *Regeneration and Change* energy rang true upon this 4 Personal Day.

What is interesting to note about MORGAN STANLEY alone is their tremendous attention to detail and ability to analyze energy that guides them through the 7, which we see both in their 16 Karmic Path and the 34 Lifepath of the company. I still wonder what the 16's *The Shattered Citadel* may bring to them in the future, but let's hope they remain in the eye of the storm by continuing to rely on the 34's *Discrimination and Analysis* (the same meaning as the 25) that grants "wisdom gained through careful observation of people and things, and worldly success by learning through experience. The judgment is excellent."[52] While they may have certainly lost money, they are one of the sharper players in their field. Anytime you see Neptune in completion, with it's opposing energy of Virgo, these energies rarely miss any of those detail-oriented beats.

MORGAN STANLEY is a 44 Name Expression of *Partnerships*, and it shows. Here we again see the energy of Saturn in its most masterful form. In as much as making more money may still accompany the moves of this company, they are doing something smart that keeps them adhering to that wisdom, sound judgment, and learning through their experiences. An 8 entity, like people, are best known to grow more robust as they mature, and it seems so far that MORGAN STANLEY is living up to it's karmic responsibility somehow. While the potential in their original name denotes they could be SET TO LOSE TONS, I'll take it that, since this company survived the wrath of Saturn in its own Sun Sign, they just MAY NOT LOSE TONS if they continue to play by the rules of integrity and don't give in to making any greedy errors in how they wish to earn.

## MORGAN STANLEY

- ☉ YES STRONG ANALYST TALENTS GO ON AT MORGAN STANLEY
- ☉ YES ARE SENT TO EARN NEAR A REAL MASTERY
- ☉ STRANGELY ARE NOT SET TO LOSE TONS AS MOST MEN ARE SMART ONES
- ☉ YES ARE SENT AS A MONEY MAGNET EONS ON TO EARN NEAR TONS
- ☉ STRONGLY MEN EARN A REAL GREAT SALARY YEARLY
- ☉ YEAR TO YEAR, MORE ORNATELY EARNS ARE SET IN REAL STONE
- ☉ A REAL MONETARY MAGNET TO MASTERLY GO ON, GO EONS ON
- ☉ ARE REAL SMART MONEY MANAGERS SET TO LAST
- ☉ AS A MONEY MANGLE STORM GOES ON, A MORAL SMART RE-LEARN GOES ON
- ☉ YES SENT TO LAST AS A REAL MONEY MAESTRO NEAR LONG EARNS

MORGAN STANLEY SMITH BARNEY now carries a Name Expression of the 59/14's *Movement–Challenge*. Well, it certainly sharpens their ability to apply logic to the situation. The 14 does grant that moving of the masses understanding, as: "Magnetic communication with the public through writing, publishing and all media-related matters is associated with the 14. Periodic changes in business and partnerships of all kinds are usually beneficial. Dealing with speculative matters brings luck, likewise movement and travel associated with combinations of people and nations can be fortunate."[53] Yet, the 14 does warn: "However, both gains and losses are sometimes temporary, due to the strong currents of change, which are ever-present."[54] As often as these banking companies seem to need to formulate new ones and buy up the underdogs, I'll bank on it that this Mercurial Name Expression will serve our analysts just fine. Lucky for them, the chairman, JAMES P. GORMAN, EARNS AS A MEGA MAJOR PRO MORGAN MAN and is all too familiar with this energy, being born on 14 July 1958. Cancers surely know how to handle money, most likely holding on to it with those pinching claws of theirs. For the sake of the future, let's just hope Mr. Gorman is charitable with his wealth along his own 35/8 Lifepath:

## MORGAN STANLEY SMITH BARNEY

- YES THIS ENTITY ARRANGEMENT CAME TO BE IN EARLY O' NINE
- THIS TRANSLATES TO A BIG BIG GAIN AS MORGAN STANLEY GETS MORE STABLE
- YES THIS STRENGTHENS THEIR MASTER ANALYST ABILITY MORE
- A REAL SYMMETRY IS SEEN AS THESE MEN BRING MORE SMARTS TOGETHER
- OH YEAH YES THEY ARE SET TO SEE SOME BIG REAL ESTATE GAINS AGAIN LATER
- THEIR STRATEGIES ARE NOT IN SHENANIGANS AS THEY EARN
- THEY ARE BEST TO REINSTATE A REAL INTEGRITY TO MONEY
- THEIR MAIN MAN IS GORMAN, ON HIS EIGHT TRAIL
- AS MONEY IS IN A REGRESSION, THESE MEN STILL EARN LARGE SALARIES
- THEY ARE SEEN TO GROSS IN THE TONS AS THIS BIG GIANT MONEY MONSTER

The media ceaselessly has surged on about the continual economic pitfalls and reassessments, and just two months after Morgan Stanley became a larger giant in 2009, Venus had been doing her Retrograde dance in the zodiac skies, adding more fuel to the financial fire and meltdowns. It was during March 2009 that it totally became official we were in that ugly word: a RECESSION: I SEE IN NO SINCERE SCENE; I SEE NO SCORES, I SEE NO ENCORES, I SEE NO SINCERE CORE; I SEE CRISES RISE.

Knowing the realities of a VENUS RETROGRADE period, where REVENUES NEAR GREED SEE SURGENT OVERTURNS, it should not have been a surprise that the "notorious" AIG had once again been under the political and financial microscope in those recent weeks. Most analysts agree they were another one of the major contributors to the economic downward spiral. Have you let in a little love of seeing the real worth of what the upward spirals of Lexigrams undoubtedly can provide for you? The spiritual value alone can be astounding in its truth. Before we get to all the analysis on this one, let's first check out the uncanny wisdom of the true tale from within the name that this entity known as AIG had manifested:

### AMERICAN INTERNATIONAL GROUP, INC.

- ⊚ IN MAR<u>C</u>H O'NINE A REAL INTERNAL LIE COME OUT TO EMOTE MOANING & MOURNING
- ⊚ MEANT TO TERMINATE AT A TIME PLUTO ENTER INTO CAPRICORN
- ⊚ TO GET A MAIN POLITICIAN ATTENTION PROCLAIMING ONE OPINION CLAIM TO NOT TO PERMIT IT TO GO ON

- ONCE IN A GREATER RUIN IT NOT TO RETURN TO A RELIANT MONETARIAL AREA
- A CREATOR LET A TOP LIAR CONTROL IT
- MEANT TO REAP IN A TOP EARNING
- NOT ABLE TO RETAIN A GENUINE ARRANGEMENT OR GO ON IN TIME
- TOP CEO'S PLAN IT IN A LARGE MIRAGE LIE
- TOP CEO' S ORIENT IN A GIANT LIE TO EARN
- IT INITIATE ON A MEGA INTERNAL LIE TO CAPTURE A REAL LARGE CLIENT ATTENTION
- RAN IN A PLAN TO MANIPULATE A CLIENT
- NOT TO PROTECT A CLIENT IN A LONG TERM GAIN
- LOANER PROGRAM NOT ABLE TO GET A LONG TERM GOAL RETURN
- TO RUIN A LARGE "CLEAN" REPUTATION
- IT RETURN TO A MAIN COMPETITION IN ANOTHER NAME LATER ON
- GO ON...TIME TO RENAME IT IN O'NINE, GET IT IN A MAIN MERGER OR...TERMINATE IT! LET THE LION OUT, GET A NAME RENEW!

This seems to reveal some truth of the matter, wouldn't one say? I don't think they've thought of a new name yet, as they should have. Trusting this name to manage money may not be the best choice. Even AIG's Name Expression breaks down to the 11, representing *A Lion Muzzled—A Clenched Fist*—a master number, yes, but one filled with covered trails, treachery, conflicting desires, and emotional turmoil as the results of improper choices.

Further evidence leading to the immediate restructuring of AIG was easily seen right in it's natal astrological chart. Founded on 19 December 1919 in Shanghai, China, AIG's natal 06-degree Pluto in Cancer was in a heavy opposition from the current transiting Pluto in the Career House at 03 degrees Capricorn. Regeneration is requested, while the potential for hidden parts of the corporation to be revealed are bound to occur. Whenever the currently transiting Pluto may be opposing or squaring itself in any natal chart, one can expect the changes at hand to be difficult, yet fully necessary to have rebirth occur. Saturn and Uranus were opposing each other as their current transits fell within AIG's 6th House of being of service and the 12th of the subconscious process. Fascinating that a corporation founded in 1919 can still have the handy tool of astrology to verify there surely is a reason why the way AIG serves others was under serious scrutiny. Equally, with this heavy opposition, whatever hidden lies have been a part of this process will be brought to the light of day—it's karmic retribution time whenever Saturn and Uranus are involved.

Looking to the numbers, it is no coincidence AIG was circulating through none other than a 5 Personal Year. Ultimately stemming from the new beginnings that were laid down over the course of December 2005 to December 2006, AIG was meant to see major movement and permanent change occur on the stage of corporate life throughout 2009. As much as there was a trail of exposure leading up to March's dreary report for AIG, it was within an 8 Personal Month under a Venus Retrograde that their fate was sealed. Undoubtedly, they could have seen a pleasant forecast bringing them gains and a rich harvest, but instead the Universe manifested the opposing outcome due to their internal structure collapsing from the roots of AIG's flimsy foundation. As the "solution" of the government bail out rescued AIG, this Lion is still on the loose, so seriously, look out.

Even though we may too be tired of hearing of the car industries' financial woes—make no mistake that 2007-to-2010 transit of Saturn in Virgo had everything to do with the readjusting in all transportation and service-oriented areas. Another addition to the ill-fated bankruptcy list, GENERAL MOTORS was founded 16 September 1908 and, just like our former Morgan Stanley friends, follows a 34 Lifepath of *Discrimination and Analysis.* While we saw Morgan Stanley seemingly come out victorious under such a passage, what makes GM different? Well, you see GM, by all astrological measures, just hadn't done it's homework as well as Morgan Stanley had, and in a period when kar-mic responsibility had come to visit and reorganized a few things for this global company, they instead saw the 16's promise of being "a Tower struck by lightning, from which a man is falling, with a crown on his head. It warns of a strange fatality, also of danger of accidents and the defeat of one's plans."[55]

As GM celebrated its New Year in 2008, it entered a 26/8 Personal Year of *Partnerships,* advising to proceed with caution in any pairing throughout the year. The sin-gular 8's energy denotes the potential for advancements, honor and recognition, along with material gains from the last 7 years work. However, if the right choices lead-ing up to this point have not been made, the very opposite affects may unfold in an 8 Personal Year. The date 01 June 2009 marked the beginning of a 5 Personal Month within their 8 Year for GM—where the 5's energy of permanent changes sure brought in just a bit more movement than they probably desired. On a 6 Personal Day, where legalities can ideally be addressed, the world learned that GM had joined the list of economic examples of what not to do to gain genuine long-term success.

Touching back to astrology, GM's current transits at that time saw Saturn in Virgo square to their natal Pluto in Gemini—equally lending to the explanation of the hardship it had announced. When stern Saturn is squaring off to transformational Pluto, destitution is an easy outcome if responsibility has not been adhered to. Couple this aspect with the current Saturn-ruled 8 Personal Year from the 2008-to-2009 cycle, and it is all about "doing the right thing"... or else!

Blockages appeared in other areas for this former giant. GM's natal Mars sat at 14 degrees Virgo, just as our Sun was about to square these very same degrees in its current transit through Gemini. The current transit of Saturn was only 1 degree off its natal Mars at 15 degrees Virgo. Woah. Definitely the time had come for GM to do some serious reassessments in their drives, vision and ability to pioneer.

Now, of course, Lexigrams have their usual uncanny tale to tell about this business entity. From the start of this corporation, now more than 100 years old, there was no doubt GM was meant to rise to the status within the car industry that they did. Let's see if they'll heed to some of the story within their name to get a proper restructure to succeed. In light of the BP Oil debauchery in the Gulf, please, send your thoughts that GM pays close attention, so they can hear it definitely has something to do with being GREEN.

## GENERAL MOTORS

- SEEN AS A SMART MASTER TO START ERAS AGO
- SET TO SEE REAL SALES TO EARN MEGA
- GM'S SALES ARE REAL SET TO EARN TONS
- GM'S MEANT TO SEE MERGERS
- SOME MERGERS NOT MEANT TO GO EONS ON
- LATER AS A MEGA EARNER STORM START, GM TO SEE A RESET
- GM LEARNS A GREEN AREA A REAL SMART ONE TO GO TO
- GM MEANT TO RESET TO A GREEN AREA TO EARN
- AS GM'S GOALS GO GREEN, GM SET TO EARN MORE
- SO, "GO GREEN" GM!
- GET A MASTER GREEN RESTART...

Shifting from a company that utilizes the product our next company produces, Lexigrams once again will marvel in a not-so-happy way from their revelations. Our wonderful world at large became more than aware of the catastrophic event that unfolded from the irresponsibility of BP in the Gulf of Mexico on 20 April 2010. Known for years under the motto "Best Possible," BP adopted their tag line "Beyond Petroleum" back in 2000. Their latest name change from BP Amoco to BP p.l.c. did not to prevent the hardest fate that this company has faced—what we know as the DEEPWATER HORIZON OIL SPILL.

An OIL SPILL is always in an ILL SPOIL. The term OIL SPILL vibrates to the 20's understanding of *The Awakening*. Surely whenever these spills have unfortunately occurred, a big eye-opener follows. Sadly, these seem short-lived as the events of 20 April unfolded. It is of interest to note, on the 20th day of April 2010, this 20 energy emerged, and indeed the world had yet again been awoken (more like shaken this time) to a real truth here to resolve. The 20 is guided by the Moon, which urges nurturing and emotions to unfold. Oil spills have been happening since oil was first captured as a natural resource (BP's most recent previous spill occurred in Alaska in July 2006). Moreover, the response that typically unfolds has been paternal in nature, as the company tries to remedy the emergency at hand.

But let's get realistic here and recognize this wording is highly inappropriate for what has transpired in the disastrous situation in the Gulf. The proper term is OIL LEAK. It is what properly brings us to the understanding that OIL ILL KILL ALL ALIKE. OIL LEAK vibrates to the 22's *Submission and Caution*. Even though the 22 is a master number, it is deeply riddled with the warning: "22 is a Good Man, blinded by the folly of others, with a knapsack on his back, full of errors. In the image he seems to offer no defense against a ferocious tiger, which is about to attack him. It's a warning number of illusion and delusion. It indicates a good person (or entity) who lives in a fool's paradise; a dreamer of dreams who awakens only when surrounded by danger, when it's often too late. It warns of mistakes in judgment, of placing faith in those who are not trustworthy."[56] This seems to be a much better characterization of BP's OIL LEAK (not SPILL), which has wreaked historical havoc on, and in, the waters of the Gulf of Mexico, as well as its domino effect that will continue to unfold. Beyond Petroleum indeed.

To utilize such a title as DEEPWATER HORIZON OIL SPILL, we see that this is a Name Expression vibrating to the 31's *The Recluse–The Hermit*. While genius can be present in this number (and we are best to keep positive prayers that the genius of humans continues to come to the rescue of all things affected by it on the earth), it also carries the understanding that "the person (or entity) represented by this number is even more self-contained, self-sufficient, lonely, and isolated from others."[57] Although capped after months of irreversible damage, this seemingly unresolved disaster in the Gulf gets more and more hermit-like as the days have passed since 20 April 2010. Let's examine ways that the uncanny Lexigrams agree with the 31's reference:

## DEEPWATER HORIZON OIL SPILL

⊚ SENT ON TWO-O APRIL IN A TWO-O-TEN DATE TO A WESTERN SEA NEAR NEW ORLEANS,
TONS O' OIL PROPEL INTO THE WATER TO WHIRLPOOL ON AND ON

⊚ THIS IS AN EARTH DISASTER NOT TO END TOO SOON AS THEORIES AND THERAPIES ARE TRIED AND TRIED TO RESTRAIN IT

⊚ THE "SPILL" REAPS ON IN AN ISOLATION POSITION;

⊚ THIS IS A REAL WORLD DISHEARTEN AS WELL AS A REAL DISAPPOINT

⊚ ONE WEALTHIER WORLD OIL "STAR" IS SET TO LOSE IT ALL NOW IN A REAL SLANDER IN PENALTIES

⊚ THIS IS A RELATIONSHIP IN POLARITIES, IN OPPOSITION AS OIL TRILLIONS ARE LOST IN THE EARTH'S SEA, TO WASH ON THE SHORE

⊚ THIS OPERATION DOES NOT SEE A PRESIDENT IN REAL LEADERSHIP

⊚ THE EARTH INHERITS A PLASTERED DEPLETION

- REAL WORDS TO ALL IN THE WORLD: LET A NEW HEALER ROLE RISE AND TRANSPIRE TO END OIL AS A TOP EARNER
- AS A WORLD WE NEED TO RESPOND IN HEART AND STOP OIL REALITIES ON THE EARTH NOW
- WE ARE AS A WORLD TO PIONEER A NEW HEALER ROLE NOW

There are even more tales to be told from the BP name. With all of its greed and supposed "green growth" over the years, it changed its legal name more times than one would imagine reasonable over the last century. It began on 14 April 1909 as the Anglo-Persian Oil Company (APOC). By 1954, BRITISH PETROLEUM COMPANY became its name. Its Name Expression grants a 64/10 vibration, known as *The Wheel of Fortune*. While one can reap tremendous rewards from the 1's energy here, the 10 has these warnings: "The name will be known for good or evil, depending on the action chosen. The number 10 is capable of arousing the extreme responses of love or hate—respect or fear. There is no middle ground between honor or dishonor. Every event is self-determined. The power for manifesting creative concepts into reality is inherent, but must be used with wisdom, since the power for absolute creation contains the polarity power for absolute destruction. Self-discipline and infinite compassion must accompany the gift of the former to avoid the tragedy of the latter. Discipline must proceed Dominion."[58]

Well, although their legal title is now BP p.l.c., BRITISH PETROLEUM's poor example of discipline has certainly turned the wheel and resulted in serious destruction. It is times like these when it gets painful to know how powerful the art of Lexigrams truly can be. As we keep in mind the karma that BP has reaped for itself, it is certain as we have witnessed quite heavily within this chapter and in the preceding ones that greed never blesses anyone with genuine rewards. This is our time in history to look deep, and realize there must be a new way we can move forward to sustain life while regaining true health upon our dear planet earth.

## BRITISH PETROLEUM COMPANY

- SET TO RACE TO A TOP MOTOR OIL SPOT
- IT EARNS THE BEST TOP MONEY YEARS AND YEARS THEN TO LOSE THEIR SPOT
- YES IT IS SET TO SEE THE TOP MOST TREACHEROUS, TERRIBLE OIL PROBLEM IN HISTORY THAT SPILL ON THE USA SHORE IN APRIL YEAR O'TEN
- THE OIL PROBLEM START ONE MILE BENEATH THE SEA
- BP ORIENTS IN NO SPIRIT, MORALITY NOR HUMANITY, ONLY MONEY AMBITION
- AS THE OIL SPILLS ON, SOON, BP IS IN A MONEY CRISIS IN RUINS
- THIS PROBLEM HURTS OUR EARTH, OUR HEART, OUR CORE
- IT HURTS THE EARTH'S HEART MORE THAN ANY OTHER OIL SITUATION HAS, AS OUR TRUST IN BP IS PUT TO A STOP
- BUT, IT IS CERTAIN IN TIME THE EARTH CAN HEAL ITS HURT
- THE PEOPLE'S HEARTS MUST HOPE & PRAY TO REROUTE THEIR MOPE

- YES PEOPLE YOU CAN HATE BP BUT YOU MUST BE IN ACTION TO HEAL THIS SPOIL
- HUMANS PLEASE HEAR YOU ARE TO STOP OIL USE TO HEAL
- HUMANS YES YOU CAN USE OTHER CLEAN RESOURCE IN NATURE
- PEOPLE PLEASE UNITE, AS YES IT IS YOUR HISTORIC TRIUMPHANT TIME TO CLEAN UP YOUR RELATIONSHIP TO THE EARTH
- THERE IS A REAL TRUE RESOLUTION TO THIS TERRIBLE OIL PROBLEM
- YES YES YES YOU CAN USE NO MORE OIL AS YOU HEAL YOUR PLANET MOTHER EARTH
- TIME IS MITE HUMANS: SO TREAT THE EARTH IN SPIRITUAL RITUALS AS YOUR ANCIENT ANCESTORS TO HEAL IT BEST TO LET NATURE TRIUMPH.

In closing, when we look to the Lifepath energy of the date 20 April 2010, we arrive at the 9, *The Finalizer*. It is more certain than ever that the oil era is coming to a conclusion and a real completion. Under a 0-degree Taurus Sun representing ultimate transformation, this date equally indicates that an end must come to something dealing with nature that is desperately awaiting a rebirth. It is imperative that we shift, as this better be the last time the 20 has now truly awoken us like never before to the sad truth about the irreversible dangers of oil drilling. Let us all take in the knowledge that, when presented with CHALLENGES, we can be sure ALL CHANGES HEAL AS A CLEANSE.

The result of BP's careless acts opens the door for a massive movement to change. Even though the journey will not be short-lived, we will heal, as will our great Mother Earth.

As you turn the page to take in chapter 10, there within is some interesting advise from our Dear Indian Ancestors, as we explore what we can do to live properly in any New Age. As we have learned from the energy that lies within the names and titles that humans beings have chosen for our major companies that seem to dictate to the masses, there has been some not so happy forces created because of them. There are essential new habits the world at large needs to implement and adapt to. We must tap into the very core of our thoughts—the advice we consider, and most important, the natural energy that should be utilized, now more than ever before, to renew and ultimately survive. It is time we remember for the sake of our planet earth, as it is for any soul, that it all starts deep within our spirit. For we all, in any of our human experiences, have always been a significant part of any New Age.

# Chapter 10

## FOR ANY NEW AGE

*"Thus, language, in its origin and essence, is simply a system of signs or symbols that denote real occurrences or their echo in the human soul."* —CARL JUNG

By now, I sense you may have come to realize just how SIMPLE this uncanny art of Lexigrams truly is. And when we deal with something so SIMPLE: I IS ME, ME IS I, I SEE ME LIPS SMILE MILES. Doesn't it totally make you smile to now know you can always find out the truth of the matter whenever you'd like to journey in life? Undoubtedly, by now you can clearly see how the magic of Lexigrams validates and re-affirms how our history has unfolded till now. So, what's next, you may be asking? Using a term you have probably heard many times before, there is a "New Age" coming for us all. But it is, in fact, already here. It has always been here, within each and every HEART upon the EARTH. People who may resist our modern-day society are probably the first ones you hear responding to any kind of self-help, natural healing, or spiritual practice with "Oh, that's *sooo* NEW AGE!"—as in GEE WE WEAN AN ANEW. I don't know about you, but whether it is this present life we are currently living or any of the ONES we've lived EONS ago, they are all ONE.

We incarnate again, again, and again—as our soul comes back each time to reap more karma along its journey—to see what truly is anew in this current New Age. Undoubtedly, you know what periods in history that attract and draw you in over others. But of course your spirit has been there before! That's why these attract your interest, as that sense of familiarity is part of your entire soul's imprint. There doesn't seem to be any question that us earthlings are indeed SPIRITUAL BEINGS that ARE SENT IN TRUE SPIRIT AS STAR SUN SIGNS; ARE SENT IN BLESSINGS; ARE IN REAL TRUE GAINS; ARE BEST IN LEARNING RITUALS; ARE BEST IN A REAL BIG LITE; ARE ABLE IN PAINS, LIES, SINS, BEST IN ANGEL LISTEN RITUALS; SPIRAL STAR TRIPS LET US LEARN IN A TRUE ALIGN.

Each of us comes back every lifetime in spirit, being guided through our name, as well as the date of birth we choose. Any life, then, once more engages us to have those HUMAN EXPERIENCES wherein EACH MAN SHARE IN A MAIN CHANCE HE CAN REAP IN; HUMANS ARE NICE AS HUMANS ARE HUMANE; SEEN IN PAINS, HUMANS CAN ERASE SIN IN CRIES; HUMANS CAN EXERCISE A MAIN PEACE; HUMANS CAME IN SHARP INSANE PAINS; HUMANS CAN REAP A PACE IN PEACE AS HUMANS RINSE PAINS; HUMANS CAME IN SUN MAPS IN A MAIN SEE.

It seems to be a fantasy that we will ever live within a world that there is no pain or heartache to experience. Yet again, it is of no coincidence to note that the very words SIN and PAINS are within both of our spirit beings and human experiences. Hmmm. Interesting to note that when in PAINS: I IS IN SIN AS I IS IN A NAP. While the term pain can mean anything from physical to emotional turmoil, in this case, let's stretch our minds a little more and think of the voluntary pain within our world—the kind that people put on others without conscious thought nor respect. These inflicting people may seem all-powerful, but they are undoubtedly taking a true nap away from their spiritual core within their personal human experience. Apparently, the only "angel" they may be listening to is the one supposedly down under the ground, who has already LIVED. You know the one, who still dresses in red?

Remember those trickier Name Expressions, karmic, and Lifepath numbers we have talked about? These are the kinds of souls that come back to balance out their spirit with the chance to reap a better karma than in the previous life, but are they ever put to the most precarious test when given that chance. The boomerang game that karma undoubtedly plays ensures that if you come back to live out another incarnation that is guided by challenging numerical guidance, it is best to adhere to this ancient wisdom. Should one try to go against the responsibility to their planetary guidance, karma, and that equally misunderstood word of FATE, may have them in deep regrets about what follows AFTER things don't go well when they have made choices that aren't exactly in ALIGNMENT with their individual soul journey recommends they pick. When we tune in to ourselves, in this way, only then can one see I AM IN A MAIN GIANT GAIN, I AM IN AN ANGEL LINE, MAN MEANT TO TEAM IN A MAIN ALIGN, I GET TIME MEANT IN A MITE GATE.

Back to those times of strife and sadness: we aren't here to have a "flat line" life where it is all unfolding in bliss and flowing without CHALLENGES. It is within these, where we see with any of our human experiences, that ALL CHANGES SHALL HEAL AS A SAGE, HENCE SEE ALL CHANGE AS A HEAL, ALL ACHES HEAL, ALL ANGELS ANGLE HEALS AS A CLEANSE. With the ones we are meant to come to understand individually, we are truly sent back every time, showered in blessings, as we have the proper tools within our reach to handle, ultimately, our times of trouble in response to adversity. The star secrets at our disposal through the uncanny tales of Lexigrams, along with our planetary guidance, are all present to serve us in this and every "New Age" of which we've ever been a part.

As this book is being written, the talk about the infamous date of 21 December 2012 is definitely a topic of intrigue. I hope to be able to share some valuable insight and even further relief on the very fact that the world is hardly coming to any kind of end. But, you will see things ending in regards to what was established EONS ago connecting us all to ONE, when in comes to the deep understanding of what our wise ancestors the Mayas were truly wishing to convey to us. It seems more than apparent there is confusion surrounding the present-day society about what will actually be occurring upon this date. Rest assured, if you are in alignment with those angel gains, you for surely know we've already overcome one major scare involving a particular calendar date in the past ten years, that of Y2K (oddly enough, Y2K vibrates to a 5, with good old Mercury here to represent change). Remember how it was plastered all through the global media that the transition from 1999 to 2000 would create multitudes of problems? Think we all survived that one just fine. As we will with 21 December 2012, as our sagely Mayas knew:

## THE MAYAN CALENDAR

- ๏ MAN REALLY NEED A HEALER ERA
- ๏ LET A REAL DREAM HEAL THE EARTH
- ๏ LET THE REAL DREAM HEAL THE HATE
- ๏ LET A REAL DREAM HEAL THE HEART
- ๏ LET THE HEART HEAL AND THEN HEAL THE EARTH
- ๏ LET THE CANDLE HEAL
- ๏ LEARN THE HEART CAN HEAL
- ๏ LEARN THE HATRED CAN HEAL
- ๏ LEARN THE EARTH CAN HEAL
- ๏ HATE DARE THE MEAN MAN
- ๏ THE HEAL LEAD A REAL MAN
- ๏ THEY MADE AN END DATE YET THE HEART DREAM RALLY THE EARTH
- ๏ A HEARTEN MAN THE LEADER THAT THE EARTH NEED
- ๏ MAN: END THE HATE, END THE HATER ERA
- ๏ MAN LEARN THE HEALER HEART DREAM REACH MANY

The very title itself rings in as none other than the 14's *Movement–Challenge*, and you have learned how this number works in its mighty affects upon the masses. Here we are also looking at the pairing up of the 1's initiations, along with the 4's innovations and the possibility of the unexpected, resulting in the outward expression of the 5's ability to change. The weather is always seen to influence those guided by the 14, and for certain we are in a time when its challenges are more evident than ever before in history. Oh yes, there we go again, for wherever there is CHALLENGE, there must be a CHANGE going on. We are meant, at this time, to stand, as our individual selves in complete COOPERATION: I IN A NEAT TOP PAIR TO PARENT IT; TO OPERATE IN ONE I IN A TRAP. Now talk about challenges. So, the true question still remains: Are you ready to heal as a sage allows those angels to angle a change?

If you do a little research on the internet, you'll also find the title THE MAYA CALENDAR is also used. This is actually preferred and considered the more grammatically correct term over the word MAYAN. The game of telephone being what it is, everyone still seems to say, more often than not, *Mayan,* so this energy is still going out there to the world. Do your internet homework and see. However you choose to look at it, it is of interest to note, with this slight alternation in spelling, the Name Expression of THE MAYA CALENDAR becomes none other than that of the 18's *Spiritual–Material Conflict.* Oh boy. I'm going to let you ponder this one on your own. Whether you wish to look to the 14/5 for permanent change, or see the conclusions and endings the 18/9 ultimately can bring, don't forget our earlier discussions that reference the energy of this number that the Chaldeans deeply understood was more than pivotal in the affects it can cast upon the world. One clue to keep in mind when handling the 18: only kindness and courage matters.

In addition to their calendar, another significant part of the wisdom the Maya left us is the teaching to respect our differences while assuming a supportive and nurturing role. And we've had plenty of healers and spiritual leaders in our history who not only pave the way for our spiritual beings to find healing human experiences, but also predict and tell us about the future before it becomes our past. It will be easy to see that there indeed has always been a New Age for which people have been searching. We are meant to strive to achieve our soul's continued success, life after life. We're going to explore how certain spiritual leaders in our history have shaped the collective consciousness, but first, let's take a look at one more piece of Lexigram magic, about what we can expect in the present-day quest for a New Age.

If I may, I'm going to revert back into time to a reliable source of what still rings true to this day to sustain a respectful and honorable life for any age, at any age. I couldn't help but note the undeniable truths to be derived from the title of THE TEN COMMANDMENTS, also referred to as the DECALOGUE. No matter how anyone individually chooses to believe in their God, this original list, set forth on two stone tablets and given to Moses, is held in high regard as a moral foundation by various religions, whether Jewish, Christian, or Islamic. Now, I am not here to give you a lesson about how to honor religion (that's up to your free will), but there is no question that we've had some pretty sound advice all these years about how to live properly in any New Age.

## THE TEN COMMANDMENTS

- ๏ THESE CAME ETCHED ON STONE AS STATED TO MOSES AS SONNET
- ๏ THE DO'S AND DON'TS MAN NEEDS TO AMEND TO EONS ON
- ๏ THESE TEACH MAN THAT AN EASE METHOD CAN COME

- THESE TEN TESTAMENTS SCORE MAN ATONEMENT
- MAN MEANT TO DETACH HATES AND DEMONS TO SEE
- MAN NOT MEANT TO CONSENT TO HATE TO CONTEND
- MAN SENT NOT TO CHEAT, DO NOT CHEAT ON SHE
- SHE SENT NOT TO CHEAT, DO NOT CHEAT ON HE
- MAN MEANT TO SEE MODEST HONEST MOMENTS ECHO ON
- MAN CONDEMN THE NEED TO HATE AND CHASTEN
- MAN MEANT TO ENCHANT AS HE MEET AND HOST
- HE AND SHE MEANT TO ACT CONTENTED
- HE AND SHE MEANT TO DANCE
- MOMS AND DADS SENT TO STANDETH THE HOME
- THE HOME CHOSEN TO ENHANCE, TO EASE
- MAN NOT MEANT TO EAT MEATS NOT TO HATE
- DO NOT EAT MEAT MAN, AS THEN NO HATE COMES
- MAN MEANT TO SEE SOME TEST THAT ENACTS ESTEEM
- DONATE CASH AND SEE A HANDSOME TO COME
- MAN MEANT TO CHANT ON AND ON TO SEE EASE THEMES

As we look to the reference of DECALOGUE, we equally see more hidden goodies that apply to those Ten Commandments. A GOD GOAL; ELUDE A GOD CODE; A GLAD OLD LEGAL CODE; AN OLD GOLD CODE; CEDE A CAGED LOAD; DEAL A GOD CODE ALOUD; A GOD CODE LEAD A GLEE; COULD U LEAD A GOD CODE? GO! LEAD ALOUD A GOD CUE A CLADE CLUE; A GOD GOAL GEL any AGE, any EGO.

Now, again, I hope I didn't get too religious on anyone just now. But I must tell you another interesting word code I originally learned from Linda Goodman, and it is truly an easy one, jam-packed full of common sense. Ever notice how the very word GOD is merely DOG spelled backward? These compassionate animals are undoubtedly a gateway to understanding the unconditional energy that is behind what GOD really means. How sad that any human may choose to treat a DOG with anything but love, for have you also noticed that is always what they reflect back to you in return? Funny how whether you are looking at GOD or a DOG, the Name Expression is that of the 14's *Movement and Challenge,* which you have seen referenced in the previous pages many times. Do the masses not deal with both of these? The realms of communication that are at one's fingertips when in the presence of either can be truly overwhelming. However it personally works for you, tuning into the energy of a GOD or a DOG is an eye-opening place to regroup in.

One further mention about this whole RELIGION thing the world up till now has obviously not ceased to stop fighting about. Whether you are or are not in this incarnation, let it be known the pure intention behind RELIGION: I RING IN ONE; I LONG IN A LINGER; I IGNORE NO ONE; I REIGN IN <u>A</u> LORE ORIGIN; I IN <u>A</u> LONER LINE; I IN <u>A</u> GENII ROLE; I GO ON EON IN EON IN ONE; I GO ON IN NO LIE OR IN NO EGO. How you choose to do this is your soul's decision. Those who take religion seriously will most likely find themselves in the GLORIES of being RELIGIOUS: LORE URGES SURE SURGE US; I OIL A RULES LURE, OUR ROUSE <u>A</u> SURE SOUL GUISE; LOSE OUR EGO <u>AS</u> EGO <u>A</u> SURE SORE

LOSER; SO LOSE OUR LIES <u>A</u>S LIES SURE USE, SOIL
US. I GO SIRE <u>A</u> SURE SOUL RISE.

While religions can be found to reign all around the
world, let's journey with our spiraling Lexigram minds to
a culture whose practices surely could be classified as one
pure and sure religious soul guide that us Earthlings should
remember to keep in mind in our present New Age. The
ancient wisdom bestowed upon us from the original occu-
pants of the land that is now the United States have plenty
of needed advice to share. For THE NATIVE AMERICAN
INDIANS are not short on conversation when it comes to
knowing how to be at ONE. You don't need any kind of
religion to tell you that our Earth is in trouble, and for us
all to keep being in ONE EON with it, this culture is one
that is worth sitting down in a SILENT LISTEN to.

## THE NATIVE AMERICAN INDIANS

- SENT AS MASTER EARTH SERVICEMAN
- ARE SINCERE CREATIVE VARIANT TRADESMEN
- CAME AS INNATE DIVINE EARTH MAINTAINERS
- SEEN IN SACRED SAINTED EARTH MEDICINES
- IT IS CERTAIN THEIR HEARTS RADIATE DIRECT IN
  THE EARTH'S
- MAINTAIN IN A DISCREET SEMINAR
- SEE DREAMS AS AN INSIDE RADIANCE
- THESE MEN ARE DANCERS IN A DEAREST RAIN
- THESE MEN INCREASE THE EARTH'S HEART RATE
- THEIR SECRET IS AT THE EARTH'S HEART
- SEE THE STAR ART AS A MAIN ACTIVE SERVICE
- THE EARTH NEEDS NICE MEN IN DECENT MANNERS
- THE INDIANS' TREES, SEAS, AND STREAMS ARE
  RADIANT

- ARE VICTIMS AS THEIR AMERICA SEE INVADERS AND THEN IS REVISED AND RENAMED
- THESE HEARTS MASTERED THE EARTH'S HEART IN EARNEST
- MAN AND AMERICA NEEDS THE INDIANS' CREDITS NEAR THEM
- THESE MEN SEE AHEAD THAT AMERICA CAME AND AMERICA END
- THE INDIANS ART CENTERS THE EARTH'S HEART IT IS CERTAIN
- THIS ANCIENT MASTER DIVINE ART HAS THE NIRVANA MAN NEED

We have come so far from what the Indians innately knew to be true. In this time in our history, their knowledge is one that is calling a movement back to how they deeply understood we are to treat the earth in order to sustain life in a positive fashion for generations to come. Let's go on to investigate some more spiritual leaders that have left their undeniable mark upon leaving us plenty of wisdom to utilize for any New Age. We can still hear the soul's voice of EDGAR CAYCE—one of our most honored and respected natural healers—through the means of the legacy he has left us while incarnated as a Pisces 18. Cayce had an uncanny ability to go into entranced states and be able to see the most direct, non-evasive, and holistic way to treat people's illness and disease. This incredible gift gave him the name "The Sleeping Prophet."

I suppose we shouldn't be surprised that a Pisces would be the sign that Edgar Cayce chose for coming back down on 18 March 1877. This *Spiritual–Material Conflict* 18/9 Mars Pioneer was well ahead of his time. Innately honing in on his Neptune abilities, he became a psychic, clairvoyant, healer, and self-hypnotist along the journey of his 35/8 Lifepath of *Partnerships*. Aside from his uncanny ability to channel healing for others, as well as to see the future while in a hypnotic state, he founded the ASSOCIATION FOR RESEARCH AND ENLIGHTENMENT (ARE) in 1931. Today the ARE is located in Virginia and has centers all throughout the world. Hmmm... wonder if this might be a good place to go for some healing? Let's find out!

## ASSOCIATION FOR RESEARCH AND ENLIGHTENMENT

- EARTHLINGS THIS IS THE REAL MAGNIFICENT HEALER SPOT
- THE INFORMATION HERE IS NOT ENTERTAINMENT, IT IS REAL SMART
- THESE ANCIENT HOLISTIC HEALTH TREATMENTS ARE GREAT HEALERS
- THESE ARE CHANNELED FROM THE LATE GREAT "FISH" EC
- THESE TRANSLATE TO MODERN HEALTH TRADITIONS IN TOTAL HEALS
- ONE GREAT METHOD IS HEATED CASTOR OIL TO HEAL INSIDE DISEASE
- LISTEN IN SILENCE TO THE EARTH FOR MORE REAL ENCHANTMENT
- THESE HEALER METHODS ARE RICH IN THEIR TEACHINGS
- THIS IS AN ORGANISATION SET TO LAST EONS ON
- AS THIS ORGANISATION CAME FROM EONS AGO IN ATLANTIS

⊙ SO RESIGN AND REALIGN IN TIME AND HEAR
THESE GREAT MESSAGES

To this day, there are millions of Cayce followers of his
philosophies of natural healing versus modern medicine.
Aside from the miraculous castor oil packs that have incredible healing affects upon the human body, his remedies
have been endlessly known to manifest miracles for those
who are otherwise claimed by normal medical doctors to
be in complete "decay," or in such DISEASE, that A DIE
EASES AS A<u>N</u> AIDE; AS IDEA'S SEEDS DIE I DIE; I SEE
EASE AS I DIE. It seems apparent once our ideas no longer
flow and get planted as seeds, thus do we ease in closer to
die. Cayce once said, "Spirit is the life. Mind is the builder.
Physical is the result." It was a statement on the relationship
of holistic health to one's spiritual life.

True to his Pisces 18 soul, his Karmic Path of the 18/9
resulted in his drive to seek and remain on the spiritual path,
while denying getting addicted to the material side of life.
His 35/8 Lifepath requested this be done responsibly and
ambitiously. The 8's energy is well known to deal with material rewards, but the material that Cayce undoubtedly gave
to the world in abundance was an invaluable and intellectual wealth that stems from the 8's wisdom and stability.
The very name EDGAR vibes to the 15's *Magician*, who is
known to have special gifts through the voice to bring forth
needed balance, while EDGAR CAYCE, as a full Name
Expression, was none other than the 10's *Wheel of Fortune*.
The 10 always brings upon strong cycles of rebirth, which
Cayce continuously brought to others through his career.
Along with the help of the Sun's guidance over the singular

1, it kept plenty of people needing to be warmed by Cayce's healing light, as he attracted thousands in need of his insight.

As always with a short name, Cayce was a very private man and did not allow too much exploration into his own self, and this was further intensified by being guided by his Pisces Sun, who always enjoy a solo swim. Yet, Lexigrams once again, oddly enough, wish to share some key revelations indicating some clues of the presence Cayce was to this world:

### EDGAR CAYCE

- ◉ EDGAR A DEAR
- ◉ EDGAR A READY EAR, A READY EYE
- ◉ EDGAR A EAGER READER
- ◉ EDGAR CARRY A READY CREED
- ◉ EDGAR CARRY A READY ADAGE
- ◉ EDGAR ACCEDE A CARE
- ◉ EDGAR GEARED A GRACE
- ◉ EDGAR READY A DAY A YEAR
- ◉ EDGAR DARE A DECAY

Sixteen years earlier, on 27 February 1861, another paramount Pisces 9 that also left his spiritual footprint deeply upon the future of Earthlings was RUDOLF STEINER. Neptune- and Mars-ruled Steiner was a man of much depths and many levels. Not only was he a Pisces, he was also one guided by the leadership of Mars through both his Karmic and Lifepaths of the 27's *The Sceptre,* of which the Chaldeans were aware: "This is an excellent, harmonious and fortunate number of courage and power, with a touch of enchantment. It blesses the person or entity it represents with a promise of authority and command. It guarantees that great rewards will come from the productive labors, the intellect, and the imagination. All of these creative faculties have sown good seeds which are to reap a rich harvest. People or entities represented by the 27 should always carry out their own original plans and ideas, and not be intimidated or influenced by the diverse opinions or opposition of others."[59]

The singular 9 and Pisces influence found Steiner compelled to lead the spiritual realms that engaged his intellect and imagination on all levels, while remaining a mystical seeker in his life. There wasn't an area of philosophy, literature, education, the arts, writing, social thinking, or esoteric quest that he didn't touch. Indeed, he was a man who came to be a leader for the world and the Universe at large.

There is an interesting discrepancy about Steiner's true date of birth. Some claim he was born on the 25th. Yet, the Moon sign differences from the 25th to the 27th give us a clue into Steiner's understanding of creating balance alone when it came to architecture and had to come from the Libra Moon on the 27th. When we further examine the timing in history that marked his life by matching up the numbers, and take a look at his Lexigram revelations, it seems unlikely the 25th was his actual birthday. This would have made him purely Neptunian in his influence, as not only would his Sun Sign of Pisces have the mystical urges he undoubtedly sought out, but his Karmic and Lifepaths would equally be guided by the 7's energy of *The Seeker*. This combination would more than likely make him draw further into his own inner solitude, and not take the world by the horns as Steiner so ideally displayed in his lifetime, as the blessings of the double 27's influence by far ideally describe him. He was opposed frequently for his original ideas and plans, but when you look to the present day and see the great rewards that continuously reap from his labors, there is plenty to back up what drove him to bring his spiritual knowledge to a Universal place, which was not kept quiet. I could go on and on into the why of the 27th over the 25th, but let's save this topic for another book perhaps?

Steiner is best known today as the founder of the Waldorf Education as well as coining the term ANTHROPOSOPHY. He is ultimately true to his Neptune and Mars channel as he explained Anthroposophy to be: "a path of knowledge, to guide the spiritual in the human being to the spiritual in the universe. Anthroposophists are those who experience, as an essential need of life, certain questions on the nature of the human being and the universe, just as one experiences hunger and thirst."[60] And so, this became one of the many quests that he led with fine success through his double 27 influence. Just what do Lexigrams have to say about Steiner's initiation?

### ANTHROPOSOPHY

- A TOP PRO PHOSPHOR PATH TO PATRONS
- A STAR ARTS PATH TO SOOTH
- A HAPPY STAR ART TO TROPHY ON
- APPROPOS TO HONOR A PAST STORY
- TO POST ORPHANS ON A STAR PATH
- HOORAY! A STAR PATH TO HONOR
- TO ROOT TO HONOR STAR ARTS PATHS
- TO POST TO STAR NOTARY HONORS
- PATRONS PRAY TO PAST STAR HOST
- A "TORAH" STORY NOT TO STOP, NOT TO PART

◎ A TOP TORAH STORY STAY ON AN ARTY STAR PATH TO SOAR

Does anyone else see how closely the word TORAH is to the HEART? Steiner was born in Austria, and one of his oppositions that were not to stop him from his Mars influence was in 1919, when he was accused of being an instrument of the Jews. In a time of the first World War, he still courageously led his ideas and was not easily thwarted by those that wished to put an end to the new philosophies he was unleashing. At this particular time, he had the nationalist extremists in Germany in full battle against him. But even this opposition was not to put an end to the leadership that continues to this day from:

### RUDOLF JOSEPH LORENZ STEINER

◎ RUDOLF IS SENT TO "THE S<u>C</u>EPTRE" LIFE TO "THE FISHES" SUN
◎ RUDOLF IS SEEN TO RISE TO THE TOP TRUE PIONEER ROLE
◎ RUDOLF IS SET TO SEE THE FINEST TENDER SOUL TRUTH
◎ RUDOLF'S SEEN IN THE FINE SEER ROLE
◎ RUDOLF'S SOUL RESOLUTION IS SET TO SEE IT TRUE
◎ RUDOLF SEE TO RISE TO FIND THE FINEST SPIRIT IN LIFE
◎ RUDOLF IS SET TO FIND THE UNDERLINE OF TRUE LIFE
◎ RUDOLF IS A TRUE FOUNDER OF SUPERIOR THEORIES
◎ RUDOLF IS TO REDEFINE THE FRONTIER OF LIFE TO OPEN UP THE SOUL

- RUDOLF FINDS THE FINEST SOUL ORDER TO SURRENDER TO
- RUDOLF LIFTS OUR SOUL TO FEEL IT TRUE, FEEL IT HONEST
- NO ONE IS TO STOP RUDOLF'S PLENTIFUL SOUL SOLUTIONS
- RUDOLF IS SENT TO FLOURISH THE SOUL IN FERTILE SEEDS
- RUDOLF IS TO SET THE TRUE SOUL ENTERPRISE IN STONE
- RUDOLF SEES THE SOUL IS TO RESTORE IN SOLITUDE TO REPLENISH
- EONS ON SOULS LISTEN TO STEINER'S SURETIES IN TRUE SPIRIT TO SHINE

Between the time Rudolf Steiner and Edgar Cayce were born, there was another spiritual leader who came back on 02 October 1869 to leave behind a legacy that continues on it its impeccable wisdom for this New Age. MOHANDAS KARAMCHAND GANDHI, who so appropriately lent some deep advice to "be the change you want to see in the world," in order to manifest the outer transformations necessary to ideally evolve in true spirit. Here again we find another Mars-guided 27 *The Sceptre* Lifepath native that did not listen to the opposition presented to him. As with all 9 energies channeling Mars influence, he courageously kept holding his 27 *Sceptre* torch high to bring common sense to humanity about the practice of *ahimsa*, which means to do no harm, nor kill, or physically hurt any living thing. This understanding is the very opposite of *himsa*, which represents VIOLENCE, where ONE LIVE IN NO LOVE, LIVE ON IN EVIL VOICE, LIVE ON IN VILE VICE, wherein the karmic consequences result in one suffering because of their actions. Gandhi stated and then restated as his creed "God is Truth. Truth is God."

As a pure Libra 2 soul, Gandhi came down as an old one, with no Chaldean Karmic Mystery to unwrap. As a cardinal air sign, he surely was destined for leadership on top of his 27 Lifepath, and the 2 Karmic Path granted him pure energy of the Moon's guidance of sensitivity, a paternal instinct, and imagination. 2's are known to nurture all throughout the life, and couple this energy with innate leadership and anyone can see why Gandhi was driven with a tremendous courage to spread the word about being cooperative and peaceful, to arrive at a solution for humankind's ongoing dilemma of fighting to try to solve its problems. Libras are well known to shun away from any kind of dispute, always offering a path of balance to bring calm. From his early life as a lawyer, Gandhi did with his 27 Lifepath energy seek to nurture justice, as he found himself in the realms of political leadership that would become an ideal model for us to follow if we would LISTEN carefully. It's only too bad, the world up till now has not sincerely been SILENT enough for Gandhi's wisdom, for what truth lies in his sensible statement, "An eye for an eye makes the whole world blind." Once more, we again see the wonders of Lexigrams reveal just how much Gandhi was sent to bring his needed mission to this earth.

## MOHANDAS KARAMCHAND GANDHI

- ๑ GANDHI IS A KIND CARING AIR SIGN ON A MARS ROAD
- ๑ GANDHI ANCHORS IN A HIGH HARMONIC COMMAND AND RANK

- GANDHI'S SIGN HAS A CHARMING AND RICH CHARISMA
- GANDHI IS IN A DARING DARING MIND
- GANDHI IS DASHING IN NO HAIR
- IN DARING COMINGS AS GANDHI IS IN MARCHS
- GANDHI IS IN A SHOCKING DANDI MARCH
- ORDAINS IN AN ORGANIC DOMAIN
- GANDHI IS A ROMANCING CHARMING MONARCH
- GANDHI ORDAINS KARMA IS A MAN'S MAKING
- GANDHI'S DOINGS GO ON IN A MAIN DOGMA
- HARD DRAMAS SCORN ON AS GANDHI ROAMS
- GANDHI'S MISSION IS IN A SOARING DHARMA
- GANDHI'S KINGDOM IS IN SOARING ROAMING MAKINGS
- GANDHI RINGS IN A SHARING INDIAN KHADI
- GANDHI IS HOME IN AN ASHRAM
- GANDHI COINS HIS MISSION AS "AHIMSA," NO "HIMSA" OR IN SAD SHAMING
- HARMING AN ORGANISM IS MADDING AND CHASING KARMA
- DR. KING ADDS ON GANDHIS' DOMAINS
- GANDHI MARKS GOD IS A MAIN MANKIND MAGIC DOMAIN

Let me conclude our "for any New Age" leadership with the one magical person responsible for the very reason why you are reading the book you are holding in your hands right now. This woman is considered the pioneer who initiated another wave in the New Age movement. Born 09 April 1925, you cannot find a better headstrong leader than the gifted LINDA GOODMAN. We must tip our spiritual hats to the soul responsible for coining the term

Lexigrams and revealing their mighty powers in 1987's *Star Signs*, which if you haven't yet, I highly recommend picking up a copy of and proceeding to engross yourself within its pages. Linda was incarnated to the name MARY ALICE KEMERY, and she is another true example of how, when you change your legal name, all sorts of magic can occur by choosing a vibration that works with you, not against you.

Many people do not know that Linda, or Mary at the time, decided to learn the realms of astrology only so she could become a better poet. As the original coiner of Lexigrams, Linda surely understood the revelations from her own names, which further ensured her success would reign through this choice to educate herself. In a 1 Personal Year for Goodman in 1968, she published her first book, *Sun Signs*. This became the only astrology book at that time ever to find itself on the *New York Times* bestseller list. Soon to follow in 1978 was her equally cherished tell-all creation about signs relating, entitled *Love Signs,* which also became a best seller. As Mary became Linda when she hosted a radio show called *Love Letters from Linda* back in World War II, she remained a very private person, and until her death in 1995, didn't want people to even know her year of birth. (Please do forgive me, Linda, for revealing it here, yet it is now after all these years—thanks to the internet—no longer a secret.) When an Aries 9 is born to a 30 Lifepath as Mary was that represents *The Loner— Meditation,* privacy and time alone is extremely well, valued and necessary, so their innate ability to endlessly seek higher knowledge and develop their own philosophies can be done in peace. I don't think there is any spiritual place or mystery that Linda's mind did not eventually aim itself.

A true leader through and through with the spark of the Aries flame, Linda Goodman is a true embodiment of what it means to be guided by the double influence of Mars. It is most certain she was an old soul, being born to the 9 Karmic Path on that rainy April morning she came back to the name MARY ALICE KEMERY. Before choosing Linda, what was her true soul's original intention?

### MARY ALICE KEMERY

- MARY CAME <u>IN</u> A MERRY MAR<u>S</u> RAM CARER KARMA
- MARY CAME <u>IN</u> A REAL MERCY
- MARY LIKE A CLEAR EARLIER A.M. CALM
- MARY CARRY A REAL ACE KEY CAREER
- MARY RARELY MAKE A LIE, RARELY MAKE MALICE
- MARY LIKE MAIL, MARY RARELY LACK MAIL
- MARY CAME A<u>S</u> A REAL MIRACLE MAKER
- MARY A REAL CALM KARMIC MAKER
- MARY RECLAIM A KARMIC MARK
- MARY A YEARLY KARMIC REELER
- MARY CLAIM A RARE RELIC REALM MARY RELAY/ MAKE A REAL CAREER
- MARY MAKE A MERRY YEARLY CAREER
- MARY MAKE A REAL MERRY RH<u>Y</u>ME LYRIC
- MARY CLEARLY LIKE A EERIE "CREEK" CREAKY AREA
- MARY AIM IN A CLEAR REALM RELIC CAREER ALL LIKE

After living for years in New York City, you'll learn when you read (or go for a reread of) *Star Signs* that Linda moved to Cripple CREEK, Colorado, where she remained in her well-known and haunted EERIE CREAKY house, formerly owned by Nikola Telsa on 315 Carr Avenue until her passing. (It's no coincidence that this was a 9-vibing residence, in a town where gold and many treasures thrived during the rush many years before.) Here we have yet another pure example, as the many others preceding it within the pages you've already read, of how, even though we can choose to change a name, your tale can surely be told from the birth name. Even with being the solitary person as Mary came here to be, she definitely was here as A KARMIC REELER with her deep and innate understanding of it. Her CAREER in A RARE RELIC REALM is responsible for changing the face of astrology with her RAM CARER KARMA, while we least forget her ability to write a real MERRY RHYME LYRIC with her outstanding work of seemingly endless poetry, *Goobers*, published in 1989. It is a certainty Linda RARELY LACK MAIL once her best sellers came to be. Oh, and by the way, in case you didn't know one more interesting fact, one of Linda's favorite sayings was "Expect A MIRACLE."

But, as names are changed, it is interesting that the rewards the name LINDA GOODMAN brought to the plate. While Linda deeply understood the importance of one's Name Expression, her original birth Name Expression was the 13's *Regeneration and Change*. Not, by any means, a negative number, but even as much as the 13's genius was inherently present all along Linda's successful career, this cipher can bring along its fair share of the unexpected. So instead, as LINDA GOODMAN, Linda claimed another 9 notch and intensified her attraction to lead her Universal cause all the more. Definitely an important choice that had to do with reclaiming those karmic miracles that she originally came here to do.

## LINDA GOODMAN

- LINDA IN A MAGI GOAL IN A MAIN DOGMA
- LINDA A DO ALL GAL IN A MAIN GOOD
- LINDA IN MAIL AGAIN AND AGAIN
- LINDA IN A MAIN MIND IN A MAIN GAIN
- LINDA LAND IN A MAIN OLD ODD DIAMOND/OIL/ GOLD MIDLAND
- LINDA LOOM AND LONG IN A MAIN MOON MOOD
- LINDA IN NO MILD MIND, A MIND IN NO LAG
- LINDA IN A MAIN NAMING ALIGN
- LINDA GOAL AND ALIGN IN A MAIN DOMAIN
- LINDA IN A GLAD MIND DOING GOAL AGAIN AND AGAIN
- LINDA AIM ON AND ON AND ON IN A MAIN MAGI AGO MIND
- LINDA AMONG A MAIN MIND DOMAIN
- LINDA AID ALL IN A MAIN GOOD MIND
- LINDA ALIGN IN A MAIN GOD
- LINDA ALIGN IN A MAIN ALMA MAGI IDOL

So... with all of that now having been said and spiraled, I leave you now to pause for a moment and ponder one question before you turn the page to start applying your own spiraling Lexigram talents in your everyday life. Are you ready FOR ANY NEW AGE?

# PART III:

# APPLYING THE KNOWLEDGE

# THE CONCLUSION

# Chapter 11

## YOUR SIXTH SENSE OPENED

*"There is nothing that cannot be accomplished, there is nothing that cannot be known, by the power of the word. Therefore the principal and central theme of esotericism and mysticism is the word."* —HAZRAT INAYAT KHAN

Whenever you are dealing with the ELEVEN, you'll find that there will be an EVEN to be gained. One thing Lexigrams surely do for us is aid in bringing a deeper understanding that brings a needed balance to our lives. For whatever reason it works in the seemingly magical and intuitive way that it does, you've got a genuine gift at your fingertips now that you've put another notch in your SIXTH SENSE: I SEE THE TENSE SIXTEEN; I SHINE IN THIS SENSES THESIS; I SEE THIS IN THESE SENSE TIES; I EXIST IN SENSE; I SITE IT IN THE SEXES, IN THE EXIST; I THEN SIT IN THE SIXTEEN SHINE; I EXIT, I NIX THE SIN; NEXT I NET THE SEE IN THE SEEN. We've discussed numerous times the meaning the Chaldeans so profoundly grasped about the SIXTEEN. It is interesting to find it staring right at us when we ponder the SIXTH SENSE, for we do need to be in the eye of the storm when utilizing it fully. You can't tap into it without the spiritual intention the 16 requests, for otherwise, you'll be falling far down off your tower and get further swept up into those hurricane winds. Not fun for anyone who is seeking clarity and insight in life.

Undoubtedly, your mind has been very exercised, fully stretched, and is completely untangled from any kind of LIMITED THINKING as you've absorbed chapter after chapter of more than enough circumstantial and historical evidence to validate that Lexigrams are nothing to be taken lightly, and are quite serious in their messages they wish to bestow upon us all. When it comes to utilizing that sixth sense any human can utilize, it certainly seems best to stay very clear of any kind of LIMITED THINKING: I TEND IN A THIN TIGHT LINE TILTING IN A LIE; I LET THE LIGHT DIE, I LET THE IGNITE DIE, I LET THE DELIGHT DIE, I LET ME TIMING MINGLE IN A MELTING LINK. Again, where's the fun in the journey of exploration here?

So, just where do we go from here? Now that you have this knowledge at your disposal, let me tell you my story of how this all began, and what will probably start to happen to you now that this valuable star secret is no longer one. When I first learned about Lexigrams from one of our New Age leaders, Linda Goodman, I was at a very pivotal point in my present incarnation, that of my first Saturn Return. For anyone, this is the time we are within the ages of 28 to 30 years old. It is the very first time in our lives that the current transit of Saturn returns all the way back to the exact same sign it was in when we decided to come back for another go at this human experience as we spiritually align in another natal birth chart. Saturn, as we have discussed, is a very slow, responsible and lesson-learning kind of planet. Now, if you are still under the age of 28 and reading this, you'll be surely forewarned of this upcoming time in your life. For those of you 30-plus, you know exactly what I am talking about. The first Saturn Return is all about clearing out what doesn't work in your life, and tuning into a true trust in yourself like you have never felt up until that point. And should you not be willing to let go of things that you no longer need to move into the more mature, full character of yourself to keep evolving optimally, Saturn casts down some rather intense lessons to learn at this time.

Anyway, so there I was, about to embark upon this fairly tricky transit in my own life. This was in the summer of 2001, as I was equally finishing my first numerical period cycle, and breaking into a whole new one. For some souls, the Saturn Return and first numerical period shift open simultaneously, according to how it works out mathematically by the Lifepath, and mine was surely in an incredible alignment. One thing Linda always said was to not take her word for it that these ancient wisdoms actually work to provide invaluable insight. I was indeed at that time seeking something new to fulfill my life, and I innately understood there was a different path I was about to take. I decided to listen to what she said. I started testing the validity of Lexigrams. What started to occur blew my mind in ways that I couldn't have even possibly expected.

In the summer of 2001, I was residing in the East Village and would spend plenty of time walking around, as most native New Yorkers find themselves doing. At this point, I couldn't have anticipated how tapping into this sixth sense of Lexigrams would truly begin to affect and move my life. One day, I was out running errands and came across an ATLANTIC Travel store sign. I remember this was the first time I ever just "randomly" got hit with a "spiral." Linda, too, said that once this starts occurring, it is best to keep a pen and notepad with you at all times, because you definitely don't want to forget any of the brilliant things that will want to be remembered. I equally pass this advice strongly along to you, and in this present day and age, I am sure your Blackberry or iPhone will come in handy all the more for these emergency "spirals." So... back to the travel store. I keep on just strolling on down the street, and catch the thought, THE ATLANTIC OCEAN. Then, it HIT me like a ton of bricks. Oh my God! THE TITANTIC HIT ICE... LATE IN THE NITE.... AN OCEAN EAT THE TITANTIC! Well now, I guess the people who named the *Titanic* didn't know anything at all about Lexigrams.

At this same time, I had the INCREDIBLE experience of being a member of a gospel choir of more than 155 singers, and was fortunate to have already made it to Carnegie Hall in my very first concert with the group. Talk about INCREDIBLE! It was for certain I was IN A NICE CREED RELIC RIDE, I CRIED IN A REEL, I BE IN A NICER LINE. The fearless, savvy, witty, and endlessly entertaining leader of our group was a man named MICHAEL DAVID BROWN. Okay, I thought, here's a name of someone I know I can explore. Let's see... Again! WHAM-O! CHOIR... MIRACLE... LEADER... MARBLE! Now, at this time, David was the youth minister at MARBLE Collegiate Church on 29th and 5th Avenue in New York City. The divine choir that he led and I was honored to have found was a community one, and one lucky enough to grace one of the most sought-out stages in the world. I kept going... CHILDREN...

LIBRA... (David's birthday is 14 October, but of course a Libra!) Then the words came through: HE CAN LEAD A REAL WONDER...DIVINE...LOVE! I kept thinking: This is totally crazy; surely just all a coincidence... I mean, really, are you kidding? This actually works with names so clearly? So I took all the anagrams I had just made and connected them into phrases as I eagerly began to spiral.

### MICHAEL DAVID BROWN

- HE CAME IN A MIRACLE LIBRA LINE TO HEAL IN
- HE WILL LEAD A DIVINE CHOIR OVER AND OVER
- HE WILL EARN AND LEAD CHILDREN IN A MARBLE LOCALE
- HE WILL LEAD ALL IN A REAL LOVE AND HEALER CROWN
- DAVID CAME IN A REAL WONDER ALL LOVE

Wow...this is beyond intense, was all I kept thinking. This was also the time I was at my beginnings of exploring Name Expressions and seeing how these numerical vibrations held validity in the particular subject's life. I questioned the differences between the Western system, A-Z, and the way Linda had said you'll undoubtedly find the Chaldean Hebrew Kabala Alphabet match-up one to be more accurate in its insight when examining any entity. I soon began to look at our letters through this language of numbers, and absorbed the Chaldeans letter-to-number 8 natural note understanding. It was no wonder to me David's birth Name Expression is the 6, as through the balancing acts of Venus, this is undeniably done with love. Then I got some more spirals... DAVID CAME IN A REAL BALANCED NAME IN LOVE. More WOW... I was becoming further and further convinced that the subjects of Astrology, Numerology, and by far these uncanny Lexigrams were indeed like looking into a very crystal clear ball as Goodman so perfectly understood.

I decided to move along to my own family, as I figured, well, I surely know all the details to validate their possible revelations! Hmmm... coming from a pretty small one with both my Mom and I being only children, I chose first to see what truths are within my dear grandmother's name from my mom's side. She was born 31 January 1920 to the name KATHLEEN MARY SOUR, which a couple years later was legally amended to KATHLEEN QUINN SAURS. As we have seen, even with name changes, the birth name tells the true soul story as it was originally planned, while within what we may choose to then express ourselves equally will manifest their energies as well. Kathleen was later converted to Kitty as a nickname, who became "Grammie" to me. But what did KATHLEEN MARY SOUR have to tell me?

- ☉ SET TO MARRY HER SOUL MATE EARL KERN LATER ON
- ☉ SHE LEARNS AS A TRUE SMART STYLER SALESMAN AT MARSH'S
- ☉ ALL MEN'S EYES REST ON KATHLEEN
- ☉ NOT REAL MATERNAL TO KATHRYN AS HER MOTHER, A KARMA SORT OUT
- ☉ SENT AS A TRUE MASTER AT THE HOME'S NATURAL SOUL

Now, I know you don't know my Grammie like I do, but it surely was fascinating to unveil these truths within her name. My Poppie's name, but of course, is EARL KERN. My Grammie was the manager of the ladies' department in a store called MARSH'S, where she also modeled for them, and, well, many a man's eyes found pleasure in looking at my Grammie! Sadly, my mom KATHRYN, also KATHY, grew up not being exactly as close to her mother, and at this point in life, it's no secret this was a natural part of how my Grammie's innate and quite intense Aquarian 31 energy chose to express itself. But, this was their KARMA to work out this time around, and no one else's. All of my life, my Grammie's HOME always had A TRUE MASTER NATURAL feel to it, as she never-ever stops being an inventor and bringer of new life to its presence.

Then I took a look at the name that became Grammie's legal Name Expression as a child, and more interesting things popped out to speak their truths:

## KATHLEEN QUINN SAURS

- ◎ SHE SEES A QUEEN TITLE IN HER TEENS
- ◎ HAS HER HEART TAKEN IN AN EARL KERN
- ◎ THERE IS A TRUE SATURN/URANUS LINK SHE & EARL ARE IN
- ◎ SHE IS QUITE THE QUIET TALKER AS SHE LISTENS
- ◎ HER AQUARIAN UNIQUENESS REQUESTS SHE IS IN AN INNATE TRUE THANKS

As gorgeous as my Grammie just so happens to be, she did find herself while in her TEENS in high school to be crowned the Prom QUEEN. Although she and my Poppie are 10 years apart in age, her heart still decided it was meant to follow in the SATURN/URANUS LINK. As Linda has so strongly implanted in my brain, the karmic connections between those born to a Saturn- or Uranus-guided Karmic Path are nothing but a further source of cosmic intrigue. While Grammie was born to the 31/4, my Poppie's Karmic Path is that of the 8, being born on 08 May 1910. Soul mates indeed. But my Poppie was the true TALKER of the two of them, as my Grammie certainly is QUITE QUIET AS SHE LISTENS. That has all to do as well with her 31 Karmic Path, as we have already learned how it grants the soul born to it with the desires to stay more behind the scenes, in a hermit-like way. But my UNIQUE AQUARIAN Grammie will most certainly talk anytime she is in TRUE THANKS, as this quality is, by and large, one of the INNATE virtues I have learned from her. (And you, too, Mom!)

I think one of the favorite things I realized at this time was how my Poppie's name EARL spells REAL. I actually don't even have to tell you anything more about the revelations from his full name at birth, EARL WILSON KERN, because it is so plain and simple how REAL EARL truly was. But, because it so aligns with the truth that was to unfold in his life, I'll continue on with what was opening within my own sixth sense at the beginning stages of sharpening my Lexigram talents along with the tying in of the Universe's wisdom. My Poppie was the very family member I was blessed to learn the practice of patience from—and I couldn't have a better teacher than a Taurus 8, whose Sun Sign and Karmic Path equally bestow a soul to possess this trait. Now, there are a great many things I have learned from my Dear Poppie, but let's find out more about the interesting tales that wish to be told from his name.

### EARL WILSON KERN

- EARL IS SLOW AS EARL IS REAL WISE
- ALL KNOW AS ALL LIKE EARL'S REAL WILL
- EARLIER EARL REARS A LEO ALONE, ALSO A LEO NINE
- EARL IS A WISE LEARNER IN A REAL REASON
- EARL EARNS & WORKS IN SWINE, SNOW, ALSO IN LAWN RENEWALS
- EARL IS A REAL WISE WORKER, EARNER, AND OWNER
- EARL IS A WINNER AS HE KNOWS AN INNER ANSWER

Well, I have yet to meet someone as WISE as my Poppie in the way he did practically everything so SLOW. I can't even think of a person who didn't LIKE EARL'S REAL WILL. I, as a LEO NINE, spent a lot of time as one of the LEOS he REARed, the first of whom was my mother Kathy, also a Leo. We already talked about that part of the family history, but yes indeed, my Mom and Poppie were thick as thieves, and not that he was completely ALONE in the task, yet, again it's no secret how close their bond was, while she and Grammie butted Aquarian and Leo heads together all too often. No doubt Poppie took on life with A REAL REASON AS A WISE LEARNER, with that 8 Karmic Path side of him, and he always walked away learning a lesson, rare to repeat his mistakes. Never afraid of REAL WORK, he was raised on a farm, spent years developing other people's, before working as a caretaker, wherein whether it was IN SNOW or IN LAWN RENEWALS, his steadfast and reliable flow of income prevailed to become AN OWNER. Long before he was my hero, my Poppie indeed was A REAL WINNER that knew AN INNER ANSWER.

It was becoming more and more apparent how much Lexigrams can provide us all with the inner answers we seek. While I was eagerly exploring the realms of my family and the people I knew in the summer of 2001, as it came to a close there was something quite serious about to historically unfold that would send me on a completely different track. I don't think I'll ever erase the experience of 11 September 2001 from my mind, as living in the East Village at that time had me all too close to the catastrophic event that forever changed everyone's world. I used to be able to see the THE WORLD TRADE CENTER from the top of my 5-story walk-up on 5th street, where I had spent many an hour over the years. I would have never guessed on the evening of the 10th, while spending a little time trying to see the stars among all the white light pollution, that I had taken in the Twin Towers for the very last time, gleaming in their nighttime brilliance.

As the nightmare now called 9/11 began, it was after the initial shock calmed down that I was able to listen to my inner voice that prodded me to seek out something the media was not sharing with us.

### THE WORLD TRADE CENTER

- A NORTHERN WONDER NOT HERE TO ATTRACT ON AND ON
- ON A CLEAR DAWN ON A LATER ONE-ONE DATE IN TWO-O-O-ONE, NEAR TEN TO NINE A REAL DREADED TERROR DREW NEAR DOWN TOWN
- THE TWO TOWERS LOCATED DOWN TOWN ARE THEN TOTALED, LOWERED TO A REAL HOT HEATED END A HATRED TORRENTED CON ACT ORDERED

- NOW NOT A REAL CENTER, NOT A REAL WORLD ORDER, NO DECENT REAL TRADE TO ATTRACT
- THE TERROR DOWN TOWN NEEDED A LOT O' WATER TO DROWN
- NO DECENT TRADE WENT ON HERE TOWARD A REAL WORLD TO HEAL THE EARTH
- THE CENTER HAD NO HEART THAT CARED TO CREATE AN END TO HATE
- NO REWARD CAN HEAL THE TATTERED CORE
- WE NEED TO HEAL THE HATE THAT THE WORLD AND EARTH CANNOT DROWN ALONE
- WE ARE DARED TO CREATE A NEW WORLD THAT CAN DROWN HATE
- WE ARE TO CROWN A NEW WORLD THAT CAN CREATE A REAL EARTHEN HEALER ROLE THAT LET THE HEART LEAD NOT HATE
- THE WORLD NEED TO LEARN A REAL TOLERANCE TO RELATE TO;
- WE NEED TO ADHERE TO A NEW WORLD ORDER THAT END HATE

This was the first time I got very, very interesting messages as I have discovered them to find me as these Lexigrams will begin, too, to speak to you through. Very soon after this, I got to a point that I finally knew it wasn't wise anymore to take in so much news from the television. It seemed no matter what I would see flashing upon the headlines as the ticker tape flied by underneath, as the media relentlessly tried to stuff our heads with more up-to-date and LIVE information, I could find the truth of the matter going on. I soon used my own sixth sense to unveil just how EVIL and VILE it all truly is. But still, when those seemingly unbelievable events are leaked out, there is something to rely on as a message that the art of Lexigrams truly wanted me to unravel.

But let's not get all freaked out about the "bad stuff." Remembering that not everything one can indeed spell from a given name will turn into reality, let's see how Lexigrams may, however, be waiting to bestow some unexpected joy on a soul. Jumping ahead a couple years, I was reading a copy of the *New York Post* on 09 July 2004, wherein I saw how a woman named GERALDINE WILLIAMS, who at 68 just had won the $294 million Mega Millions jackpot in Braintree, MA. There my head went off again: GERALDINE IS SEEN IN A REAL MEGA MEGA MEGA WIN! I wasn't successful in ever locating her birth date or true middle name on my searches, but I had an inclination that, if her middle name were ROSE, we'd have more details than GERALDINE WINS MILLIONS. With or without the O, I do wonder what Jupiter was up to at that time in her charts otherwise. One might well presume the planet of luck and fortune was indeed in a lucky spot.

Now, there's winner's luck and a certain other kind of "luck" and fortune that can watch over people, I have come to learn. By and large, another unforgettable event of great magnitude since 9/11 was the devastating tsunami that hit in Thailand on 26 December 2004, the result of a severe earthquake in the Indian Ocean. Now, while thousands of innocent lives where taken by this unconceivable natural disaster, there was one celebrity that caught plenty of attention in the aftermath, a top-notch model who had graced the cover of *Sports Illustrated* since 2001, at the tender age of 22. This amazing story of survival totally caught my Lexigram fixation in a wild way, the tale that PETRA NEMCOVA's name was awaiting to tell. Nemcova was vacationing over the holiday with her fiancé and top-of-his-game photographer SIMON ATLEE, whose name you'll also find a not so happy tale to tell, in that he unfortunately did not survive the choice of being in Thailand upon that date.

Petra's emotional story became plastered all over the mainstream news as at least one of miraculous proportions, with the exception of her beloved Atlee's fate. Thanks to the saving grace of a palm tree, she rested many hours in it after being swept up in the vigorous rush of the tsunami's waves, her body severed at the pelvis, till she was rescued. Keeping in mind that she was still only 25 at the time, the 24 June 1979 birth date's promise worked in two ways, in that her current 18 Personal Year of *Spiritual–Material Conflict* at the time tells us how, during that month she was to sacrifice, as she saw something concluded and finalized within the 9's guiding energy over her year.

Following a 38 Lifepath of *Grace Under Pressure*, emotional situations through the 2 often find her along the life (of which being charitable will ease this burden). Yet Petra is protected by undeniable blessings, being on the 24's *Love Money Creativity* Karmic Path, one of which is the undeniable power of love as Venus's urge through the 6 requests. So, why would fate intervene and allow the outcome of Petra to survive and not Simon?

## PETRA NEMCOVA

- ◉ NEAR A TOP TEN COVER ART
- ◉ AN OCEAN OVERCAME PETRA
- ◉ AN OCEAN CAN TRAP PETRA
- ◉ PETRA CAN COPE

- A TREE CARE OVER PETRA
- PETRA MEANT TO RECOVER
- NOT MEANT TO RECOVER A MAN
- AN OCEAN EVAPORATE A CAMERA MAN
- NOT MEANT TO RECOVER A ROMANCE
- PETRA CAN REENACT AN OCEAN EVENT OVER & OVER
- PETRA CAN MOVE ON TO PEACE

### SIMON ATLEE

- SIMON IS A TAME MAN IN A SMILE
- SIMON IS NOT A MEAN MAN
- SIMON IS LOST IN A MAIN SEA
- A MAIN SEA EAT SIMON
- SIMON NOT MEANT TO MATE TO LAST
- SIMON LOST TO A MAIN TSUNAMI
- SIMON IS MEANT TO SEE EONS AT SEA

Whether you are looking at events of seemingly unbelievable proportions, or something in the news that the media wears out by the time the story fades, undoubtedly you can turn off the TV and take the matter at hand and see for yourself what's really going on. We can be forever GRATEFUL to the sixth sense that our dear Lexigrams undoubtedly are here to provide for us. For then: LET A TRUE, ULTRA, REGAL ART RULE U; LET RAGE, FEAR FALTER; LET UR TEARFUL ALERT RULE U; GET A FRUGAL URGE, GET GRATEFUL! What I have equally come to understand when events and things happen that make the "big news," if one chooses to tap into some spiraling, there are truly deeper messages we are meant to receive. Yes, we will usually learn the actual truth of the matter, but in such a case as the World Trade Center and the next example that spoke to me in this very way, you'll see how for whatever reasons, the derivations within large-scale events are sent for a higher purpose to awaken us. The United States was stunned on 16 April 2007, when, with incredible sadness, the VIRGINIA TECH tragedy became the pulse of the news cycle.

To be honest, I had totally chosen to stop focusing on the news at this point, rejecting the obvious negativity it always seems to prevail. Whatever called upon me to focus upon the Virginia Tech tragedy was another investigation that shocked me to no end. In all I have up till now been able to share with you about the endless mysteries swirling around us through the Universe above, I believe this occurrence is one of the most revealing horrific events that is asking us to truly be aware, and not ignore what our star secrets can ultimately share with us to avoid outcomes such as this in the future.

My first thoughts came and spiraled one of the many profound messages you will find in the words VIRGINIA TECH, and I imagine you would also agree, I GRIEVE IN A GREAT RAIN...As much as I wanted to ignore it (and there are many things I may have denied receiving messages from due to my news resistance over the years), something compelled me to look into these Lexigrams. What came to me was even more than the actual occurrence. Undoubtedly, it became more than apparent to pay close attention to the revelations within this name. The collective—and in particular the piece of it residing within the United States—was sure meant to digest these messages in the aftermath:

## VIRGINIA TECH

- AN EIGHTEEN/NINE NATIVE IGNITE A TRAGIC ARCHIVE IN A VARIANT HATE
- IT AIN'T IN A GRACE, IT GRAVITATE IN A GREAT VAIN
- IT IN AN ANGER, A RAGE, A GREAT RAIN
- IT REIGN IN AN IRATE HATE, IT CREATE A GREAT CERTAIN CHANGE
- IT TEACH REIGN CAN'T EARN, CAN'T REACT IN HATE
- IT TEACH THE EARTH CAN'T GAIN IN HATE
- IT TEACH THE EARTH CAN'T THRIVE IN HATE
- IT TEACH THE EARTH CAN'T ACHIEVE IN HATE
- THE EIGHTEEN/NINE REACT IN A CRAVE IN HATE, REACHING
- THE EARTH GATHER IN A GREAT GRIEVING
- THE EARTH CAN REGAIN, INVITE IN AN ETHNIC GRACE
- THE EARTH CAN ENRICH IN A RIGHT CARING ETHNIC CHANGE
- IT CREATE AGAIN A GIANT TV GAIN

For those who may not know, the gunman, CHO SEUNG HU, was born on the EIGHTEENTH of January in 1984. This granted him a Saturn-ruled Capricorn Sun with a Mars-ruled 18/9 *Spiritual–Material Conflict* Karmic Path. Cho was on the Lifepath of the 32/5, representing Mercury's influence of change, movement, and communication, indicating the native's actions in the lifetime affect masses of people. The videos he sent to NBC between the shootings have revealed to the masses that he compared himself to Jesus, and the 18 is directly referred to by the ancient Chaldeans as one where "extreme caution and care must be taken to meet the challenges and dangers of this Compound number. Those born on the 18th day of any month have chosen themselves (on the higher level of self), between incarnations, this channel of birth (as did Jesus) as the greatest of all testings of the soul for worthiness."[61] While 18 can be all about love, there are great warnings within the Chaldean's 18 message to beware of reacting in life with rage and anger to the apparent obstacles presented to them. When Mars energy is not nurtured with courage—conflict, penetration and aggressive action are the natural reactions.

With a 32/5 Lifepath of *Communication*, Cho's rash actions reached the masses on a level that bewildered and incredibly troubled many, and, unfortunately, it will never be forgotten. This heavy combination of Mars and Mercury does not always relate well within the soul, and the negative polarity of fiery Mars prevailed in Cho's choice to react in conflict. As he lived out the last days of his Lifepath, Mercury's typically grounded and logical messenger energy resulted in the opposing polarity of confused, restless and scattered behavior. As many psychologists struggled to understand, the energies from within the identity of his Capricorn soul did not exhibit the usual wise, responsible, and stable energy known to these Saturn natives.

The numerical expression of Cho's full name, CHO SEUNG HU, again indicates the influence of the 12, *The Sacrifice–The Victim*. The energy of the 12 is directly related to the 18, in the same respect of how he compared himself to Jesus. Jesus dealt with the energies of the vibrations of the 3, 6, and 9 in his short lifetime. What is even more intriguing is Cho's first name alone also vibrates to the 6, as well as one of the names upon his tattoo. There is no doubt Cho struggled within his own understanding of what Jesus was truly all about, for the unfortunate outcome, unlike Jesus, is that Cho was not "the figure 2 of the kneeling, submissive student,"[62] which the 12's meaning so deeply urges the native to do. Along with the 18's energy, he forgot to learn the lesson of how to react to life's pressure: with love. Eerily enough, the characters in Cho's full name reveal why he did not:

### CHO SEUNG HU

- CHO'S HUGE EGO CHOSE GUNS
- OUCH HE USE GUNS HE SHUN CHOSEN ONES
- HE HONE ON GUNS, GOSH CHOSEN ONES GUSH, GO HUSH
- ONCE HE CHOSE NO HUGS, NO SONG
- HE ECHOS ONE SEC HE USE GUNS ON CUE
- OHH HE CONS US
- HE GONE EONS ON
- SO NO SON, NO ONE GOES ON
- SO HE, NO ONE HE CHOSE GOES ON
- SO SUCH CHO'S EGO CHOSE ENOUGH

The media revealed at this time that Cho had a tattoo, which had the following name upon it, which, same as the name Virginia Tech, carries the 10's transformative *Wheel of Fortune* Name Expression.

### ISMAIL AX

- I AIMS IN AX ILLS
- I AM AN ILL AXIS
- I AM M.I.A.

- ◉ IN AN ILL I SLAM ALL
- ◉ ALAS I MAIL ALL ILLS
- ◉ I MIX AIMS
- ◉ I AM LAX
- ◉ I AM ILL
- ◉ I AM ALL'S ALIAS

When one is guided by the 10, as VIRGINA TECH and ISMAIL AX are, I repeat here again the full meaning of the 10, for it is worth the reread in full reference to absorbing what went on that tragic day in April 2007. *"10 is a number of rise and fall, according to personal desire. It will be known for good or evil, depending on the action chosen. 10 is capable of arousing the extreme responses of love or hate—respect or fear. There is no middle ground between honor or dishonor. Every event is self-determined. 10 is the symbol of LOve and LIght, which create all that can be imagined, and also contains the code: Image 10 Ordain. Image it and it shall be. Ordain it and it will materialize. The power for manifesting creative concepts into reality is inherent, but must be used with wisdom, since the power for absolute creation contains the polarity power for absolute destruction. Self-discipline and infinite compassion must accompany the gift of the former to avoid the tragedy of the latter. Discipline must precede Dominion. Unfortunately, some 10 people fail to realize their power potential, and consequently harbor deep-seated feelings of frustration, causing them to feel unfulfilled, and to occasionally behave in a somewhat proud and arrogant manner to cover such unnecessary feelings of inferiority."*[63]

It is more apparent than ever that there is inherent wisdom in the Chaldean's ancient teachings that still apply to life in this modern age. Coupled with the equally intuitive knowledge our star secrets can provide for us, there is undeniable insight that truly is meant to serve us all. As we continue to coexist in a fast-paced world, no doubt the collective is being asked to slow down and take the time to know thyself, and be aware of the choices we make. We always have the personal option to make positive choices, and not gravitate to negative ones. Interestingly enough, the Universal Numerical Energy for $4+1+6+2+0+0+7$ was none other than the 20's understanding of *The Awakening*. But I'll give you another one to ponder now: Has the world learned a valuable lesson from the revelations at Virginia Tech?

Now, what is obviously more fun is hearing about GOOD NEWS, as the world continues to turn daily in its media-filled chatter. Even though it seemingly is a rare occasion, don't you just feel when you hear some that GOD SWOONED DOWN, SOON GOD ENDOWS NOW, GOD SENDS SONGS, WE OWN DO GOOD ENDS NOW. Wow. I really love it when that good news from a name or word ultimately prevails.

Speaking of good news, I can't help but slip in just a couple Lexigram truths in kind regards to England. There is a new Duke and Dutchess of Cambridge who wed on 29 April 2011, Britain's Prince William and Kate. This is where we surely see some "fate" falling into some divine timing. The very fact that the new royal couple waited until their first Saturn Returns to decide to tie the knot, surely was an undeniably wise choice for England's future leadership. Born on 9 January 1982, KATE MIDDLETON is primed TO TAKE A MAIN LEAD IN TIME through her

Capricorn and 9 Karmic Path guidance, which grants her the innate ability to lead. Aside from her obvious charm and impeccably classic look, one should not wonder why Prince William (a Cancer Sun Sign like his mom) chose Kate to be his beloved, as her Lexigrams equally agree with his decision.

## CATHERINE ELIZABETH MIDDLETON

- A MILLIONAIRE "COMMONER" TO REALIZE A RARE DREAM
- MEANT TO BE MARRIED TO A REAL NICE CANCER MAN, ONE THAT HAD A REAL NICE CANCER MOM DIE IN A CAR
- CATHERINE CAME TO EARTH TO BECOME A LEADER IN A GREAT HEART
- CATHERINE TO BECOME ANOTHER ETERNALIZED NAME IN TIME

One thing I hope you have learned by now about the magic of Lexigrams is how much they put one in AWARENESS: WE ARE A SEER NEAR A RARE ANSWER; WE SEE RARE ANSWERS; AS WE SEE, WE ARE NEAR A RENEW; AS WE ERASE WARS WE NEAR EASE. Then, once all is aware, your soul can join up in REALIGNING: I REIGN IN A REAL LARGE GAIN, ENLARGING IN A REAL INNER LEARN, ANGLING IN A REAL REGAIN, A REGAL AGILE ANGEL RINGING NEAR; AN ANGEL LINGER NEAR, I IN A LARGE INNER GAIN, I IN AN AGILE LEARNING AGE, I IN A REAL REGAINING ERA, I IN A GINGER REALIGN.

Which brings us now to a place where we can feel secure to take on Lexigrams as true:

## RESOLUTIONS

- I UNITE IT IN ONE SOLUTION
- I IS RESOLUTE TO RISE TO IT
- TRUE SOULS UNITE IT IN ONE
- I RE-ROUTE ROUTINES, I NOTE TRUE OUTLINES
- I LET IN TRUE SOUL RULES NOT TO LOSE
- SUNRISE TO SUNSET I UNITE IT, SOON I UNITE TO ONE TRUE SOUL
- I SURE IS IN SERIOUS RESULTS
- I ORIENT IT INTO ONE TRUE SOUL LINE
- I LOSE LIES TO UNTIE, TO LOOSEN TRUE LIES
- I LISTEN IN TO OUR SOULS' TUNE
- I LISTEN IN A SILENT SOUL UNITE

For then, as it is for anyone, you are primed and ready for the *REAL:*

## REVOLUTION

- TO UNITE IN LOVE, NOT TO UNITE IN EVIL
- IN TUNE TO LET LOVE LIVE ON
- LET LOVE RULE NOT EVIL
- TRUE LOVE RULE OVER EVIL
- TO NUTURE IN LOVE, LET LOVE REIN IN TRUE ROUTINE
- LOVE OUTLIVE EVIL, VOTE IN A LOVE VIRTUE
- VETO EVIL, VETO RUIN, VETO RIOT
- UNVIEL LOVE TO RULE TRUE
- LET IN EVIL, ONE IN TOIL
- NOT TO REVOLT IN EVIL TO EVOLVE
- LET VIOLENT RULE OUT TO NOT RUIN IT
- LET IT IN…LET TRUE LOVE IN TO RULE ON

- UNTIL LOVE RULE OVER EVIL U LET VILE IN TO TURN U
- TO ORIENT OUR EVOLUTION TURN TO LOVE
- LET TRUE LOVE IN: LET IT LIVE ON EON IN, EON OUT

With the pure power of Love, no doubt you will positively align and realign your spiritual being and allow your soul to become a strong:

## REVOLUTIONARY

- TRUE LOVE OUTLIVE ANY EVIL RITUAL
- I UNITE IT IN A RELIANT LOVE NOT EVIL
- I TUNE IN TO A LOVE REALITY TO LIVE IT RITE YEAR IN, YEAR OUT
- LET IN A REAL LOVE ROUTINE TO LIVE IT REAL
- YEAR TO YEAR, ANY YEAR I OVERTLY VOTE IN TRUE LOVE
- YOU! TURN INTO LOVE TO UNITE IT IN ONE LOVE REVOLUTION
- ORNATELY, NATIVELY, LIVE YOUR LOVE IN VARIETY

I don't know about you, but I sure do think being a revolutionary soul may be just what they mean when anyone tells you that you need to LIVE YOUR LIFE. I'll share this last piece of my Lexigram experience before I go. During a moment when I was in need of reflection, I came across a message that spoke to me precisely when I needed it most, yet when I least expected it to show up. I am always in the belief that wherever we may find ourselves in life, even at times of great sorrow, if we just notice one mystery waiting to be found surrounding us, there is one ready to share something we personally need to understand precisely at that moment.

This is one of multitudes upon multitudes of times when, since opening my sixth sense to the art of Lexigrams, I become ever-more blown away with their uncanny abilities in my own life. With your sixth sense opened, they will now bestow these same gifts to you. During the process of this book coming to completion, I have been spending part of my time outside of New York City with my beloved Grammie, whom is not exempt from the wisdoms of Lexigrams that you learned about earlier. Since she had a stroke in December of 2006, it's been my ultimate pleasure to be able to lend her support and company. On one of my trips back down to do business in NYC, I was having a very hard time switching gears from the country chill to the city pace, so, as I often do when needing a hefty dose of reflection, I took pause for a long walk.

There was a lot this particular week had brought to the surface. There were plenty of things I was feeling confused about within these years between caring for a dear family member and keeping a budding career going simultaneously. Before returning to New York City that trip, my Grammie and I talked pretty deeply about life—hers, my mother's, and mine—and the one thing she made very clear to me by the end of this conversation was: to live mine. It was a beautiful message, but I was still quite torn for a seemingly endless period after our talk to be able to fully grasp her words, and not feel there was more I should be doing for her.

My route back to NYC down the Taconic State Parkway, to my eventual walk to clear my head around Union Square, resulted in much contemplation and answer-seeking, not to mention tear-stopping. I wound up at a resting place on Union Square and Broadway, overlooking the windows above the American Outfitters storefront. I found a message not only for me at the time, but one it only seemed apropos to share with you all. I knew right then in my heart that Grammie's words were so very real, and just as Lexigrams are here to do for us, there is a deep message to adhere to within. I must have sat down at least 5 minutes before realizing what truth was awaiting to be told to me above American Outfitters store, where I seemed to magically see the words:

LIVE YOUR LIFE

This is where even the simplest things like a phrase we come across in our everyday life can tell us what we need to hear, as you are now ready to discover just how Lexigrams work in the most profound and mysterious ways. You will always now have, at your fingertips and under your star secrets thinking cap, a way to look at the world like you never have before, as you continuously unravel the complexities of the English language. I'll totally warn you now, it can become come addicting, but what a functional form of it! The brain workout and spiritual pleasure it will undeniable give your seeking soul will fill you up with that necessary and vital LOVE that is so important for you to EVOLVE. So, I absolutely know you, My Dear Reader, are more than ready. It's time for you to spiral. Go on now and...

**LIVE YOUR LIFE**

- ๏ FLY, YOU'RE FREE
- ๏ IF YOU LOVE YOUR LIFE YOU'RE FREE
- ๏ FREE FEEL FOREVER
- ๏ IF YOU'RE VILE OR LIE YOU'RE EVIL

- I LOVE YOU FOREVER
- LIVE LIFE LIVELY
- YOU'RE VERY FREE
- YOUR LIFE RELIVE 'OLE YORE FEEL
- YOU LIVE A LOVELY FULL LIFE
- EVERY LOVE REFILL, REFUEL LIFE
- I VERIFY LIFE LOVELIER IF FULL, FULLER
- FREELY RELIEF REFILL LOVE FULLY
- RELY LIFE VERY FREELY
- LOVE FULLY IF YOU RULE
- ROLL OVER LURE OR FURY
- RELY LOVE FOR YOU FOREVER…

> With LOVE to EVOLVE,
> *Namaste,*
> *Sharita*

# NOTES

1. Linda Goodman, *Linda Good-man's Star Signs*, p. 329–330.
2. Ibid., p. 336.
3. Ibid., p. 335.
4. Ibid., pp. 203–204.
5. Helen Keller, *The Story of My Life*, chapter 4.
6. Dorothy Herrmann, *Helen Keller: A Life*, p. 337.
7. Linda Goodman, *Linda Good-man's Star Signs*, p. 203.
8. Ibid., pp. 198–199.
9. Ibid., p. 199.
10. Ibid., p. 196.
11. Ibid., p. 204.
12. Ibid., pp. 196–197.
13. Ibid., p. 205.
14. Ibid., pp. 198–199.
15. Ibid., p. 199.
16. Ibid., p. 199.
17. Ibid., p. 203.
18. Ibid., pp. 199–200.
19. Ibid., p. 204.
20. Ibid., pp. 204–205.
21. Ibid., p. 200.
22. Ibid., p. 202.
23. Ibid., p. 197.
24. Ibid., p. 198.
25. Ibid., p. 199.
26. Ibid., p. 202.
27. Ibid., p. 196.
28. Ibid., p. 198.
29. Ibid., pp. 196–197.
30. Ibid., p. 197.
31. Ibid., p. 205.
32. Ibid., p. 197.
33. Ibid., p. 197.
34. Ibid., p. 200.
35. Ibid., p. 206.
36. Ibid., p. 199.
37. Ibid., p. 207.
38. Ibid., p. 197.
39. Ibid., p. 203.
40. Ibid., p. 203.
41. Ibid., p. 197.
42. Ibid., p. 206.
43. Ibid., p. 203.
44. Ibid., p. 205.
45. Ibid., p. 203.
46. Ibid., pp. 198–199.
47. Ibid., p. 196.
48. Ibid., p. 203.
49. Ibid., p.198.
50. Ibid., p. 201.
51. Ibid., p. 202.
52. Ibid., p. 203.
53. Ibid., p. 197
54. Ibid., p. 197.
55. Ibid., p. 198.
56. Ibid., pp. 201–202.
57. Ibid., p.205.
58. Ibid., p. 196.
59. Ibid., pp. 203–204.
60. Rudolf Steiner, *Anthroposoph-ical Leading Thoughts*, 1904.
61. Linda Goodman, *Linda Good-man's Star Signs*, p. 200.
62. Ibid., p. 197.
63. Ibid., p. 196.

# REFERENCES

Goodman, Linda, *Linda Goodman's Star Signs,* New York: St. Martin's, 1988.

Herrmann, Dorothy, *Helen Keller: A Life,* Chicago: University of Chicago, 1998.

Internet (about Rudolf Steiner): http://www.steinerbooks.org/aboutrudolf.html.

Jung, Carl Gustav, *Symbols of Transformation,* New York: Princeton University Press, 1956.

Keller, Helen, *The Story of My Life,* New York: Doubleday, 1903.

Khan, Hazrat Inayat, *The Music of Life,* New Lebanon, NY: Omega Uniform Edition, 1988.

Ruiz, Don Miguel, *The Four Agreements,* San Rafael, CA: Amber-Allen, 1997.

Steiner, Rudolf, *Anthroposophical Leading Thoughts,* London: Rudolf Steiner Press, 1904.

Since the age of 7, Sharita remembers being attracted to reading the horoscope section of the newspaper. Raised in the beauty of Upstate New York, she went on to be an honors graduate of SUNY Oneonta with a Bachelor of Science in Theater. Her studies include acting, singing, drawing, writing and a formal and extensive education in astrology, numerology, and metaphysics.

Called to be of service to others, she credits much of this inspiration and knowledge to the teachings of the Astrologer and Poet Linda Goodman. Goodman's teachings introduced the insight of how deeply astrology, numerology and lexigrams are connected. Sharita discovered that Goodman's revelations were accurate when applied to any person or entity. She has concluded that in order to gain complete insight, these three intertwining subjects must be interpreted together.

Since establishing *Sharita's Star Secrets,* Sharita is now considered a "Psychic of the Planets," wherein she channels the energies from one's name and date of birth to furnish various extensive readings tailored to true personal insight and development. She produces *What's Your Sign? I Have Your Number!,* a radio show heard on WBCR-LP, 97.7FM, Great Barrington, MA, which discusses the intricate link of astrology and numerology with notable special guests and through the profiles of featured talent.

Sharita writes monthly and bimonthly columns for both the *Millbrook Independent* and the *Utica Phoenix,* providing sound advice for readers with "The Zodiac Month Ahead," as well as her intuitive and original "Lunar-O-Scope." Along with her one-on-one consultations, she has developed the Star Learning Series, in which she teaches classes and lectures about the wonders of our planets and the magic of Lexigrams. She can be found as a psychic reader and teacher at The Awareness Shop, considered one of New York's finest metaphysical stores.

Currently residing between New York City and her country home in Chatham, New York, *It's All in the Name* is her first book and captures her passion of Lexigrams alongside Astrology and Numerology. For more information, please visit Sharita's website www.sharitastar.com.

9 780983 198406